Becoming Modern Women

Becoming Modern Women

LOVE AND FEMALE IDENTITY
IN PREWAR JAPANESE
LITERATURE AND CULTURE

Michiko Suzuki

STANFORD UNIVERSITY PRESS
STANFORD, CALIFORNIA

Stanford University Press
Stanford, California

Library of Congress Cataloging-in-Publication Data

Suzuki, Michiko.
  Becoming modern women : love and female identity in prewar Japanese literature and
culture / Michiko Suzuki.
    p. cm.
  Includes bibliographical references and index.
  ISBN 978-0-8047-6197-0 (cloth : alk. paper)--ISBN 978-0-8047-6198-7 (pbk. : alk. paper)
  1. Japanese fiction--Women authors--History and criticism. 2. Japanese fiction--20th
century--History and criticism. 3. Women in literature. 4. Love in literature. I. Title.
  PL725.S89 2009
  895.6'093522--dc22   2009026081

Typeset by Bruce Lundquist in 11/14 Adobe Garamond

For My Parents

Contents

Acknowledgments   ix

Note on Names and Terms   xi

I.   INTRODUCTION   I

     Becoming Female in Modernity   4

     Woman, Selfhood, and Love   6

     A Brief History of Love   8

     Bluestocking and Hiratsuka Raichō   10

     Modern Love Ideology   13

     Organization of *Becoming Modern Women*   15

PART ONE | GIRLS AND VIRGINS

2.   SAME-SEX LOVE   23

     Introduction   23

     Sexology Discourse   25

     Bluestocking Discourse   29

     Girls' Culture and Yoshiya Nobuko   32

3.   YOSHIYA NOBUKO
      AND THE ROMANCE OF SISTERHOOD   34

     Introduction   34

     Flower Tales: Girls and Adolescent Love   35

     Two Virgins in the Attic: Alternative Adulthood   42

     Becoming a Virgin: Rewriting Female Development   50

     "Abnormal" Virgins and Pure Wives:
     The Future of Same-Sex Love   54

PART TWO | THE WIFE'S PROGRESS

4.   LOVE MARRIAGE IDEOLOGY   65
     Introduction   65
     Love Marriage Ideology: Hiratsuka Raichō and Ellen Key   68
     Kuriyagawa Hakuson and the Byakuren Incident   70
     Love Marriage Ideology, Women Writers, and
     Miyamoto Yuriko   75

5.   MIYAMOTO YURIKO
     AND THE NOBUKO NARRATIVES   79
     Introduction   79
     Nobuko's Progress and Love Marriage Discourse   81
     Marriage as Disease, Divorce as Cure   91
     Erasing Love Marriage: The Bolshevik Wife   99

PART THREE | REINVENTING MOTHERHOOD

6.   MATERNAL LOVE   107
     Introduction   107
     Hiratsuka Raichō and Takamure Itsue   108
     Nationalism and Feminism   113
     Maternal Love, Women Writers, and Okamoto Kanoko   115

7.   OKAMOTO KANOKO
     AND THE MYTHIC MOTHER   118
     Introduction   118
     From "Mother and Child" to *Wheel of Life*   120
     Becoming a Female *Marebito*   124
     National Mythopoesis: Ataka's Tale   129
     Becoming an *Ur Mutter*   135
     Recreating Maternal Love   141

     CONCLUSION   147

Notes   153
Bibliography   197
Index   217

Acknowledgments

Many years have gone by since I began working on this project, and many people have helped bring this book into existence. I have been inspired and encouraged by my teachers, colleagues, friends, and family; it is impossible to list everyone here, but I am truly grateful for their support. I am especially indebted to my mentors at Stanford University. In particular, I thank Jim Reichert and Susan Matisoff, who helped me to reconsider various aspects of my work with insightful comments and critique. Their guidance in matters both intellectual and practical continues to be invaluable. Peter Duus has also provided me with constant support and encouragement. During my early graduate years I was fortunate to be able to study with Professor Makoto Ueda. At Stanford's East Asian Library, Naomi Kotake's expertise and generosity greatly helped facilitate my research.

I am grateful to professors in Japan who kindly provided assistance during the research process. I especially thank Professors Komori Yōichi, Toshiko Ellis, and Takada Yasunari, who generously shared their valuable time and allowed me access to resources while I conducted research at the University of Tokyo. My gratitude also goes to Kate Ellwood, who enabled me to work with materials held at Waseda University.

I appreciate the support of my colleagues at Indiana University. In particular, I thank Edie Sarra and Dick Rubinger, who have provided advice and encouragement for this project. I also thank Bob Eno, Sara Friedman, Sumie Jones, Tom Keirstead (now at the University of Toronto), Wen-ling Liu, Mike Robinson, and Heidi Ross.

Many colleagues and friends helped me in a variety of ways while I worked on this project. My gratitude goes especially to Abe Sachiko, Suzy Cincone, Claire Cuccio, Sabine Durant, Bernard Faure, Derk Frerichs, Hank Glassman, Bettina Gramlich-Oka, Henk Maier, Kumamoto Eliza,

Michele Mason, Mizumura Minae, Elizabeth Oyler, Sabine Roth, Reiko Shinno, Bob Tierney, and Leslie Winston. Special thanks go to Annette Keogh and Leslea Haravon-Collins, who have supported me in this process from beginning to end.

I am grateful to Stanford University Press—especially to Stacy Wagner for her enthusiasm and insight. I am extremely appreciative of the perceptive comments offered by the readers of this manuscript. Sarah M. Strong's feedback has been invaluable, and I thank Mariana Raykov and Jessica Walsh for assistance during the production process. Several sections of this book have appeared in earlier forms as part of other articles. Where appropriate, I provide previous publication information at the beginning of each endnote section.

I received institutional funding and fellowships at various stages of my endeavor. I thank Indiana University's Department of East Asian Languages and Cultures, the East Asian Studies Center, the Office of the Vice Provost for Research, and the Office of the Vice President for International Affairs. Prior to my employment at Indiana University I also received research support from Dickinson College and the Japan Society for the Promotion of Science. At Stanford University I received a doctoral scholarship as well as additional fellowships from the Stanford Humanities Center, the Center for East Asian Studies, and the Institute for International Studies.

My family, both the Fosters and the Suzukis, were understanding and helpful while I worked on what must have seemed to them to be a never-ending project. Thank you, Jerry Foster, for your hospitality and your intellectual curiosity that I can only hope to emulate. I wish this book would have appeared in time for Joan, but I know she approves nevertheless. I also thank Ken'ichirō Suzuki, Adam Foster, and Ann Ayton. Most of all, I thank Tatsuo and Yumi Suzuki, my wonderful parents. Their unwavering support for whatever I do has sustained me over the years. I have learned much from their belief in learning, their love of history and literature, and their zest for life. I dedicate this book to them.

Finally, Michael Dylan Foster has patiently read each draft of this book, engaged me in debate, and offered valuable critique at every step. My work, to say nothing of every other aspect of my life, has been enriched by his presence. There are simply no words available for me to use to adequately express my thanks, but I think he knows how I feel.

Note on Names and Terms

Throughout this book I use the Japanese order for proper names (family name first). In referring to individuals, I use the family name, except in the case of Yanagihara Byakuren, whom I call Byakuren (her penname) to avoid confusion. I do not use macrons for place names that are in standard English-language dictionaries, such as Tokyo. All other Japanese terms are italicized and use macrons or double vowels to indicate long vowels (ō, ū, aa, ee, ii). In Buddhist names and terms I use macrons not used elsewhere (ā, ī). All cited Japanese publications are published in Tokyo unless otherwise noted. All translations are mine unless otherwise indicated.

Becoming Modern Women

Introduction

In a 1903 work titled *The Evolution of the Japanese*, American missionary
Sidney Gulick (1860–1945) praises Japan as a model nation that is making
dynamic progress. His sentiments reflect the early twentieth-century worldview in which evolutionary progress and development were key notions.
From a Social Darwinist perspective, both individual and nation were to
follow a trajectory of maturation, moving toward a better future and a
higher state of existence. Gulick writes:

> New Japan is in a state of rapid growth. She is in a critical period, resembling
> a youth, just coming to manhood, when all the powers of growth are most
> vigorous. . . . In the course of four or five short years the green boy develops
> into a refined and noble man; the thoughtless girl ripens into the full matu-
> rity of womanhood and of motherhood. These are the years of special inter-
> est to those who would observe nature in her time of most critical activity.
>
> Not otherwise is it in the life of nations. There are times when their
> growth is phenomenally rapid; when their latent qualities are developed;
> when their growth can be watched with special ease and delight, because so
> rapid. . . . Such, I take it, is the condition of Japan to-day. . . . Her intellect,
> hitherto largely dormant, is but now awaking. Her ambition is equaled only

by her self-reliance. . . . The growth of the past half-century is only the beginning of what we may expect to see.

Gulick, who later became an important Japan specialist, highlights the
nation's rapid development by emphasizing the advancement of Japanese
women. In "Old Japan," he notes, a woman was not given "such liberty as is
essential to the full development of her powers." He suggests that the condition and position of Japanese women have improved, and that this change
can be considered one exemplary feature of progress for "New Japan."[1] This
close association of woman and nation is typical of civilization discourse;
the woman's status reflects the level of the nation's enlightenment and becomes a gauge for assessing its process of growth.[2] Ultimately, however, even
though it invokes Japanese women as an important means for measuring
national progress, Gulick's work does not present the women's own perspectives, self-reflections, or narratives.

When I set out to write *Becoming Modern Women*, I began with the desire
to understand how Japanese women imagined their growth and changing
identities within modernity. How did they negotiate their national and gendered identities and strategize in creating narratives of self-representation?
In the early to mid-twentieth century, which was shaped by visions of progress and faith in evolutionary transformation, how did Japanese women
articulate themselves as mirroring modernity, as dynamic sites of coming-
into-being in time and space? In the Western literary context, the *bildungsroman*, a fictional narrative of self-development and self-discovery, is often
described as the "symbolic form" of modernity.[3] Yet even when writing
in the dominant genre of the semiautobiographical I-novel (*watakushi
shōsetsu, shishōsetsu*), Japanese women writers did not always use straightforward coming-of-age narratives to explore the connection of modernity
and gender. Instead, they often used a particular concept—love—to talk
about woman as modern process. Regardless of its representation—as success, failure, promise, or disillusionment—the experience of love led to the
attainment of an identity resonant with a changing Japan. Although it was
not the only notion through which women explored their evolving, modern
identities, love was a critical concept within the cultural imaginary and vital
for the construction of both woman and nation.

With this in mind, *Becoming Modern Women* examines narratives by
women in conjunction with various discourses about love in order to
interrogate the process of becoming a modern female in Japan from the

1910s through the 1930s, the "prewar period" that preceded the Pacific War (1941–1945).[4] Since the mid-nineteenth century, love had been viewed as a Western ideal with which to measure individual and national advancements. This is not to say that in Japan there were no expressions of physical and emotional attachment in human relationships prior to its opening to the West, but this new understanding of love, associated with Christianity, was a radical departure from the Confucian ideals of traditional Japanese society. Heterosexual romantic love in particular quickly became valued, in secular terms, as a necessary experience for the modern Japanese self. The nation and its people were to progress not only through modernization in the public sphere but also in their private emotions and personal experiences. Notions of modernity and progress were thus embedded in discussions of love, literary and otherwise, from the very beginning of Japan's modern period.

During the first half of the twentieth century in Japan, I suggest, various ideas about love coalesced to create a modern image of the process of growth and development for women. This ideal process was conceptualized as an evolutionary trajectory. The girl would first experience "innocent" same-sex love romance; then, as she matured, she would move on to "real" (heterosexual) love, to be consummated in a love-based marriage; finally, she would become a mother and attain maternal love, the highest love of all. Although traditional idealized identities for women, such as "Good Wife, Wise Mother" (ryōsai kenbo), had been promulgated before, they were set, distinct identities. It was only after the early feminist movement of the 1910s and the blossoming of media culture that female identity came to be widely understood as a dynamic *process* reflecting the progress of modernity and shaped by experiences of love.

The narratives I examine in this book use contemporary ideas about love and womanhood but at the same time criticize and challenge such normative trajectories of female development. Understandably, not all women accepted or praised this concept of love's "evolution"; ideas about love were treated in a variety of ways. In my analyses, I consider the rich and complex texts by women as part of the broader publication boom of the 1910s through 1930s. These narratives were shaped by early feminist writing as well as by discourses about love from a wide range of media—popular magazines, sexology books, newspapers, bestselling love treatises, and new academic fields such as native ethnology and women's history. Although I do not suggest that love was the only means by which actual or fictional women became modern in prewar Japan, it was a critical idea and practice in the articulation of such a process. By investigating the interplay of women's writing and love discourses within the contexts of their production, *Becoming Modern Women* shows the ways in which modern Japanese female identity was constructed, questioned, and rewritten during the prewar period. This exploration illuminates the intersection of gender and modernity and opens a new window into Japanese culture in the seminal years before World War II.

Becoming Female in Modernity

How do we understand the woman in modernity? In both the West and Japan, the woman is a flexible symbol, malleable within the context of her representation. She is often depicted as the embodiment of modernity, but she is also used to signify its Other. She is a "modern" figure that mirrors seismic shifts in values and technologies; at the same time she is a "premodern" figure of innocence and nostalgia, providing stability in an unpredictable world. Often she is a representation of gendered "sites" that produce or interrogate the meaning of modernity, such as the non-West, popular culture, the everyday, the spectacle, language, the city or country, and consumption.[5]

In Japan, the woman became important as a sign of such ambivalent simultaneity during the Meiji period (1868–1912). It was, however, during the prewar decades of the 1910s through 1930s, the Taishō (1912–1926) and early Shōwa (1926–1989) periods, that the most dramatic changes occurred and the relationship between modernity and gender became increasingly complex. Indeed, the eclipse of Meiji civilization (*bunmei*) by Taishō culture (*bunka*) has been discussed as the emergence of a feminized culture; the idea of modernism (*modanizumu*) or the modern (*modan*) has also been gendered female, evoking the ephemerality of *modernité*, the fragmentary aspects of modernist art, the spread of mass culture, the disruptions of individualism, and the fantasy of consumerism.[6]

Such emphasis on the relationship between woman and the prewar period has been productive for feminist inquiry; scholars have illuminated the significant presence of female images and voices and the dramatic transformations of women in Japanese society and culture. These studies have often evoked modern female identity as representing change, a radical shift or decentering that challenges the social landscape. Although my own inquiry emerges from such validations of the prewar woman, I focus on change that is directional and cumulative. The modern female I pursue inscribes herself as an intrinsic part of modernity, becoming a modern Japanese woman through progress and growth.

This becoming can be understood in relation to Miriam Silverberg's concept of Japanese modernity as "constructionist."[7] In my view, the awareness of modernity as a dynamic process of being-in-construction was an important part of female identity; prewar women fashioned themselves as active participants in modernity by taking part in the process of continual progress and change. This self-image is clearly articulated by Hiratsuka Raichō (1886–1971), one of the most influential feminists in Japan. In 1911 she wrote in *Seitō* (Bluestocking, 1911–1916), the first Japanese feminist journal:

The flow of life progresses moment by moment. Now the people of the world have finally burst forth beyond known human boundaries and are making an intense effort day and night . . . to evolve beyond the humanity of today. We are no longer the set, unchanging beings conceived of by people of past ages. We are rich in changes, full of promise with the ability to evolve endlessly into the future, to become more beautiful, stronger, larger and superior day by day. The laws of nature cannot be so unfair as to say that only women are an exception to this rule of evolution, and are unable even now to become a part of humanity. It is clear that we must use our will to accelerate and strengthen the power of our progress.[8]

Hiratsuka describes "the women of today" as barely sentient beings "just newly awakened from a state . . . of infancy," who need to "move forward" resolutely with "an attitude that focuses on the self" (*shugateki taido*). She comments that she does not think the insistence on the "self" should always be the ultimate goal for a woman's journey forward, but she is convinced that for now it is a crucial stage in human life and a step that must be taken for "becoming a true person" (*honto no mono ni naru koto*).[9] Although "men" (*danshi*) are considered "human beings" (*hito*), "women" (*onna*) are still considered inferior. It is thus of the utmost importance for women to achieve true personhood.[10]

In Hiratsuka's words, Japanese women have awakened and are evolving "endlessly into the future." This reframing of female identity as process highlights the hope that women will "catch up" to the state of normative (male) personhood—a desire for progress articulated through the notion of equality and later refined through the idea of difference. This identity is also shaped by the time and space of nationhood. Progress is a goal not only for the nonnormative (female) sex but also for nations and races that need to evolve—the nonnormative (non-Western) spaces considered inferior to the West. Although we no longer conceive of it in this way, during the early twentieth century Japanese modernity was commonly seen as "spatially peripheral to, and temporally lagging behind, the West."[11] This perspective contributed to Japanese women's desire to progress, to mature and develop in tandem with Japanese men, but also with their more advanced sisters around the world. The goal and directionality of female progress were integral to prewar sexual politics and the contested meaning of a modern, developing Japan.

Woman, Selfhood, and Love

By rejecting the idea that women are inferior and unchanging, Hiratsuka validates demands for both external social progress (women's rights) and internal progress (realization of selfhood). Unable to participate in the political process and being without full legal rights, women under the 1898 Civil Code were subject to the authority of their fathers, husbands, and sons; but even with their lower status codified in this way, Japanese women were transforming themselves in the public sphere throughout the 1910s, 1920s, and 1930s, not only in their writing but also in labor, in popular and consumer cultures, and in feminist and proletarian movements. Scholars of this period have shown that female identities such as New Woman (*atarashii onna*), Modern Girl (*modan gaaru*, *moga*), working woman (*shokugyō fujin*), factory worker (*jokō*), housewife (*shufu*), and café waitress (*jokyū*) rose to cultural prominence, thus highlighting the radical changes that were taking place in society.[12]

Along with the advent of such distinct identities for women, female identity itself was also changing, being reconfigured as a trajectory "continually in process, an identity that is performed and actualized over time within given social constraints."[13] Newly emergent discourses and social changes from the 1910s made concrete the idea of female identity as a developmental trajectory. Instead of a simple two-stage shift from girlhood to adulthood, the female lifecycle became more complex as a result of the new educational system, ideas of sexual development, delayed age for entry into marriage, and even the emergence of age-specific media such as magazines for adolescents.[14]

Most important for Hiratsuka's view of female progress, however, was the cultivation of interiority, the completion of true "self" (*jiga*).[15] As Karatani Kōjin has argued, the "discovery of the self" was made possible through *genbun itchi* (unification of written and spoken language), which created the idea of the "inner self."[16] Beginning in the Taishō period, "selfhood," as both a place of departure and a coveted goal, was increasingly emphasized as integral to the modern experience along with the rise of democracy, liberal humanism, and key concepts such as culturalism (*kyōyō shugi*), personalism (*jinkaku shugi*), and self-cultivation (*shūyō*).[17] The prominent literary group *Shirakaba ha* (White Birch School) is representative of this cultural milieu; it placed a premium value on selfhood, and believed that "the goal of life was to pursue, to develop, and to express one's self."[18]

For women, as for men, the discovery of a true self and the fulfillment of its potential was a significant way of constructing a modern identity. In creating the feminist journal *Bluestocking*, Hiratsuka Raichō used the White Birch School's publication, *Shirakaba* (White birch, 1910–1923), as a model and stressed the importance of self in becoming a legitimate part of modernity and the greater human race.[19] Despite, or perhaps because of, women's lack of political or legal authority, internal transformation was highly valued. Hiratsuka's 1911 statement about female agency and evolution is significant because it represents wide-ranging changes taking place in everyday life and thought. Women were recreating themselves, using what Foucault calls "technologies of the self," transforming their "bodies and souls, thoughts, conduct, and way of being" through "their own means or with the help of others" in order to attain a higher state of existence.[20] This notion of self-development remained crucial throughout the prewar period; even after the allure of liberal individualism waned and many turned to Marxism and later nationalism, the pursuit and establishment of true self continued to define the idea of the modern man and woman.[21]

During this time, love was considered an important "technology of the self" that enabled women to grow and attain their true selves. From a twenty-first-century perspective, the idea of love itself may seem clichéd, vague, or too subjective to be conceptualized as a critical means of identity formation. Yet during the prewar period, the extent to which discourses about different forms of love pervaded society was truly remarkable; they shaped ideas about the modern self, about sex and gender differences, and even about national identity. Although not always manifest as a "class discourse" per se, love in this context can be viewed as what Fredric Jameson calls an *ideologeme*, a minimal unit that shapes ideology, a "pseudoidea—a conceptual or belief system, an abstract value, an opinion or prejudice."[22] A range of ideologies about modernity, gender, and progress were produced and reproduced around the concept of love.

For women, love was particularly important, not only because it allowed them to express agency separate from the dictates of the family system (*ie seido*) and social convention, but also because it enabled them to visualize a new process of becoming female. In Hiratsuka Raichō's letter entitled "Dokuritsu suru ni tsuite ryōshin ni" ("To My Parents on Becoming Independent," 1914), published in *Bluestocking*, she explains to her parents why she is leaving home to start a new life with Okumura Hiroshi (1891–1964), her lover and future husband:

> I have been faced with this choice—to nurture our love, or to destroy it, one or the other. And this time I have decided to boldly explore the former path, with all the power available to me. Due to my predisposition and character, there is much contradiction and anxiety in affirming love, but I have chosen to vanquish such fears, and to nurture and sustain the love that has taken root between us. I am determined to pursue this, to see how this love will develop, where it will take me, what unknown world will unfold in front of my eyes, how my thought and life will change.[23]

The reverence that Hiratsuka expresses toward the love she shares with Okumura, described here with the terms "*ai*" and "*ren'ai*," may seem melodramatic and excessive at first glance. Yet love was a critical means of articulating identity, a crucial catalyst for female development and self-discovery. During the early part of the twentieth century, love—its dreams and disillusionments, its various forms and expressions—was a vital concept for female writers as they explored the notion of becoming women both modern and Japanese.

A Brief History of Love

Love had been considered a gauge for measuring both individual and national advancement since the early Meiji period. Initially introduced as *rabu*, a new, Western ideal rooted in Christianity, it was juxtaposed as superior to *iro* and *koi*, traditional notions that emphasized sensuality and carnal desire. Saeki Junko notes that this new love, "born of a true and upright spirit," was associated with progress and viewed as a vehicle for the development and enlightenment of the Japanese people.²⁴ In the words of missionary Sidney Gulick, love is "that which to Western ears is the sweetest word in the English language, the foundation of happiness in the home, the only true bond between husband and wife, parents and children."²⁵ The Christian-humanist journal *Jogaku zasshi* (Journal of female learning, 1885–1904), published by Iwamoto Yoshiharu (1863–1942), played a central role in promoting such love as an ideal.²⁶

Love was soon to become valued, however, within a broader, secular context, not so much for its Christian qualities but as the foundation for male-female romance. In the late nineteenth century, the word *ai* was already used to signify various kinds of love beyond the narrowly defined Christian or spiritual love.²⁷ *Ai* is embedded in the compound *ren'ai* (romantic love), a word popularized during the late 1880s and 1890s to refer to heterosexual love; *ai* and *ren'ai* from this point on were (and are) often used interchangeably.²⁸ We also find *ai* in terms such as *dōseiai* (same-sex love) and *boseiai* (maternal love), both compound words created during the prewar period and now a part of the standard Japanese lexicon.²⁹ Throughout the 1910s to 1930s, writers explored modern identity using such different concepts of love as these, treating them as central to their own lives as well as to their literary creations.

The pivotal text that presents love as a modern experience is the 1892 essay "Ensei shika to josei" (Disillusioned poets and women) by writer Kitamura Tōkoku (1868–1894), published in the *Journal of Female Learning*. Often cited as a seminal text in the history of modern Japanese literature, Kitamura's essay articulates for the first time the idea that *ren'ai* is the most important aspect of human existence. He opens with the now famous lines, *"Love is the key to life's secrets. Love exists first, then there is life. If one takes away love, what is the meaning of life?"* Such thinking is a radical departure from the traditional Confucian worldview, and it inspired a whole generation of writers and thinkers with its shocking new perspective. Although Kitamura's essay goes on to cover a range of ideas, it clearly establishes love as central to human identity and as enabling the individual to attain selfhood and place in society:

> Love leads to self-sacrifice, but at the same time, it is a clear mirror that reveals one's "true self" [ware naru "onore"]. It is only once a man and a woman experience mutual love that the truth about society can be known. Even minute insects cannot function when they are isolated from each other. Society is

made up of humans coming together, and only by relying on and embracing each other can it be built and sustained. This fact can be understood only by taking the first step of experiencing mutual love. *When a person lives alone in isolation, there is nothing that makes him a part of society. It is only when a partnership is created that this unit becomes a part of society, and one is able to see oneself clearly in relation to society.*[30]

Although Kitamura's discussion here is rendered in gender-neutral terms, it is evident from the context that he is thinking specifically of male identity. Love as a "clear mirror" establishes a man's "true self" and reveals to him his place within the world; because love embodies an idealized relationship, its pursuit leads to the advancement of individual and society. At the same time, in the essay this encomium is juxtaposed with a sense of the difficulty of attaining love, especially within the institution of marriage. The articulation of love as the key for self-discovery, expressed simultaneously with doubt about love's ability to be realized in the real world, can be found in numerous works of Meiji literature.

Women writers of the Meiji period also responded to the concepts of *ai* and *ren'ai*. Even an early story such as "Koware yubiwa" ("The Broken Ring," 1891) by Shimizu Shikin (1868–1933), published in the *Journal of Female Learning*, already explores the literary possibilities for a resistant female voice that emerges through disillusionment in love.[31] A more optimistic view of love is presented in *Midaregami* (Tangled hair, 1901), the romantic poetry collection by Yosano Akiko (1878–1942), recognized for invoking love and sensuality to celebrate female identity.[32] It was not until the 1911 publication of *Bluestocking*, however, that the experience of love was explicitly theorized as a vital component of the development, growth, and discovery of a woman's true self. This publication not only was important for the feminist movement, but it also established a foundation for understanding woman, identity, and love in the prewar period.

Bluestocking *and Hiratsuka Raichō*

Bluestocking was published by Seitōsha (Bluestocking Society), a literary group founded by Hiratsuka Raichō and others who saw the need to further women's literature and achieve female liberation through writing. Featuring stories, poems, and essays as well as translations of famous foreign works, *Bluestocking* was the first Japanese journal written and published by

women. In the inaugural issue, Hiratsuka articulates the group's objective
to restore dignity and power to women:

> In the beginning, woman was indeed the sun. She was the true person.
>   Now woman is the moon. She is the moon with a sickly, pale face, who
> relies on others to live, and shines by others' light.
>   Now we must regain our sun that has been hidden from us.[33]

Although at its peak the publication sold only three thousand copies per
month, the Bluestocking women were by no means an obscure group.[34]
These New Women (*atarashii onna*) received a great deal of attention for
their writings, debates, and public appearances, and they enjoyed a prevalent place within the cultural imaginary.[35]

In recent years a great deal of critical work on *Bluestocking* has been published, prompted by the growing interest in Japanese women's literature,
history, and women's studies. Through detailed study of *Bluestocking* writers, literature, and debates, as well as of the concept of the New Woman,
scholars have reassessed the journal's role in the early feminist movement
as well as in the later rise of nationalism.[36] We are now able to see that this
multivalent journal reflects a range of ideological positions and that its critical ramifications extend beyond the limited period of its publication history. The writings about love and female identity presented in this journal,
however, have not yet been fully recognized as an integral part of prewar
discourse despite their wide-reaching influence throughout the period.

Arguably the most famous feminist of twentieth-century Japan, Hiratsuka was the leader responsible for publishing *Bluestocking* from its incep-
tion until 1915.[37] Unlike Kitamura Tōkoku, she did not produce a single
essay that prompted a paradigm shift; rather, her works played a profound
and continuous role in the discursive formation of the modern female self.
She published in *Bluestocking* as well as in other venues, and her ideas about
love and women evolved with the times and with her experiences. Because
her ideas were in flux during the 1910s through the 1930s, it has perhaps
been easy for critics to dismiss them as being too subjective or inconsequential. Yet these shifts in her thinking actually offer valuable insight not only
into Hiratsuka's personal convictions but also into vital trends within the
larger sociohistorical conversation. Kitamura's thoughts on love can be read
in terms of both the private and the public—on the one hand expressing
dismay at the failure of his own love-based marriage while on the other hand
simultaneously articulating a central concern of the Meiji literati regarding

the modern man and love. Hiratsuka's texts document a woman's search for her own identity through love while at the same time illuminating the broader relationship between modernity and gender in prewar culture.

Because of her watershed conceptualization of love and female progress, as well as the way her writings reflect and shape contemporary discourses about women, the figure of Hiratsuka Raichō serves as a touchstone and guide through the various discourses in *Becoming Modern Women*. A graduate of Nihon joshi daigaku (Japan Women's University), Hiratsuka first gained public notoriety in 1908 when she ran away with writer Morita Sōhei (1881–1949), supposedly to attempt a double suicide; this incident was fictionalized by Morita in his successful newspaper serial entitled *Baien* (Cinder and smoke, 1909).[38] Hiratsuka furthered her reputation as a radical New Woman by establishing the Bluestocking Society in 1911, and in 1912 she openly discussed a same-sex love affair with Otake Kōkichi (or Tomimoto Kazue, 1893–1966), a fellow Bluestocking member. After meeting artist Okumura Hiroshi, the younger man who would eventually become her lifelong partner, however, Hiratsuka prioritized heterosexual love. Her ideas about love and marriage that emerged from this time were published in *Bluestocking* as well as in other journals and newspapers. Subsequently, she wrote vociferously about maternal love, particularly after experiencing childbirth in 1915; this form of love became central to her thought throughout the 1920s and 1930s.

Strongly influenced by Western feminist texts and her own experiences, Hiratsuka's ideas established a foundation for discussions of heterosexual love and love-based marriage. In addition, her writings about female same-sex love are intricately related to the rise of sexology discourse during the 1910s and 1920s, and her praise of maternal love from the mid-1920s to 1930s is shaped by discourses of nationalism. Although no single individual can completely embody a historical era, I agree with Rita Felski that "accounts of the modern age . . . typically achieve some kind of formal coherence by dramatizing and personifying historical processes; individual or collective human subjects are endowed with symbolic importance as exemplary bearers of temporal meaning."[39] I do not claim that Hiratsuka is a representative voice for all women in prewar Japan, but the female authors and their writings about love that I examine are clearly in profound conversation with the discourses produced by or around this prominent writer and theorist. Her varied writing about love provides a useful optic through which to view other women writers' works and the larger historical context.

Modern Love Ideology

In *Bluestocking*, Hiratsuka established the notion that love (*ai*, *ren'ai*) is intrinsic to female self-development and the discovery of a woman's true self.[40] This love is considered a fusion of both spiritual and sexual love. Throughout this book I call these critical ideas *modern love ideology*. Although Japanese critics sometimes use this term (*kindai ren'ai ideorogii*) to refer to either the emphasis on love as an ideal or the promotion of marrying for love, I use it specifically to refer to the notion that true love is an amalgamation of spiritual and sexual love, and that this love is the basis for female development.[41] This highly influential idea was adapted from the works of Swedish feminist Ellen Key (1849–1926), specifically, *Ren'ai to kekkon* (*Love and Marriage*, English edition 1911). An important text for early twentieth-century feminist movements in Japan and the West, it was the basis for Hiratsuka's ideas on love, marriage, and motherhood.[42] She read *Love and Marriage* in the English edition, then translated several chapters into Japanese and published them in *Bluestocking* from 1913 to 1914. Although male critics had already introduced some ideas from *Love and Marriage* in other journals by this time, Hiratsuka was the first to translate this influential work.[43]

Hiratsuka notes in her memoirs that her own process of growth as a person through her romance with Okumura was framed and illuminated by the ideas found in *Love and Marriage*. In fact, by treating Key's work as a kind of primer on love, Hiratsuka seems to have transposed the "correct" reading of love onto her relationship with Okumura, even as she explored this new experience. She writes:

> While my own experience of love [*ren'ai*] moved rapidly forward, I was simultaneously translating Ellen Key. This fact, I believe, had a greater meaning for me than simply introducing Key's writing. At a time when love and marriage were becoming real, inescapable, pressing issues, coming across Key was in fact like finding a light that shone brightly on a world of love unknown to me and could be described as a revelation from heaven. . . . It [Key's work] looked at love in terms of development and taught me an endless number of things at a time when I was completely ignorant about love—about the different stages of the process and the differences between male and female love—it could be described as a treasury of issues about love.[44]

Hiratsuka's translations of *Love and Marriage* are recognized as important *Bluestocking* texts, but critics have not fully addressed their content and their impact on the broader Japanese culture. Through Hiratsuka's introduction and elucidation of Key's work, love was presented as the ideal means to progress as an individual and as a society. Key criticizes the traditional marriage system arranged by families on the basis of class, and praises unions founded on true love. Although this view is very similar to the Japanese Christian humanists' idea of love as a sign of progress, Key refutes the notion that this love needs to be sanctioned by religious authority or the legal framework of marriage. Love—that is, this new male-female relationship—takes the individual to a new, evolved state of self-awareness. Key asserts that "a woman's essential ego must be brought out by love before she can do anything great for others or for herself."[45] She further notes that "in moving forward, step by step on the path of selfhood, the first consideration is love and its proper way."[46]

The two central aspects of modern love ideology, as articulated in the work of Key and Hiratsuka, can be delineated as follows. First, love is integral to female selfhood, a process of self-development ultimately leading to one's true identity. This focus on the individual and the project of aiming for a higher state or better future, or both, reflects Key's fundamental position as an evolutionist-humanist; the underlying assumption is that both individuals and society are progressing toward betterment.[47] In her view, both the individual and the human race can become whole and attain completion through love.[48] This combination of the ideas of progress, love, and selfhood appealed to Hiratsuka as she attempted to articulate a strategy for Japanese women and girls to express and realize their true modern identity.

Second, love is both a spiritual and a sexual experience that completes the individual (*rei-niku itchi;* unification of spirit and flesh). Key's point is that true love, rather than following a hierarchical framework in which spiritual or platonic love is superior to sexual love, must combine both elements. This idea of love became an ideal that helped to define and shape sex/gender difference and equality; although men were understood to experience love first through sexual desires and women were perceived to feel spiritual love before awakening to sexual love, both men and women had to experience spiritual *and* sexual love in order to progress and attain a modern self.[49] Strongly promoted by Hiratsuka, the unification of spirit and flesh in love became fundamental to the understanding of ideal modern love and an important part of the prewar cultural consciousness.[50]

Organization of Becoming Modern Women

Becoming Modern Women examines narratives by three important women writers: Yoshiya Nobuko (1896–1973), Miyamoto Yuriko (1899–1951), and Okamoto Kanoko (1889–1939). It explores how their works engage with modern love ideology and other discourses on love. By investigating their texts in this way, I attempt to negotiate two different approaches to women's writing. On the one hand, I highlight these authors' shared interest in feminist thought, illustrating their overlapping concerns and questions about modern female identity. My goal is to remap lost connections and recover common discursive fields in works by and about women. On the other hand, however, I also demonstrate that women's writing is not a hermetically closed genre, limited in scope or topic, influenced only by other women's texts and employing set literary styles and strategies.[51] Literature is a heterogeneous and porous site that is in conversation with a range of ideologies, texts, and discourses. I analyze, therefore, how these authors employ a wide array of contemporaneous discourses and media events in order to challenge, criticize, and rewrite modern love ideology and the normative process of development. I approach women's literature as part of a broader realm of cultural production in which meaning is created through contestation and hybridization.

The authors examined here work within very different genres. Yoshiya is considered a writer of popular fiction (*tsūzoku shōsetsu*) and girls' fiction (*shōjo shōsetsu*); Miyamoto is seen as a serious writer of proletarian literature (*puroretaria bungaku*); Okamoto is known as a *tanka* poet and Buddhist scholar, and her fiction is often associated with the nationalistic Japan Romantic School (*Nihon roman ha*). My analyses of these authors do not rely on the unifying trope of the semiautobiographical I-novel; on the contrary, I particularly avoid interpreting their works from this perspective. It is true that these authors often use what Tomi Suzuki calls the "literary and ideological paradigm" of the I-novel; that is, although not necessarily categorized as I-novels in the narrow or formal sense of the term, many of these works are part of a literary mode in which texts are considered a reflection of authorial reality. Although some works are clearly "self-conscious I-novels" that presuppose "autobiographical assumptions on the part of the reader," my interpretations do not focus on whether or not the texts articulate "real" female experience.[52] The relationship between the woman writer's own self-image and the textual representation of female identity is not a simple one and has broad implications for interrogating the tension between woman-hood and the idea of authorship; this is not my area of inquiry.[53] I do, to an extent, discuss the lives of women—the authors as well as Hiratsuka and other feminists—but my goal is not to unearth the exact relationship between fictional protagonist and real author. Rather, my project here is to explore how these texts use ideas about love to construct discursively a mod-ern, developing female identity.

Becoming Modern Women analyzes these writers' works in relation to dis-courses that pertain to same-sex love, love marriage, and maternal love. The three sections of the book discuss each of these forms of love respectively and are loosely framed by the decades of the 1910s, 1920s, and 1930s. The first section looks at same-sex love discourses that emerged from the 1910s and at how Yoshiya Nobuko strategically employed these ideas during her prewar writing career. The second section examines love marriage discourses and their prominence during the 1920s, using them to reread Miyamoto Yuriko's famous "Nobuko" texts and in turn garner insight into broader social concerns of the day. The third section interrogates the idea of mater-nal love and its significance during the 1930s and explores how Okamoto Kanoko rewrites this idea in her texts about motherhood. By highlighting each form of love in correspondence with the 1910s, 1920s, and 1930s I am not suggesting that only one type of love was the subject of discussion in each of these decades. Rather, by pairing each type of love with the histori-cal and discursive context in which it resonated most significantly, I show how ideas about love changed and interacted with each other throughout the period. Although I recognize that decades and even markers such as Meiji, Taishō, and Shōwa go only so far in delineating the tenor of cultural trends and historical shifts, the organization here is intended to be a useful map with which to revisit the prewar landscape.

Part One, "Girls and Virgins," is composed of two chapters. Chapter Two, "Same-Sex Love," looks at this love in the context of the 1910s: the rise of sexology discourse, media discussions of female-female love, *Bluestocking* writing, and young girls' culture (*shōjo bunka*). Same-sex love was construed in dualistic terms, as a pure, platonic attachment common between young schoolgirls or as a sexual deviance practiced between women (perverse ex-perimentation, congenital inversion, or both). These divergent ways of un-derstanding same-sex love enabled a flexible interpretation of its role within the female developmental process. Although it is impossible to delineate completely what *same-sex love* means within any given context, I use this term in keeping with early to mid-twentieth-century usage. It is also now standard practice to use this term as opposed to *lesbianism* or *homosexuality*, because these latter terms carry with them their own meanings and nuances that have been shaped within current discourse. Also, I should note that although sexuality is not an explicit focus of this book, it is certainly relevant to a number of the same-sex discourses I explore.

In Chapter Three, "Yoshiya Nobuko and the Romance of Sisterhood," I argue that Yoshiya's prewar fiction validates same-sex love through an engagement with modern love ideology. Exploring a number of her novels and stories from girls' magazines, private pamphlets, and popular women's magazines, I illuminate her use of female-female love. Yoshiya published in the last two issues of *Bluestocking* and had direct contact with Hiratsuka Raichō, having studied the English edition of *Love and Marriage* in the same reading group. Rather than interpreting Yoshiya's fiction as a commentary on her own life with her female partner, I show how she co-opts sexological and feminist discourses to rewrite ideas about female identity, inscribing same-sex love into mainstream notions of female development. Her works, such as the bestselling girls' fiction *Hanamonogatari* (Flower tales, 1916–1924), transformed society's view of girlhood as well as of same-sex romance and sexuality.

Part Two is titled "The Wife's Progress." Chapter Four, "Love Marriage Ideology," explains how love marriage (*ren'ai kekkon*, a marriage based on mutual love and initiated by the partners themselves) became an important means by which to attain a modern identity within the 1920s cultural imaginary. Stemming from modern love ideology, this idea, often called "(*modern) love marriage* ideology" ([*kindai*] *ren'ai kekkon ideorogii*), stressed the importance not so much of love itself but of *marrying for love*. This ideology posits that love attains its fullest potential within marriage, so the love marriage rather than the traditional arranged marriage is the best way for men and women to complete their selves.[54] Although traditional forms of wedlock continued to be the most prevalent in actual practice throughout the prewar period, an astounding number of texts about love marriage—from fiction and essays to explicatory love treatises—were published and consumed during this time. The 1920s were marked by the popularization of love marriage discourse through landmark works such as Kuriyagawa Hakuson's (1880–1923) *Kindai no ren'ai kan* (Views of love in the modern era, 1921), and by a number of public scandals, ranging from love suicides to high-profile extramarital romances.

Chapter Five, "Miyamoto Yuriko and the Nobuko Narratives," focuses on Miyamoto's canonical work, *Nobuko*. I offer a new way to approach this text, by examining both the 1924–1926 serialization and the standard 1928 book edition in light of contemporary ideas about love, marriage, and divorce. I also discuss the two sequels that feature the same protagonist, which are set during the 1920s and 1930s but written in the postwar period. Miyamoto was not a member of the Bluestocking Society—she was only twelve years old when the society was formed—but she read works by both Hiratsuka and Key, and commentary on their ideas is found in her diaries and critical work on literary history. *Nobuko* has been read primarily as an I-novel mirroring Miyamoto's disillusionment with her own love marriage to her first husband, but it has never been fully analyzed within the discursive and historical context of the time. Her rejection and reinscription of modern love ideology is part of the broader intellectual shift from liberal humanism to socialism as the ideal means of national advancement.

Part Three is "Reinventing Motherhood." Chapter Six, "Maternal Love," looks at how feminist and nationalist discourses converged during the 1930s to articulate a new model of female self rooted in motherhood and maternal love. These topics were of considerable interest for the general public. A few months before the beginning of the China War in 1937, writer Sata Ineko (1904–1998) noted that there was a publishing boom for works theorizing about motherhood, a trend reminiscent of earlier demand for books about romantic love and theories on youth.[55] Within modern love ideology, the attainment of maternal love and the identity of a mother had always been crucial for the fruition of romantic love, but during the mid-1920s to 1930s there was a profound shift in Hiratsuka's understanding of love and womanhood, as well as in the thought of feminist Takamure Itsue (1894–1964), who considered herself Hiratsuka's disciple. Maternal love became a mystical notion, an intrinsic part of female identity; it was no longer something gained through the physical experience of motherhood but rather a natural instinct that existed *a priori* in all females. The idea that the pursuit of modern identity as a process would ultimately lead to the superceding of linearity, to the discovery of a mythic self existing outside of time, radically altered the understanding of both women and nation, and indeed the very concept of progress, in the years immediately preceding the Pacific War.

In Chapter Seven, "Okamoto Kanoko and the Mythic Mother," I examine Okamoto's works through notions of maternal love and modern love ideology. I particularly focus on *Shōjō ruten* (Wheel of life, 1939), one of her longest novels, as a validation of woman as an integral part of Japanese history and national identity. Okamoto met Hiratsuka in 1907, when they were both studying Western literature at the home of writer and translator Baba Kochō (1869–1940).[56] Okamoto began her career as a *tanka* poet and joined the Bluestocking Society in 1911; she wrote poetry and letters for *Bluestocking* and her first poetry collection was published by the Society in 1912. Although her poems, written during the 1910s and 1920s, are known for their focus on heterosexual love, Okamoto's fictional narratives, a genre she began publishing only in the last few years of her life, are remembered for their exploration of maternal love and female identity. Rather than reading these works as reflecting her love for her son, Okamoto Tarō (1911–1996), I demonstrate that Okamoto's construction of a modern female self, a figure far more powerful than men, emerges as a result of her engagement with contemporaneous writings on maternal love, native ethnology (*minzokugaku*), and historiography. In particular, I examine the idea of transcendence in her interpretation of maternal love, and her subversive rewriting of nationalism. Okamoto makes use of various discourses that endorse maternal love while offering a new vision of motherhood as the goal for female maturity.

By examining how love, shaped within specific sociohistorical contexts, plays a pivotal role in productions of the modern female self, *Becoming Modern Women* introduces a new way of viewing the complex relationship between gender and modernity. The processes of love, woman, and nation intersect in a variety of unexpected yet vital ways. By critically exploring such connections, I hope to illuminate both literary and cultural discourses and, by extension, the changing landscape of prewar Japan.

PART ONE

Girls and Virgins

Same-Sex Love

Introduction

Female-female love as a practice did not begin suddenly during the modern period, but in the early twentieth century it became a prominent topic of discussion and debate in Japan. The rise of same-sex love discourse occurred with the creation of the schoolgirl (*jogakusei*), a modern female identity that emerged from new institutions: the higher girls' school (*kōtō jogakkō*) and the women's college. With the passage of the 1899 Higher Girls' School Act (*kōtō jogakkō rei*), schools for secondary education were established throughout Japan and their numbers increased dramatically from the late 1910s to the mid-1920s;[1] and in 1901, Japan Women's University was established in Tokyo as the first women's college for higher girls' school graduates. As many works of Meiji literature indicate, schoolgirls captured the cultural imagination as potential partners in romantic (heterosexual) love.[2] From the 1910s through the 1930s, however, they were also seen as practitioners of same-sex love, confined as they were in sexually segregated environments and discouraged from socializing with young men. Indeed, a popular writer suggested in 1926 that "same-sex love play" (*dōsei no koi ome gokko*) among schoolgirls started with the establishment of the first women's college.[3] Also, with the proliferation of higher girls' schools and schoolgirls during the prewar period, the term "same-sex love" (*dōseiai*), used for both sexes, came to be associated especially with female-female relationships.[4]

In addition to *dōseiai*, a number of other words for female same-sex love—including *ome* and *esu* (or *S*)—were created or developed within the higher girls' school context.[5] The meanings and nuances associated with these and other terms shifted during the period, but broadly speaking, same-sex love was construed through what might be called a dualistic continuum: on the one hand, there was the adolescent romantic friendship, pure and platonic; on the other, there was the sexual deviancy practiced by degenerates and so-called "inverts" (*seiteki tentōsha*), born with an "inverted" masculine nature, whose desire was for members of the same sex. This continuum, based on a binary of "normal" and "abnormal," reflects an effort to understand a complex phenomenon inevitably intertwined with questions of environmental influence, congenital character, the length and nature of the emotion or practice, the age of the lovers, and the process of female sexual development.

Cultural critics of modern Japanese sexuality agree that the key incident that brought female same-sex love to national attention occurred in 1911, when two higher girls' school graduates in Niigata Prefecture committed a love suicide (*shinjū, jōshi*).[6] These two girls from upper middle-class families killed themselves because their love for one another could not be sustained in the heterosexual world outside school. Immediately after their suicide, a flurry of articles attempting to explicate such relationships appeared in the media. One such commentary from *Fujo shinbun* (Women's newspaper), for instance, offers a typical gauge for understanding same-sex love:

> As a result of our studies, we can say that there are two kinds of same-sex love [*dōsei no ai*]. One is a passionate form of pure friendship, whereas the other is the so-called *ome* relationship [*ome no kankei*], which is a kind of female husband-and-wife couple. The former . . . is a case in which the females make a vow of sisterhood, and promise to be with each other in life or death. This is nothing more than a passionate friendship, and there is nothing in this relationship that is shameful or despicable. Thus, in this case, the love is a mutual love but is no more than an *extremely close friendship* [*kyokudo no nakayoshi*]. . . . But as for the latter *ome* relationship, this is truly a strange phenomenon . . . and it is probably a phenomenon of disease.

The romantic friendship was "pure," whereas the *ome* relationship was based on "bodily degeneracy" (*nikuteki daraku*) and characterized as an abnormality in which a "woman of a masculine character [*danseiteki seikaku kyōgū no joshi*] controls the other woman."[7]

After this famous love suicide, intimacy among young women came to be considered potentially dangerous, particularly because it was recognized that even "pure" passionate friendships could lead to the undesirable outcome of love suicide.[8] In the unequivocally "sick" *ome* relationship, the masculine woman was viewed with great fear, as having the power to corrupt and transmit same-sex desire to the nonmasculine (and therefore "normal") woman. The *Women's Newspaper* article, for example, expresses incredulous wonder that the nonmasculine woman seems to be "truly in love" in such a relationship.[9] Although female-female love as a whole caused some level of unease and increased scrutiny, discourses about such relationships tended to be polarized throughout the period, most often oscillating between ideas of purity and innocence and those of sexuality and deviance.

During the prewar period, same-sex love discourse became an important part of society's understanding of young women in general, in addition to its views on the specific figure of the schoolgirl. This is not to say that female-female love suddenly became a dominant practice for all girls and women. Rather, ideas of "normal" romantic friendship and "abnormal" same-sex desire, as well as ideas about the connection between gender and sex (femininity and masculinity), helped form the concept of the young female, and even determined correct and incorrect trajectories for her process of growth and development.

Sexology Discourse

The views of female-female love as both "normal" and "abnormal" developed concurrently with the rise of sexology discourse since the 1910s. Sexology, the field of scientific inquiry into the "truth about sex,"[10] was originally established during the 1900s in Germany and quickly spread to other parts of the world.[11] In Japan, sexology was a subject of academic and popular interest throughout the prewar period; the publication of various books and articles by both Western and Japanese sexologists contributed to a so-called sexology boom.[12] Female same-sex desire and practice were important areas of sexological inquiry, part of its endeavor to understand the "truth" about modern female sexuality and identity.

In Japan, the major works of Western sexology that included discussions of female same-sex love, such as *Psychopathia Sexualis* (1886) by Richard von Krafft-Ebing (1840–1902) and *Studies in the Psychology of Sex* (1897) by Havelock Ellis (1859–1939), circulated widely in translation.[13] Japanese sexologists such as Habuto Eiji, Yamamoto Senji, and Yasuda Tokutarō also wrote about female-female love in a number of venues, from mainstream magazines to academic books.[14] In addition to sexologists, women writers and feminists also disseminated sexological discourse. In 1914, for example, *Bluestocking* published the first Japanese abbreviated translation of "Sexual Inversion in Women," a chapter from Ellis' *Studies in the Psychology of Sex*, with a foreword by Hiratsuka Raichō.[15] Edward Carpenter's (1844–1929) *The Intermediate Sex* (1908), another influential work that includes a discussion of female same-sex relationships, was translated by socialist feminist Yamakawa Kikue (1890–1980) and published in a magazine in 1914 and in book form in 1919.[16]

Within sexology discourse in general, same-sex relationships between girls were more likely to be perceived as platonic, innocent friendships, and thus "normal." Such female ties were considered an expected outcome of a sexually segregated society; in other words, the girls were seen as simply expressing their affectionate, emotive natures and budding sexuality (unperceived by themselves) within a same-sex environment. Havelock Ellis, who observes that these "ardent attachments" can be "found in all countries where girls are segregated for educational purposes," characterizes these relationships as normal love, stressing that most girls grow out of such "Platonic" emotions when they leave school, and thus such a relationship "cannot be regarded as an absolute expression of real congenital perversion of the sex-instinct."[17] The young virgin was typically seen as a sexual tabula rasa, without desire until first incited by a man. As expressed by romantic poet and *Bluestocking* contributor Yosano Akiko in 1917, it is "a woman's biological and psychological reality" to have no awareness of sexual desire until a man approaches her.[18] Thus, although some higher girls' schools discouraged younger students from socializing with older ones, Numata Rippō, a prominent educator and editor of a famous girls' magazine (*shōjo zasshi*), stressed in 1916 that such preventative measures are actually unnecessary because most intense relationships between girls are harmless.[19] Sexologist Yamamoto Senji reiterated this view in 1924, and criticized educators who confused the immoral practices of male same-sex love by schoolboys, such as masturbation and sodomy, with the harmless "platonic love" practiced by schoolgirls.[20]

Sexologists also explained this love in terms of the human developmental process, highlighting youth as a transitional state of not yet full maturity. Habuto Eiji, in his 1920 classic *Ippan seiyokugaku* (General sexology), explains that adolescence is the "period of nondifferentiation" (*musabetsuki*); both girls and boys experience this time of sexual development as a time of confusion in which it is "completely normal" to manifest a "tendency toward same-sex love." Later on they transition to a "period of differentiation" (*sabetsuki*) in which "sexual desire is turned in the normal direction, toward the opposite sex."[21] In 1935, Yasuda Tokutarō, a medical doctor and sex historian, asserted that same-sex love between female students is normal, because it is "a kind of love play in adolescence, a preparatory stage that leads to future heterosexual love." He notes that many of those who practice such love later enter into normal married life. These adolescent relationships are "platonic, and there is no sexual contact [*nikutaiteki kōshō*] . . . at most, [the girls] caress each other." Although Yasuda admits that it is "difficult to determine, even in scientific terms, what we can gauge as normality and what we can gauge as abnormality," same-sex love in youth seems to have become more or less accepted as part of the normal female growth process.[22]

Sexological discourse was, in a sense, able to legitimize adolescent same-sex love as a kind of rehearsal for entry into adulthood, that is, heterosexuality and motherhood. Although such love among adolescents could be accepted as normal, adult same-sex love was considered an unnatural deviation from the proper trajectory of maturity, a failure to enter correctly into heterosexual normality. In particular, postadolescent *ome* relationships, in which masculine and feminine roles were visibly defined, were considered "abnormal same-sex love" (*hentai dōseiai*).[23] The "abnormal woman" associated with this love was discussed from a variety of perspectives: as a result of the decadent "gender ambivalence" of modernity, as an "invert" born with a congenital inner masculine self, or as a result of parent-child relationships.[24] Jennifer Robertson's work shows that the *ome* relationship was particularly taboo because the cross-gendered masculine female was a threat to social stability, to institutions such as marriage and the family system, and to the integrity of the nation state as a whole.[25] It is also important to recognize that in addition to the visual appearance of cross-gendering, the age of the participants and the context of the practice would have been additional determinants for sexologists trying to decipher the nature of the love relationship. Yasuda, for example, questions the idea that gender-role division in schoolgirl love (the presence of a "male role player" [*otokogata*] and a "female role player" [*onnagata*]) signifies sexual abnormality on the part of masculine girls; he observes that they often transform into unremarkable wives and mothers after graduation.[26] In addition to the presence of masculinity, therefore, factors such as age, the female developmental process, and the context of the love's expression also provided a gauge for sexologists to determine the "truth" about same-sex love.

Obviously such schemas for understanding the normality or abnormality of same-sex love could never be fully adequate; sexological discourse attempted to map out the complex terrain of human emotion, experience, and practice even as they were being newly articulated and perceived within modernity. Girls could potentially be actual "inverts," not going through a temporary phase; older women could maintain their pure, romantic friendships beyond the space of school. In cases of love suicide, even nonsexual romantic friendships could potentially elicit the unnatural behavior of mutual self-destruction. Sexologists, with their rigid framework of gender, often struggled to explain the non-cross-gendered relationship; they also found it difficult to differentiate love from friendship in relationships between girls and women, perceiving them in general to be very intimate in both physical and emotional terms.[27] The complexity involved in correctly interpreting female sexual practice and/or feelings of love reveals the gaps and contradictions within sexology, a discipline that was itself in flux throughout the period. Yet despite such inadequacies and the multiplicity of its "truths," sexology discourse and its attempts to define the normal and abnormal in female same-sex love played a vital role in shaping society's understanding of this form of love. Because the polarities of normality and abnormality in this love were part of a continuum, female-female love always elicited some level of suspicion and anxiety. At the same time, however, sexology and its scientific prerogative could also authorize same-sex love in certain situations, reinforcing its place in the modern landscape. Because the female sex itself was already marked with ambivalence as the Other sex—considered pure and innocent but also associated with sickness (such as menstruation), carnal instincts, and weak morals—the dual "truths" of same-sex love mirrored the difference of this Other sex, providing an important key to understanding modern female identity.

Bluestocking *Discourse*

Not only was 1911 a watershed year for the proliferation of discourses about female same-sex love in the media, but it also witnessed the establishment of the Bluestocking Society. The members, many of whom had been students at Japan Women's University, wrote for *Bluestocking*. Not surprisingly, for some of these New Women, same-sex love was a part of the search for the modern female self. Member Tamura Toshiko (1884–1945), for example, explored such relationships in a number of stories. In 1911, she won the prestigious *Osaka Asahi shinbun* award for *Akirame* (Giving up), a novel about a young female playwright who "gives up" her profession to fulfill family obligations. The protagonist feels attracted to numerous beautiful women and is adored by a younger friend who calls her "elder sister." With her sensual representations of male-female, as well as female-female, relationships, Tamura created a niche for herself in the literary world. Despite her rapid rise to fame during the early 1910s, however, she produced very little fiction after 1915 and emigrated to Canada in 1918 to be with her male lover.[28]

Interestingly, Tamura did not publish works about same-sex love in *Bluestocking*. In fact, despite its reputation as a radical magazine, this journal printed very few narratives about same-sex love; and the few stories about same-sex love that were published in *Bluestocking* express anxiety about the difference between innocent friendships and abnormal relationships. Kawada Yoshi's "Onna tomodachi" (Female friends, 1915), for example, erases the idea of love between two female characters by insisting that what they have is a friendship different from the emotion felt for a real male lover.[29] In another story, "Junjitsu no tomo" (A friend for ten days, 1915), Sugawara Hatsu writes about a brief physical relationship between two women named "P" and "K" who embrace each other and kiss. Yet even while these women conduct this experiment, they joke about whether or not this is same-sex love. It seems that P and K are keenly aware of sexological discourses that mark such physicality between adult women as abnormal. The masculine K, it turns out, has initiated relationships with other women in the past. Although the beautiful and feminine P does not denounce K as a corrupting influence, P is ultimately a detached figure who observes herself "objectively" during this "strange" encounter and later tells her story to the narrator. In the recounting of the tale, K becomes an exotic

and dangerous Other while P remains an innocent, recalling the relationship in sentimental schoolgirl terms.[30]

In the United States, the New Woman who appeared during the late
nineteenth century often chose the so-called Boston marriage, cohabiting
with a female companion and remaining a spinster. She was able to make
this choice because she was no longer obligated to marry once she achieved
economic independence through higher education.[31] In contrast, the Bluestocking women were more focused on realizing romantic love between
men and women, in an effort to move away from traditional marriages and
attain male-female equality.[32] The narratives published in *Bluestocking* rein-
force the bifurcation of "normal" and "abnormal" in same-sex love; this love
is either a normal but inferior copy of "real" heterosexual love, or an odd,
anomalous experience.

This erasure of same-sex love can be observed not only in *Bluestocking*
stories but also in the real-life relationship of Hiratsuka Raichō and Otake
Kōkichi (Tomimoto Kazue). This romance that took place in 1912 was a
public event, discussed in letters and essays published in *Bluestocking*.[33] The
two Bluestocking women candidly wrote about their feelings for each other;
particularly well known is Hiratsuka's autobiographical essay "Marumado
yori: Chigasaki e Chigasaki e (Zatsuroku)" (From the round window: To
Chigasaki, to Chigasaki [Jottings]), which discusses their intense relationship that was full of "embraces and kisses." Although Hiratsuka's relationship
with Otake, whom she called "my boy" (*watashi no shōnen*), seems to have
been a serious one, within several months of meeting Okumura Hiroshi, her
future husband, she distanced herself from Otake and ended the affair. At
the end of 1912, the brokenhearted Otake resigned from the Bluestocking
Society, and married two years later.[34]

After this incident, in *Bluestocking* Hiratsuka portrayed same-sex love in
extremely negative terms. The following year she serialized "Ichinenkan"
(One year), an essay about her "year" with Otake, in which she quotes
from actual letters and even introduces Otake's previous sexual experiences as bizarre and laughable.[35] Hiratsuka's rewriting of her relationship
with Otake as a one-sided, strange devotion on the part of a sick person is
made indisputable through her strategic use of sexology discourse. In 1914
she published "Joseikan no dōsei ren'ai" (Same-sex love between women),
an abridged translation of "Sexual Inversion in Women" from Havelock
Ellis's *Studies in the Psychology of Sex*. Hiratsuka introduces the translation
of Ellis's study with a very personal preface, noting specifically that she be-

came interested in this "odd" phenomenon of same-sex love upon meeting a sexual invert (Otake):

> Although one often hears of this thing called same-sex love being practiced in places like dormitories in girls' schools, I personally had never seen or experienced it, and thus felt half-doubtful that such a thing existed at all. It was difficult for me to find any interest in this phenomenon. However, a woman I met in my recent past—a woman who may be considered a congenital sexual invert [*sententeki no seiteki tentōsha*]—this woman made me very interested in this phenomenon. I spent about a year as the object of this woman's love.[36]

Literary critic Kurosawa Ariko astutely points out that Hiratsuka's usage of sexological terminology ("congenital sexual invert") functions to identify Otake as an abnormal Other, explainable in scientific terms and distinct from Hiratsuka's normality.[37] By identifying Otake as the invert, Hiratsuka is able to present herself as the innocent, unwitting love object. Hiratsuka also relies on the idea that strong attachments between young women are normal, especially when such relationships are transitory and make way for entry into heterosexual maturity. She explains in her 1971 autobiography that she had been "taken by Kōkichi's unique charm," but she never considered her emotions to be "feelings like the so-called same-sex love"; the limits of her feelings, she goes on, "can be seen in the honest fact that my heart subsequently turned toward Okumura."[38] As Gregory Pflugfelder points out, by the time Hiratsuka's memoirs were published in the postwar period, the notion of same-sex love had become further stigmatized.[39] To create a normative identity for herself, Hiratsuka downplays her experience with Otake and reinforces the superiority of the heterosexual love that she discovered with Okumura.

Hiratsuka's meeting with Okumura and her abandonment of same-sex love coincided with her interest in Ellen Key's writing. In 1912 she learned about Key's theories of love, and as noted in Chapter One she published Japanese translations of *Love and Marriage* in *Bluestocking* from 1913 to 1914. Key's work lacks any discussion of same-sex love and emphasizes only the importance of heterosexual love and marriage. For Hiratsuka, modern love ideology and sexology discourse justify her rejection of same-sex love. Such love is an inferior play, a copy of real (heterosexual) love, easily dismissed once the female matures. If it persists, it is an abnormality experienced only by deviants and inverts. Hiratsuka's erasure or rewriting of same-sex love represents the general treatment this love receives in *Bluestocking*. Experience of such female intimacy was permissible as long as it was contained within youth, but any further exploration was taboo. Even if a same-sex relationship had an enormous impact on one's life, it had to be abandoned in the course of becoming a "real" woman who followed the correct path of female development.

Girls' Culture and Yoshiya Nobuko

Although Hiratsuka's attitudes toward same-sex love remained negative after 1912, Yoshiya Nobuko, who shared a similar education in both sexology and women's issues, took a completely different approach. Yoshiya was a *Bluestocking* contributor who published a poem and a short story in the last two issues of the journal in 1916.[40] She also belonged to the same reading group as Hiratsuka, where both women studied the English edition of *Love and Marriage* under the tutelage of Yamada Kakichi (1865–1934) and his wife, Waka (1879–1957), Christian-feminist activists who taught many members of the Bluestocking Society.[41] In contrast to Hiratsuka's writing, *Bluestocking* fiction, and Tamura Toshiko's stories of same-sex love, Yoshiya's works employ a unique outlook, strategically highlighting same-sex love as a primary, powerful source of female identity.

During the prewar period, girls' magazines and girls' fiction played a major role in the creation and dissemination of girls' culture. Although many fads and trends for young women developed within higher girls' schools, magazines and stories targeted at girls in this age range reached a wider audience in terms of class and geography—well beyond the limited number of girls who actually attended such schools. The first girls' magazine, *Shōjokai* (Girls' realm), was published in 1902.[42] By 1914 journalist Matsuzaki Tenmin could list at least four magazines with "*shōjo*" (girl) in the title; he explained that they were read mainly by twelve- to seventeen-year-olds.[43] These magazines targeted a mainstream, popular audience and were not considered radical or intellectual-minded like *Bluestocking*. By creating a female-centered literary culture, however, they did achieve one of the goals of the Bluestocking Society and the early feminist movement. Not only did the magazines cultivate girl readers, but they also established a kind of girls' community by publishing essays, poems, and stories written by their subscribers. Through readers' columns, girls could also correspond with editors and other readers / writers.[44] A vibrant girls' culture developed around girls' magazines and fiction and, particularly with the success of Yoshiya's stories, they became important venues in which to explore same-sex love.

Only a few months after publishing in *Bluestocking*'s last issue, Yoshiya started to serialize *Hanamonogatari* (Flower tales) in the girls' magazine *Shōjo gahō* (Girls' graphic). As a former amateur contributor to media targeting girls, Yoshiya strategically employed themes and language that appealed to her audience.[45] *Flower Tales*, a series of short stories, set the standard for girls' fiction by creating a unique same-sex world. In addition to sexology and *Bluestocking* discourse, the girls' fiction genre shaped the understanding of same-sex love and its meaning for female identity from the 1910s onward. In the next chapter, I begin with a discussion of *Flower Tales* and then show how Yoshiya's usage of same-sex love evolved through various literary genres and historical contexts. Strategically using the notions of "normality" and "abnormality," Yoshiya transformed the meaning of this love and rewrote modern love ideology.

THREE

Yoshiya Nobuko
and the Romance of Sisterhood

Introduction

Yoshiya Nobuko was one of the most successful writers of popular literature in twentieth-century Japan. In 1916, at the age of twenty, she began serializing *Flower Tales*, and in 1920 she made her debut as a novelist. During the 1920s and 1930s she wrote for major newspapers and popular women's magazines, and by the late 1930s she was one of the wealthiest people in Japan, with an annual income several times that of ministers of state.[1] Her works were adapted into successful films, plays, radio dramas, and later TV programs. During the postwar years she was especially known for her historical fiction, and she remained prolific until her death in 1973 at the age of seventy-seven.[2] The recent growth of interest in popular culture in Japan has contributed to the rediscovery of Yoshiya as an author who developed the genre of girls' fiction and brought a feminist perspective to the popular family romance. She has received the most attention, however, as a writer of stories about same-sex love. Much of Yoshiya's fiction features girls and women who are strongly attached to each other, valuing above all else their love and sisterhood.

Although Yoshiya herself was never "out" in the current sense, for forty-seven years she lived openly with her lifelong female partner (and legal heir), Monma Chiyo. As a result, Yoshiya's stories of same-sex love are often considered simply an extension of her own life and sexuality or an example of non-Western lesbian literature. To appreciate fully the depth and complexity of Yoshiya's works, however, it is crucial to recognize that they are constructed through an intricate negotiation with then contemporary ideas about same-sex love. Yoshiya makes same-sex love into an integral component of female growth and self-completion, reinventing this love in light of modern love ideology. Through her vastly popular works she transforms girl, virgin, and woman into identities vital to the prewar cultural imagination.

Flower Tales: *Girls and Adolescent Love*

In 1917, romantic poet Yosano Akiko reminisced about her personal experience of adolescent same-sex love: "I strongly believe that same-sex love between schoolgirls should not be considered a case of abnormal sexual desire [*hentai seiyoku*], but I also know that same-sex love is accompanied by a strong emotional attachment even more powerful than the love [*ren'ai*] between men and women." Looking back at her love for a schoolmate that lasted from age fifteen to seventeen, Yosano expresses amazement at the extent of her passion.[3] Yoshiya Nobuko, in developing her girls' fiction, highlights this mysterious, powerful love as a valuable part of girlhood and a definitive aspect of female identity.

Yoshiya's most famous work, *Flower Tales*, is a collection of fifty-two short stories featuring just such romantic friendships. Initially serialized, as noted in the previous chapter, in the girls' magazine *Girls' Graphic*, these stories were subsequently published in book format and remained bestsellers throughout the prewar period.[4] The genre of girls' fiction was created in 1897, initially in the form of didactic stories for girls that taught them to be obedient, to be virtuous, and to contain themselves within the domestic sphere.[5] Popular plotlines for this genre fluctuated over time, but girlhood friendships eventually emerged as an important theme. Building on such girls' fiction from the late Meiji and early Taishō periods, *Flower Tales* transformed the genre, promoting female-female love as a fundamental aspect of girlhood.[6] Although ignored by literary critics as inconsequential reading material for "women and children" (*onna kodomo*), Yoshiya's stories were some of the most important cultural products of the prewar period, form-ing ideas of female youth, romance, and love.

Although the stories in *Flower Tales* are certainly not uniform, they are predominantly sentimental tales about same-sex love, often set in higher girls' schools. A typical plot features a student's crush on another student or teacher; the focus is on unrequited love or the sad ending of a relationship. Each story uses a specific type of flower as its title, main imagery, and plot device. For example, in "Shirayuri" (White lily), a story in which students have a crush on a female music teacher, the flower, and the purity and in-nocence conventionally associated with it, becomes a symbol for the teacher and her nurturing relationship with students. The wisdom that she imparts to her pupils is the importance of "the unchanging purity [*junketsu*] of the soul."[7] In *Flower Tales*, the girls' innocent emotions are highlighted, and relationships are presented in terms of distance rather than intimacy; for the most part the girls express their love through admiration from afar. This pat-tern of romanticizing distance (such as age difference, noncommunication, unrequited love) can also be found in the expression of late nineteenth- and early twentieth-century schoolgirl love in the West. As historian Martha Vicinus explains, distance was fulfilling because it heightened the sense of purity and idealism associated with this love, in contrast to undisciplined physical pleasure.[8]

As a pure, innocent love manifested only in the terminal world of school and youth, same-sex love can be celebrated openly in *Flower Tales*. By stress-ing the normality of this love, Yoshiya argues for its value. In a 1923 essay titled "Dōsei o aisuru saiwai" (The happiness of loving one of the same sex), she suggests that it is an invaluable experience that enables proper female development:

> At this time, the girl experiences an extremely close romantic friendship [*yūai*] during her schooldays, and this develops into a huge force. . . . What a pure and dear episode this is in a girl's life! . . . When this romantic friend-ship occurs between an older girl and a younger one, or between a teacher and her student, it is extremely positive in terms of educational value, and its worth is immeasurable. . . .
>
> Oh, even such a pure romantic friendship as this, bubbling forth from the beautiful, pearl-like fountain of humanity, is criticized by female educators and moralists of society as unnatural or the early signs of corruption. . . .
>
> As a result, the girls begin to doubt their feelings of love [*aijō*] and kill the beautiful, kind nature that God has given them. What a sad thing this is. This is why when they grow up and become members of society they do not

comprehend the serious meaning of "love" [*ai*] and are easily led astray by unworthy, cheap love [*ren'ai*].

Love [*ai*] must be treated as the most important, serious, profound act in life. No matter what, one must allow burgeoning love to be brought to its full growth [*kanzen na seichō*].

Yoshiya defends same-sex love by insisting that it is part of a broader notion of love, a virtue she calls "Evolution Power," using these very words in English. Female-female romance in youth should not cause educators to worry, because it is part of a greater trajectory of love. In fact, in order to discern true love in the future, to avoid being led astray by false men and their shallow promises of romantic love, all girls should experience same-sex romance. Such a relationship is crucial because "love's growth and structure" are valuable in the "building of character [*jinkaku*]."[9] In positing this view that romantic friendship is a requirement for successful human development and an important component of adolescent education, Yoshiya reiterates the opinions expressed by Edward Carpenter in a chapter of *The Intermediate Sex*. In another, much shorter version of the essay, Yoshiya mentions Carpenter's name specifically and attributes these ideas to him, perhaps intending to bolster the legitimacy of her argument by invoking an authoritative figure.[10]

By strategically stressing the idea that love changes in form along with a girl's growth, Yoshiya validates same-sex love as a required prelude for proper entry into heterosexuality. Just as pure love and carnal love are often discussed in terms of sexual difference (with females associated with spiritual love and males associated with physical love), same-sex love becomes, through this logic, a part of female virtue and even a manifestation of spirituality and innocence.[11] It is not simply to be tolerated (even if considered "normal") but to be understood as absolutely necessary. By praising same-sex love in this way, Yoshiya is also validating her own stories about girlhood romance. These tales should not be dismissed as adolescent foolishness but rather valued as a celebration of love needed for this stage of female growth.[12] *Flower Tales*, she explains, is a "bouquet," a special, romantic gift from the author to her readers that endorses their experiences as girls. The dedication of the collection reads, "The many flowers that bloom / in the dream of a young girl's days / that will never return, / these I send to you, my beloveds" (5).

By arguing that girlhood same-sex love is a manifestation of preheterosexual innocence, however, Yoshiya is not accepting the notion that it is an inferior copy of "real" (heterosexual) love. She imbues this love with so much worth that it becomes far superior to any other form of love to come in the girl's future. In *Flower Tales*, therefore, same-sex love is a unique aspect of girlhood, to be cherished; it is also an impending loss to be continuously mourned. *Flower Tales* has been called a work heralding the "birth of the 'girl' within Japanese modernity."[13] Certainly it made the constant longing for girlhood and the fear for its loss a quintessential part of female identity. The same-sex romance in these stories is heightened by motifs of illness and tragedy; love is often unrequited, and even when it is reciprocated, the relationship is terminated due to a change of heart, separation, disease, or death. The girls in *Flower Tales* are extremely melancholy, overwhelmed with tears; they are nostalgic, not only for the past but also already for their own girlhood that will inevitably come to an end. They constantly lament the loss of the same-sex world; as a character from the tale "Shiro mokuren" (White magnolia) laments after graduating from higher girls' school, "I was happiest when I was in school—having entered the real world, there is nothing but loneliness⋯⋯"(321).[14]

These dysphoric stories, on the one hand, accept same-sex love as a fleeting experience that must be contained within youth. They resonate with Terry Castle's description of the Western lesbian novel of adolescence: "To the extent that it depicts female homosexual desire as a finite phenomenon—a temporary phase in a larger pattern of heterosexual *Bildung*—the lesbian novel of adolescence is almost always dysphoric in tendency."[15] Contemporary educators and sexologists characterized girlhood, especially adolescence, as a period of danger; because of their physical and emotional development, such as menarche, girls were considered to be particularly prone to illnesses such as tuberculosis, hysteria, and depression.[16] By combining the notion of a terminal girlhood love with this understanding of adolescence, *Flower Tales* imbues same-sex relationships with tragic melodrama; the girls' overflowing tears reify society's view that such excessive bursts of sentimentality represent nothing more than an ephemeral feeling within a specific developmental period. On the other hand, these depictions of same-sex love are truly terminal in the sense that the characters rarely grow up in these stories. They are resistant figures who refuse to move on to heterosexuality; they reject society's demands for girls to mature into compliant, heterosexual Good Wives, Wise Mothers.[17]

Flower Tales makes use of mainstream assumptions about "normal" same-sex love while resisting simplistic notions of purity, innocence, and the transitory relationship. By reiterating acceptable views of sentimental friendship, these stories could be published en masse by publishers eager to supply girl readers, a newly emergent consumer base for age- and gender-specific fiction. At the same time, however, *Flower Tales* opens up resistant modes of interpretation, allowing readers to see same-sex love and girlhood in new ways, and to question compulsory heterosexual development and ideas about female youth. In other words, *Flower Tales* enriches the adolescent female-female romance with layers of meaning, portraying it as a pure, positive experience necessary to achieve a modern female identity, but also as a subversive space that articulates difference.

The narrative content (*histoire*) of these stories offers possibilities for resistance, not only through the girls' nostalgia for their youth and their refusal to grow up, but also through the tragedies (death, suicide, disease) that are repeated in every story. This excessive dysphoria can be considered, through the lens of Homi Bhabha's theorization of melancholia, not as passivity (or internal prohibition) but as resistance through repetition for subaltern voices.[18] The recurring tragic drama of "normal" same-sex love, repeated with each serial and reprint edition of *Flower Tales*, underscores the subversive aspects of girlhood and highlights the oppressive nature of a society that demands compliance through heterosexual maturity. This repetition transforms same-sex love beyond a temporary phase and redefines it as a key aspect of female identity. These stories enable girls and women to explore alternative ways of understanding such relationships without overtly transgressing the boundaries of social acceptability.

Through literary style (*discours*) as well as narrative content, the stories in *Flower Tales* depict purity and innocence while interrogating these very notions. The literary style that Yoshiya employs is known for its dense, baroque imagery and experimental construction linked with modern textual symbols such as "—," "……," "( )," "!," and "?" It is a kind of hybrid writing, freely mixing *genbun-itchi tai* (unified spoken and written language style), *bibunchō* (ornate style), and English to create a distinct writing style that even today is immediately identified with Yoshiya's girls' fiction. Although this decorative, fluid style had already been used by girls who wrote in girls' magazines of the 1900s and 1910s, Yoshiya further developed it as a distinct kind of girls' writing style.[19]

Textual symbols—in particular the dashes and six-dot ellipses—are liberally used in both description and dialogue in *Flower Tales*. Here is a sample description from "Hamanadeshiko" (Japanese pink) in which Sakiko plays the *koto*, a stringed instrument, with picks made from pink shells. The picks were a present from Masumi, a girl who was in love with Sakiko and now appears as a ghost after having committed suicide:

> A small star fell at a slant⋯⋯the moment the autumn evening wind blew in, suddenly turning out the sleeves of the beautiful child at the *koto*⋯⋯blossoms of Japanese pink scattered on the thirteen strings⋯⋯a far-off sound of the waves was heard⋯⋯Sakiko's white fingertips wavered in their movement⋯⋯how strange that her hands held petals of Japanese pinks as she played⋯⋯she could not tell which were petals⋯⋯in the front of the garden, in the soft night wind of autumn, black hair wet with dew, a standing shadowy figure—it was Masumi, the one who had given her the pink shells—Sakiko's fingers left the instrument—Masumi—she called loudly the name of that shadowy figure—. (218)

Next is an example of the use of these symbols in dialogue, from a scene in "Kibara" (Yellow rose), in which Miss Katsuragi tells her student Reiko about her admiration for the poet Sappho:

> "Miss Reiko, Sappho was a person who gave her passionate devotion to a beautiful friend of the same sex and was betrayed . . . she loved her maid Melitta deeply—but she was betrayed by this girl, Melitta too—she took her sad heart, broken from fruitless offerings of passionate devotion, threw herself into the blue ocean from the Leucadian Rock, and disappeared amid the waves—Sappho, the tragic female poet—I, I love her—."
>
> Miss Katsuragi, speaking thus, had tears shining in her eyes, full of dark passion⋯⋯
>
> "⋯⋯Miss Katsuragi! ⋯⋯" Reiko's faint voice shook, barely managing to speak these words with her quaking red lips like petals.
>
> At that moment—a bell rang out, reverberating for a long while—enfolded by the sound, the two shadows became one—(228–229)

Such use of ellipses and dashes in *Flower Tales* has been read by Hiromi Tsuchiya Dollase through the work of Julia Kristeva as a kind of *écriture feminine*.[20] In another reading, Honda Masuko has analyzed this style as a representation of girls' creative skills in the making of chains (with flowers, shells, beads, and yarn); in her view, this form is purely decorative, without meaning in terms of content.[21] It is important to recognize, however, that these symbols were actually first used by proponents of the *genbun-itchi* movement, the literati whose goal was to reproduce actual speech or thought in their writing. These authors used such visual markers to, for example, show a break or shift in the flow of articulation or internal monologue.[22] Yamada Bimyō (1868–1910), one such author closely associated with the use of new punctuation, was criticized as early as 1890 for overusing such "mechanicals" (*kikai*) as "?," "!," "……," "—," and "( )."[23] In examining these symbols, we should note the critical distinction that Suga Hidemi makes between "……" or "—" and other kinds of punctuation marks, such as the Japanese versions of the comma, period, and quotation mark, which were not yet standardized during the 1890s. Suga argues that although the comma, period, and quotation mark functioned as "logical" reading guides, the use of "……" and "—" to replicate actual thought and speech could be criticized because these marks often ended up having the opposite effect, that is, distorting the flow of the narrative and underscoring the artificiality of the text.[24] Even in these early literary uses of "……" and "—," there is (unwittingly or not) a sense of the inadequacy of language to express the "real"; the symbols on the page highlight the fact that there is always something that cannot be represented.

Gilles Deleuze's notion of "stuttering" language, a narrative that embodies the "silence," "*the outside* of language," is particularly useful in considering the use of such textual symbols in *Flower Tales*. A narrative that stutters is one that is able to place language "in perpetual disequilibrium," to create "a foreign language within language" through "a syntax in the process of becoming." This language self-reflexively presents itself as being inadequate, but it has the greatest capacity for signification compared to a perfectly ordered sentence because it can, paradoxically, articulate what it cannot say.[25] This theoretical concept of stuttering illuminates the textual form of *Flower Tales* as an encoding of girlhood and same-sex love. The narrative linking that occurs through the use of "……" and "—" connotes girlhood, a special space that is circular, closed, and separate from the heterosexual world. At the same time, however, the broken-off words and phrases ending in six-dot ellipses and dashes (in contrast to the full, grammatically stable sentence) imply incompleteness; the girls in these stories have not fully matured and are not yet complete vis-à-vis the trajectory of female growth. The open-endedness of the sentences reinforces the idea that the love here is as temporary, as unfinished, as girlhood itself, while simultaneously underscoring syntax as a coming-into-existence, suggesting multiple possibilities for interpreting girlhood love.

This expansion of meaning through textual stuttering also allows for the signification of silences, what cannot be said about this love. In the "Yellow Rose" excerpt quoted earlier, for example, the teacher explains her love for Sappho, but the six-dot ellipses and dashes suggest that the two female characters are actually talking about their love for one another, encoding an unspeakable emotion into the silences and spaces between the actual spoken words. Although their love (as articulated) is "normal," innocent, and pure, the evocative textual symbols also open the possibility for something beyond romantic friendship. While showing the incompleteness of these girls and their "temporary" love, these symbols inscribe the gaps in the fabric of the narrative; by allowing meaningful silence to break through the unblemished veneer of what is actually uttered, these textual symbols challenge readers to read beyond the surface of the text.

In both narrative content and writing style, *Flower Tales* simultaneously uses and challenges contemporary ideas about same-sex love in youth, creating a subversive space that offers multiple ways of reading this love. By highlighting girlhood as a temporary stage, *Flower Tales* reiterates the view that adolescent same-sex love is "normal" but transitory, a beautiful experience that blossoms only for a limited period. This bestselling work promotes purity and innocence, but it also uses nostalgia, melancholia, and stuttering syntax to suggest alternate ways of interpreting same-sex love, as something that endures beyond the confines of school and girlhood. By highlighting the importance of same-sex love, Yoshiya eventually suggests an alternative trajectory of female development. Just as legitimate as the trajectory endorsed by modern love ideology but without requiring male participation, this process of growth is the subject of her first novel, *Yaneura no nishojo* (Two virgins in the attic, 1920).

Two Virgins in the Attic: *Alternative Adulthood*

> Let the girl stay in her world of dreams, her gentle spirit sleeping for as long as possible. Once this spirit has developed to its fullest in this world, she will leave in beauty, like a butterfly shedding its chrysalis. . . .
>
> Of course, with the growth of her emotions, the girl will no longer be allowed to live in this sweet, soft world of shadows. . . . Descending from the light pink tower of dreams, girls are awakened by the coldness of their bare feet on the ground. They will find their selfhood [*jiga*] within themselves. . . .
>
> Selfhood—the world will now be restructured around this new discovery. . . . Selfhood becomes the fountain of all creation and worth. . . . The establishment of this selfhood, its growth and development, is the one true task given to humans in their lives.[26]

In this 1925 essay, we can see Yoshiya's vision of female growth: the girl awakens from the same-sex dreamworld to enter adulthood, a world that requires the development of selfhood. The Western fairytale trope of descending the tower often symbolizes entry into heterosexuality, but here Yoshiya emphasizes instead the girl's self-discovery. *Two Virgins in the Attic* dramatizes this awakening; the protagonist, Takimoto Akiko, finds her sense of self not by a prince's kiss but through love for another woman, her dorm mate, Akitsu Tamaki.

Yoshiya published *Two Virgins in the Attic* in 1920 as her first full-length novel in book form. Based on her own experiences living in the Tokyo YWCA dormitory as she trained to become a kindergarten teacher, this work has been interpreted as an I-novel as well as a "lesbian-feminist novel."[27] Yoshiya explains that she wrote the work in response to "an inner desire unable to be suppressed," a feeling that emerged when "*Flower Tales* was not enough to satisfy." She was prepared to publish it "even if it meant paying for it myself."[28] She did not have to resort to such measures, because she won the *Osaka Asahi shinbun* award for another novel, *Chi no hate made* (To the ends of the earth, 1920). This important prize sponsored by the nationally circulating newspaper *Osaka Asahi shinbun* was considered the stamp of approval by the literary establishment. This success enabled Yoshiya not only to receive royalties for *Two Virgins in the Attic* but also to break into adult fiction.[29]

Yoshiya continued to write girls' fiction throughout the prewar period, but *Two Virgins in the Attic* departs from the formulaic pattern of girlhood romance. Because this novel employs girls' writing style, it is often seen as part of the girls' fiction genre.[30] I would argue, however, that this text is a new endeavor for Yoshiya; she strategically uses the idea of girlhood (in terms of both *histoire* and *discours*) to create new possibilities for female development and same-sex love in the transitional stage between adolescence and full maturity. *Two Virgins in the Attic* makes the subtle message in *Flower Tales* explicit; in this text, same-sex love is an amalgamation of spiritual and sexual love that can continue into adulthood, leading to self-discovery and completion. Yoshiya openly challenges the conventional trajectory of growth by rewriting modern love ideology.

Akiko, a higher girls' school graduate, is attending a teachers' school, and Miss Akitsu (*Akitsu san*) is also a student at an advanced institution.[31] The text specifically describes Akiko as a young woman, older than a girl.[32] Despite her age, however, Akiko has no direction in life and needs to grow up and find herself; an unhappy, childlike person, she is portrayed negatively, as an individual lacking a "vital nail" (*kaname no kugi*), like a structure in danger of collapsing (409). Because Akiko is an orphan, her education is critical to her ability to support herself in the future, but she is unsuited for academics and has been a disappointment to her teachers and relatives. She is enrolled in a training school for kindergarten teachers but hates the rigorous environment and the difficult curriculum that is based on the latest Western theories in child development. It is ironic that Akiko is studying this subject, because she herself is an immature character, constantly in tears, melancholic, and nostalgic for the past. She is also incapable of talking to people, finds it difficult to eat, and at one point fails even to extinguish a dangerous fire in her room. As a tearful, passive character who cries over "the days that will never return" (368), Akiko is a typical "girl," familiar to readers of *Flower Tales*.

Her tendency to daydream is an additional sign of girlhood and alludes to Frances Hodgson Burnett's (1849–1924) *A Little Princess* (1905), known to Japanese readers as *Shōkōjo*. In the first part of *Two Virgins in the Attic*, Akiko spends a great deal of time daydreaming on the top floor of the "YWA" dormitory, in her "ATTIC" room, a place that allows her to escape the realities of life.[33] This portrayal of Akiko echoes that of Sara Crewe, the heroine of *A Little Princess*, who attends a boarding school, becomes orphaned and penniless, and is sent to live in the attic as a servant. It is her imagination nurtured in the attic that allows Sara to survive and to maintain her self-identity as a "little princess" regardless of her altered circumstances. This girls' fiction was extremely popular in Japan, as evidenced by its numerous different translations and imprints.[34] Yoshiya herself notes that during her girlhood years, she considered Burnett, along with Louisa May Alcott, her "ideal woman."[35]

These echoes of *A Little Princess* in *Two Virgins in the Attic* pay homage to Burnett and identify Akiko as someone who (despite her actual age) acts like a quintessential girl. Imagination was considered a central part of girlhood and girls' culture. Although youth in general is commonly associated with a dreamy escape from reality, gender roles in the early twentieth century made it easier for boys to be depicted as physically active in their growth process, while girls were expected to be passive and withdrawn. Boys, it was assumed, would gain experience by actively exploring the world at large, while girls' limited sphere of existence discouraged them from gaining such first-hand knowledge. Girls' magazines and girls' fiction enabled girls who were encouraged to stay rooted within the home to expand their imaginations and to read and write about things unrelated to their own experiences.[36]

For Akiko, the "ATTIC" is a sanctuary that allows her to dream; it is an exotic non-Japanese space, triangular in shape, with blue walls and laden with cut *tatami* mats that look like a "rough carpet woven with grass and hide . . . used by natives in the southern islands" (376). In this space, separate from the everyday world, Akiko becomes increasingly fascinated by Miss Akitsu, who lives in the adjoining room. Akiko is attracted to a beautiful yet emotionally distant object of love in a typical adolescent pattern of same-sex love; she is the classic figure of the younger girl who adores her older lover from afar. The love Akiko feels is like that found in many *Flower Tales* stories in which the admirer cannot express her feelings directly but exhibits overwhelming symptoms of lovesickness.

Akiko's "girlness" is marked not only by melancholy, imagination, and the same-sex love presented in the narrative, but also through the language of the text. *Two Virgins in the Attic* is Yoshiya's only full-length novel to employ extensively the kind of girls' writing style found in *Flower Tales*. Here is a balcony scene in which the two women are drying their hair in the night air. The narrative style highlights the melodrama:

> . . . the ocean—the ocean of evening—and the sound echoing from afar is the melody of the night ocean inviting melancholy upon the sea-wandering sailor—or is it the echo of waves, the sound of the breaking tide—
> Akiko felt that she herself was now on the deck of a ship, being showered with moonlight as it traversed the dark ocean of night— . . .
> Miss Akitsu placed on her palm a small glass bottle filled with amber liquid, and squeezed the rubber globe at the mouth of the bottle, releasing a mist of fragrance into the air······she perfumed Akiko's hair with the mist······in the moonlight, the mist of perfume took on faint colors of the rainbow and disappeared behind the two maidens' hair······ (430)

The sense of protraction and circularity conveyed by the dashes and the six-dot ellipses textually reproduces Akiko's stay in the world of dreams; the incompleteness of the sentences suggests that she is still in the process of growing up and finding her true self. While underscoring Akiko's love as the pure love of girlhood, this textual encoding simultaneously raises the question of Akiko's development—when will she awaken and accept the normative life course of heterosexuality and marriage? On the one hand, the silences that the narrative creates through its "stuttering" suggest distance and melancholy. Akiko is unable to say "that one sentence, 'I long for you,'" and repeatedly writes Miss Akitsu's name on the attic walls with her tears: "Alas, no matter how many times she wrote out the letters with her finger, they had no way of leaving a trace, and disappeared fleetingly" (436). On the other hand, these silences also imply the taboo element of this love, a permanent, adult love that refuses to be terminated.[37]

Akiko's thoughts about normative adult life are extremely negative; she associates this world with the scenes of violence she witnesses daily on her way to school, scenes of men and boys laughing and pushing women and children off crowded trains to make room for themselves. These scenes disturb her so much that she changes her daily commute, walking part of the way rather than taking the train. That is, she chooses to go her own way, symbolically refusing to follow the path laid out for her. After Akiko realizes that she loves Miss Akitsu, the language describing her feelings shifts, articulating the forbidden nature of this desire. Her longing is described as "a secret and maddening desire" and "a crippled love" (*katawa no ai*) (431). Referring to her love in this way is a form of self-denigration, but it also suggests that Akiko needs to be made whole through the reciprocation of this love. The silence, or the missing thing, is no longer just girlish infatuation but is a matter of serious consequence, involving bodies and physical desire.

Akiko is ultimately able to break out of the girlish association of same-sex love when she publicly rejects her belief in God. The novel explains that Akiko grew up in a Baptist household, but even as a child she had an aversion to gloomy images of Christ and was severely scolded for replacing his picture with that of a young female dancer. Although Yoshiya herself was not a Christian, she often used Christian motifs (churches, nuns, missionaries, the Virgin, and Christian schools) in her girls' fiction to provide an exotic, Westernized flavor and to highlight the pure, innocent nature of girls and girlhood.[38] In such a context, there is no evident conflict between the girls' love for each other and Christianity; but as suggested by the lack of a *C* in YWA, *Two Virgins in the Attic* sets same-sex love in direct opposition to this religion. Akiko must overcome Christian teachings and its practice in the dormitory in order to acknowledge her true self. She admires Miss Akitsu, who openly rebels, refusing to attend church or to keep the Sabbath. It is only when Akiko is able to renounce her faith that she finally achieves the ability to "speak," to choose Miss Akitsu (and forbidden same-sex love) over the figure of Christ.

During the Sunday night meetings, the lodgers are expected to discuss individually their efforts to strengthen their belief in God, but when Akiko's turn comes, she "stutters," blurting out her disbelief: "I—I—if I see—

God—in front of my eyes—for certain—I will believe immediately—"
(444). This outburst prompts laughter from others, who consider her childish and immature, but Miss Akitsu, "an assertive, powerful, beautiful her-
etic," is moved by her honesty and after the meeting embraces Akiko with
passion:

> ⋯⋯A warm body closely approached Akiko from behind⋯⋯a gen-
> tle, supple arm tightly grasped Akiko's shivering shoulders with a soft,
> quick passion⋯⋯sharp, excited breaths touched Akiko's cheeks in
> waves⋯⋯fragments of words arose and were gasped forth, shivering, halting,
> full of gaps⋯⋯
> "You⋯⋯you are⋯⋯what⋯⋯a pure and honest⋯⋯person⋯⋯you
> are⋯⋯"
> ⋯⋯Akiko felt her forehead burn⋯⋯hot, fragrant lips were pressed to
> Akiko's forehead covered by her hair, kisses wet with tears⋯⋯ (448)

The "stuttering" speaks of the unspeakable aspect of this love, but once
Akiko's feelings are reciprocated, the pattern of distance disappears; she
ceases to be the melancholy admirer whose love remains unfulfilled. The
women begin sharing their rooms, making one the bedroom, the other
the study. In portraying this "adult" same-sex love, the text makes a point
of underscoring its sexual aspect. The description of the lovers sharing a
bed uses girls' writing style to evoke the romance associated with girlhood,
while simultaneously conveying the "silence" of its erotic content:

> ⋯⋯Miss Akitsu's linen nightgown had a faint fragrance like magnol-
> ias⋯⋯eventually, this fragrance transferred itself to the sleeves of Akiko's flan-
> nel nightwear⋯⋯thus in the night, the bed fragrant with a scent reminiscent
> of magnolias⋯⋯their arms were entwined⋯⋯their breasts enfolding softly
> beating hearts also pressed close⋯⋯as if their souls disappeared together into
> a sweet dream with no beginning or end⋯⋯soft, supple touches⋯⋯kisses
> like dewy, red petals that tremble and melt together⋯⋯slow undulating
> waves that softly and gently flow, sink and float, disappear, melt together
> and overflow⋯⋯. (451)

Two Virgins in the Attic is distinct from girls' fiction in its emphasis on
the physical dimensions of same-sex love. Rather than graduating from a
platonic, same-sex love to achieve heterosexual maturity, Akiko and Miss
Akitsu experience sensuality. By writing such an unacceptable scene of
adult love in the acceptable language of girls' writing, Yoshiya avoids censure and rejects the view that such love is "abnormal." This approach can

be interpreted as a result of the lack of stylistic tradition for depicting love scenes between females, but it is also a strategic choice, invoking the purity associated with *Flower Tales* to claim legitimacy for their love. The narrative shows the merging of innocent spiritual love and physical sexual love, a powerful reframing of same-sex love through modern love ideology.

As if to emphasize Akiko's development and discovery of identity through this love, the motifs and language of the text change after the two characters begin to live together. Tears, melancholy, nostalgia, and imagination decrease as motifs, and the narrative style shifts to a more standard, dialogue-centered form. Akiko becomes capable of expressing herself more clearly; she is more active, interacts with other people, and leaves her attic room to explore the city. By attaining a fulfilling love that is not limited to girlhood, Akiko is able to mature and gain self-knowledge. This positive presentation of adult same-sex love directly challenges the mainstream idea that such practice, often found in groups of females living and working together, can only be detrimental to one's physical and mental health.[39]

In *Two Virgins in the Attic* it is the *failure* of same-sex love to be realized that leads to pain and even violence. Akiko experiences a crisis when Ban Kinu, Miss Akitsu's former schoolmate who is now unhappily married, begins to visit and send telegrams and letters to Miss Akitsu. Akiko becomes dissatisfied and jealous because Miss Akitsu does not explain the nature of this relationship. In contrast to Kinu, who constantly sends missives, Akiko is still unable to vocalize directly or write out "I love you" (*Anata o aishimasu*, 480). In struggling to articulate her desperation at the imagined loss of her lover, Akiko becomes violent; she strikes another student for entering her room and even hits Miss Akitsu in an act of silent pleading ("Please think of me again—I cannot live without you—," 505).

The novel suggests that it is not same-sex love *per se* that is dangerous. Rather, the danger lies in the inability of this love to be fully realized, sustained, and articulated; the danger is the continued silence. When she believes her love is lost, Akiko regresses, acting much like her old inarticulate and childish self. Although she manages to graduate, she spends every day alone in her room, staring into empty space. In the end, the love triangle is resolved when Akiko is dismissed from the dormitory because of her violent actions, and the two lovers begin to communicate and acknowledge their desire to continue living together in the world outside the attic rooms.

In the final scene, it is revealed that Kinu, disillusioned by marriage, had been asking Miss Akitsu to commit love suicide with her, but Miss Akitsu had refused this request because she was in love with Akiko. Instead of choosing death, a destructive resolution for same-sex love, Akiko and Miss Akitsu choose a path that is neither deadly nor debilitating but that allows them to grow and find their true selves:

> Was Akiko able to have such a thing as "selfhood" [*jiga*]—did she have such a thing? . . .
> Her heart's vital nail was not missing at all. Was she not a girl with a "selfhood" more reckless than others, a strong, persistent "selfhood"? . . .
> "Can there be life as individuals without selfhood?—No, there cannot—," Miss Akitsu proclaimed. "Miss Takimoto, the two of us must become strong women. If they want us to leave the attic, we should leave today or tomorrow. There are other places the two of us can go. . . . From now, let us live as strong people, making this place our starting point. What does it matter if we go against society or morals? The way we choose to live our lives is for us to decide. There must be a way that we can follow. Let us find our destinies together, a path that only the two of us will follow—from now—" (511)

Their self-discovery and the love they acknowledge for each other go hand in hand. This awakening enables the two women to leave the attic with confidence, and the novel concludes on a hopeful and positive note:

> (Our attic)
> Farewell! . . .
> The attic that became a blue cradle that nurtured the (fate) of the two maidens!
> Farewell—
>
> Thus—the two virgins, Akitsu Tamaki and Takimoto Akiko, left together, leaving a goodbye kiss on the attic's blue wall.
> Pursuing their new fate!
> Searching for their path to follow! (512)[40]

Two Virgins in the Attic portrays same-sex love as an integral aspect of self-discovery and progress, not as something transitory, platonic, distant, or dangerous. This is a radical characterization of same-sex love that had not been attempted in sexology, feminist writing, or girls' fiction. As a spiritual and sexual experience integral to one's identity, this love becomes a legitimate equivalent of the heterosexual love so praised by modern love ideology.

Becoming a Virgin: Rewriting Female Development

The link between *Two Virgins in the Attic* and the Bluestocking Society has been illuminated by the work of critic Yoshikawa Toyoko, who interprets this novel as a *roman à clef*. She suggests that the clique to which Akiko and Miss Akitsu belong, called the "female society of the Black Hand" ("Black Hand" *no onna kessha*, 464), evokes the Bluestocking Society; and that the self-assured masculine leader of this group, Miss Kudō, is modeled after Hiratsuka Raichō. Yoshikawa sees Kudō as a typical popular-fiction character whose function is to voice discontent toward society on behalf of the oppressed female readership. She thus views this character as a positive figure who boldly challenges male-dominated society.[41] In my own reading, however, Kudō tells a darker story, which is evident when we focus on her disempowerment and subsequent death brought about through heterosexual love.

The bespectacled Kudō, wearing low wooden clogs and a divided *hakama* skirt slung low in an unmaidenly fashion, is reminiscent of Hiratsuka's description of herself as a young woman.[42] She is a masculine, physically strong character who uses male forms of speech. Like Miss Akitsu and Akiko, she is a rebel with a strong sense of self who refuses to attend church, but once she falls in love with a struggling painter named Mr. N, she begins to act in an overly feminine manner and becomes a weak figure who is hardly able to complete a sentence. Later in the narrative, Kudō falls ill and eventually dies from pneumonia (491). The ironic implication here is that growing up into heterosexuality is debilitating and even deadly; there is also an implicit warning against betraying one's true self. If Kudō is indeed modeled on Hiratsuka, Yoshiya is criticizing Hiratsuka's rejection of same-sex love. Although Kudō matures "correctly" by falling in love with N (who may represent Hiratsuka's husband, artist Okumura Hiroshi), she dies as a result; it is heterosexual romance, not adult same-sex love, that proves dangerous for this character.

Two Virgins in the Attic is very much aware of the transitional state of these characters as young women entering adulthood. One of the women in the group explains the normative growth process; she says she was initially sad to have left her girlhood years behind but now realizes that if she was "full of sweet dreams like a seventeen- or eighteen-year-old," she would not be able to appreciate men like N and his art. Referring to twenty as the transitional age when one visible sign of girlhood, *"kata-age"* (shoulder tucks in which the kimono sleeves are sewn in at the shoulder to make them shorter), is removed, she observes, "women become true human beings after twenty . . . after twenty, women's love becomes serious, something we can even risk our lives for!" (469–470). Love associated with girlhood is ignored while heterosexual love is portrayed as a legitimate experience that allows one to become truly human. Yet for Kudō, heterosexual love leads to illness and death, suggesting perhaps that this was a rejection of her true identity. For Akiko and Miss Akitsu, who deviate from the normative heterosexual trajectory but stay true to themselves, it is their love that enables self-development and triumphant entry into the greater outside world.

The notion that same-sex love can enable self-completion is further emphasized in the novel's reiteration of the term *virgin* to identify Akiko and Miss Akitsu. In the title, the two are described as "*shojo*," a word that can be translated as "virgin" or "maiden." This identity is also stressed in the climactic ending, in which they are repeatedly called "*shojo*" as well as "*musume*" and "*otome*" (both of which can also be translated as "maiden").[43] The term *shojo* identifies the characters as young and unmarried, but its meaning is more complex than might at first appear. Although it is difficult to specify the exact age range, a "virgin" (*shojo*) is commonly considered older than a "girl" (*shōjo*) and is mature enough to marry. Such a distinction reflects the emergence of a new vocabulary for the female growth process. To be sure, the girl / virgin differentiation was never a rigid one during the late 1910s and early 1920s—and it continued to be demarcated with relative flexibility even through the 1930s, depending on the context of its use. That there was a distinction in terms of age, however, was clearly recognized in both popular and dominant discourses.

Being a virgin, however, also meant something more than just being older than a girl. The novel makes use of another contemporaneous shift in the cultural meaning of virginity. In the early Meiji period, the word "*shojo*" had simply meant "an unmarried female who lives in her parents' house."[44] By the time Yoshiya was writing *Two Virgins in the Attic*, however, this definition had been replaced with the idea of a virginity determined by the female body and sexuality. A virgin was not only older than a girl and unmarried, but she also had to be sexually innocent with an intact hymen.[45] By the mid-1930s, the girl / virgin distinction in sexological and medical terms focused on menarche; being a virgin in this sense can be seen as the ability for the female body to have sexual relations and reproduce.[46] In terms of the normative female life cycle, the virgin embodied female sexual maturity—the potential for reproduction—in combination with the lack of actual sexual experience.

Historians and cultural critics ascribe this shift in the definition of *shojo* to a number of causes, but they generally agree on the importance of three factors. The first factor is the flowering of both popular and academic discourses on sexology in the 1910s. The second is the creation and development of "virgin groups" (*shojokai*) throughout rural Japan during the 1910s. These groups were part of the government's effort to create female subjects dutiful to the state and were meant to supplement girls' education after primary school. Virgin groups were intended for unmarried females from ages twelve to twenty-five and, by stressing the prescriptive nature of their name, encouraged young women to keep themselves pure, to eschew premarital sex.[47]

The third factor, closely associated with the Bluestocking Society, is the series of public discussions about virginity and chastity started by Bluestocking writers in 1914. These debates were well known as the Virginity Debates (*shojo ronsō*) or Chastity Debates (*teisō ronsō*). Ikuta Hanayo (1889–1970) instigated the discussion with her essay "Taberu koto to teisō to" (About survival and chastity, 1914), which claims that virginity and chastity were less important than being able to feed oneself, a conclusion she drew from her own experiences as a poverty-stricken writer. This idea was refuted by Yasuda Satsuki (1887–1933), who, writing in *Bluestocking*, severely criticized Ikuta for giving up her virtue, arguing that a woman's honor or chastity (*misao*) is her entire being and identity.[48] As the debate continued in a number of journals and mainstream newspapers, both male and female intellectuals jumped into the fray, exploring virginity and chastity from a variety of perspectives. The Virginity Debates widely disseminated the newly emerging concept of virginity as defined by the female body and sexuality.[49]

During the 1910s and 1920s, virginity became an important aspect of discourse on the female self. Sociologist Muta Kazue notes that the concept of virginity became a means for females to claim their own sexuality and identity.[50] Kawamura Kunimitsu also points out that starting in the early 1920s, unmarried contributors to magazines began to identify themselves as "virgin" rather than as "female" (*onna*) or "I" (*watakushi*). "Virgin" became a coveted, empowering identity, because it presented the young woman in question as pure and virtuous, in both a physical as well as a spiritual sense.[51] At the same time, the term was also restrictive, because it objectified female sexuality and enforced sexual innocence.[52]

Hiratsuka's views during the Virginity Debates were relatively moderate; unlike many of the participants, she recognized that virginity was a requirement forced on women by patriarchal society. At the same time, however, she valued virginity highly, as something that should be preserved for future participation in the ideal heterosexual love relationship. She commented in 1915 that virginity is the primary factor in "whether or not one can enable and complete love [ren'ai], the central sustenance of a woman's existence; whether or not one can allow a healthy and natural development of sexual life, the center of a woman's life; and even whether or not one can be happy in one's life as a whole, as a woman." Thus, the loss (or giving up) of virginity is a momentous decision that should occur only in a true merging of spiritual and sexual love.[53]

In *Two Virgins in the Attic*, the labeling of the two women as virgins disturbs the very notion of virginity and its relationship to modern love ideology. Akiko and Miss Akitsu refuse the possibility of men intervening in their future, but they find true (spiritual and sexual) love between themselves—indeed, they choose to be virgins forever. In addition to rejecting compulsory heterosexuality, the novel interrogates the reliance on heterosexual, phallocentric paradigms to understand female identity.[54] It even calls into question the definition of virginity itself, usually understood as lost or identified through male presence. The most overt message here, however, is that virginity is not a transitory identity to be lost in due time. As can be seen in the sentiment expressed in the popular women's magazine *Shufu no tomo* (Friend of the housewife), the idea of permanent virginity challenged the normative growth process and went against social expectations. If a woman is over twenty-five years of age, she "is no longer called virgin [shojo], though she is still pure. She is called unmarried person [mikonsha], and her prime will eventually pass away and she will unfortunately become an old maid [rōjo]."[55] The uplifting ending of Yoshiya's novel, in which two virgins find their true "selves" through same-sex love, radically questions the notion that virginity must be lost in order for female identity to be completed and legitimated.

In an essay published in 1928, Yoshiya describes the standard female life course as a painful process: marriage straps "submission, obedience, obligation, and responsibility" on the wife's back, and once the woman is a mother, "'maternal love,' that heavy millstone, is further tied around her frail neck. And thus youth passes in an instant—Alas!"[56] Akiko and Miss Akitsu can escape this path by choosing to remain virgins and gain a sense of their identity through their love. This is a permanent and fulfilling love associated with the purity of their identity as virgins—yet it is different from both the platonic friendship of girlhood and the "abnormal" adult same-sex love. The developmental trajectory from "girl" to "virgin" depicted in this novel configures same-sex love as a part of modern love ideology, and allows successful female maturity without male intervention.

"Abnormal" Virgins and Pure Wives: The Future of Same-Sex Love

By 1920, when *Two Virgins in the Attic* was published, Yoshiya already had a strong following of girl readers. The story of Akiko and Miss Akitsu, while employing girls' motifs and writing style, builds on this audience, inviting "virgins" and women to continue reading works by their favorite author. By positing same-sex love as a factor necessary for growth and self-completion, the novel makes a powerful statement, offering an alternative path for an expanded female readership. Although the novel ends with a sense of optimism about entering the wider world, we are nevertheless forced to ponder the fate of these two women.[57] What will happen to their love outside the attic rooms? Will they be able to stay together? Fifteen years after the novel's first appearance, Shinchōsha, the publisher of the 1935 *Yoshiya Nobuko zenshū* (Collected works of Yoshiya Nobuko) was still unable to describe it openly as a story about adult same-sex love. It is circuitously portrayed in ad copy as a work in which "the two [virgins] become tied to each other by a subtle feeling that resembles the same-sex love of their youthful days."[58] By noting only the *resemblance* to same-sex love and associating it with purity and innocence, the advertisement glosses over the central message of the story.

After publishing *Two Virgins in the Attic*, Yoshiya wrote only a handful of stories directly touching on adult same-sex love. The longest and most dramatic of these is titled "Aru orokashiki mono no hanashi" (A tale of a certain foolish person, 1925), which features Takigawa Akiko, a character with the same first name as and a last name similar to that of the protagonist in *Two Virgins in the Attic*. This story was serialized in *Kuroshōbi* (Black rose), a monthly "pamphlet" that Yoshiya published from January to August 1925. One of only three private magazines published by individual women during the prewar period, *Black Rose* featured Yoshiya's short stories and essays, and a discussion forum for her fans.[59] As Yoshiya explains in the inaugural issue, she wanted a medium that would allow artistic freedom and independent expression (1:67–68). Certainly *Black Rose* was a radical work that featured stories and essays criticizing patriarchy and sexism, and even overtly defending same-sex love.[60] The title was not one of the flowers featured in *Flower Tales* and can be read as a symbol of rebellion, an embracing of the "darkness" and "negativity" that male-centered society associates with female identity.[61] In fact, the subversive stance of the magazine probably led to its early termination after only eight issues.[62]

"A Tale of a Certain Foolish Person" is not exactly a sequel to *Two Virgins in the Attic*, but it tells the story of Akiko, a twenty-two-year-old higher girls' school teacher, who falls desperately in love with Kazuko, her nineteen-year-old pupil. Akiko recognizes that she has a tendency to fall in love with beautiful young females. It is explained that in the past, as a student in a teachers' school in Tokyo, Akiko had a mutual relationship with a dorm mate—but this person (in order to save her own reputation) had betrayed Akiko's "sincere passionate love" by reporting to the dorm mistress that Akiko was "making threats, insistently demanding something more than friendship" (1:10). This bitter experience had made Akiko determined to escape the attraction she feels toward women. After becoming a teacher in a remote girls' school, however, she ends up falling in love again, this time with her student, Kazuko, who in turn has a crush on her. This story takes *Two Virgins in the Attic* a step further, into explicitly grappling with issues associated with adult "abnormal" same-sex love. It is also a darker portrayal of the realities of pursuing same-sex love within society.

The setting and the motifs, at least on the surface, are reminiscent of those in *Flower Tales*. In particular, the plot shares close similarities with "Yellow Rose," the story quoted earlier of a student-teacher romance that is curtailed when the student graduates and her marriage is arranged. Akiko and Kazuko's relationship in "A Tale of a Certain Foolish Person" takes place in a higher girls' school, and it is constructed through platonic distance. Akiko never directly expresses her love for Kazuko and the extent of their relationship is writing letters and visiting each other. Despite such purity and innocence, however, Akiko self-identifies as an abnormal female and chastises herself for her love of women:

> Why am I this way? If I keep this up I will never be able to return to the true path of nature [*shizen no hondō*] for as long as I live. I really must make an effort, I must take this seriously and tackle it *steadily*. [She admonishes herself:] Aren't you already twenty-two years old? How long are you going to keep dreaming *strange* "abnormal" dreams [*hen na "abnormal" na yume*]? (1:21)[63]

"Abnormal" is written in English here, echoing texts such as Havelock Ellis's "Sexual Inversion in Women" that attempt to identify and distinguish between "normal" and "abnormal" same-sex love. Ellis notes that most love relationships between girls stem from a "normal instinct" (*nōmaru no honnō*) even when they involve "mutual touching and kissing." Although he depicts postschool love relationships as being in a somewhat grey area, he suggests that for the "truly inverted woman" (*hontō ni sei no tentō shita onna*), attraction to women and rejection of men can be considered "sexual abnormality" (*seiteki hentai*).[64]

Akiko identifies herself as being "abnormal" in this way because she always falls in love (*ren'ai*) with someone of the same sex and has never felt any interest in men. She describes her love for women as "an unnatural passion" (*hanshizen no jōnetsu*) but notes that for her to force herself to love men would be "even more unnatural" (1:21–22). Although Akiko starts out by berating herself, she ultimately challenges the idea that adult female-female love is "strange." She overrides the natural / unnatural, normal / abnormal divide and defends same-sex love by discussing the different "paths" of life for a woman: "It cannot be denied that mutual male-female love is the primary true way of humanity [*jinrui no daiichi no hondō*]. But there must be a secondary path [*daini no michi*]; is this not a path that should be allowed for the small number who walk the way of same-sex love?" (1:23).

Akiko is not a stereotype of the evil invert, feared for her promiscuity and her power to tempt and corrupt the innocent. Rather, she is reluctant to become close to Kazuko, because she does not want to involve her in this difficult "secondary way" (2:28). By presenting Akiko's "abnormality" in this manner, the text actually legitimizes her desires: Akiko's sexual orientation is permanent and congenital, not a decadent choice. Similar to *The Well of Loneliness* (1928), the classic British lesbian novel by Radclyffe Hall, "A Tale of a Certain Foolish Person" chooses to depict the protagonist as possessing an innate state that cannot be altered. By discussing Akiko in terms of abnormality, therefore, this story (like *The Well of Loneliness*) gives scientific validity to her character, demanding recognition and acceptance for her natural state in loving another female.[65]

Although it may be difficult for us today to accept or understand the use of *abnormality* to authenticate same-sex love, historian Lillian Faderman notes that such sexological discourse was liberating for many early twentieth-century women in the West; by embracing this validation of difference, they were able to reject the notion that heterosexuality and marriage were the only options for normative maturity.[66] Edward Carpenter explains in *The Intermediate Sex* that in earlier studies, "love-sentiment towards one of the same sex was always associated with degeneracy or disease," but with developments in sexology, this idea has been rejected. He says that "sexual inversion" is "in a vast number of cases quite instinctive and congenital" and is not associated with "any particular physical conformation or malformation . . . nor with any distinct disease of body or mind." He goes on to quote Havelock Ellis in calling this phenomenon "a 'sport' or variation, one of those organic aberrations [*yūkiteki hentai*] which we see throughout living nature in plants and in animals."[67] Akiko defers to the primacy of heterosexuality, but she demands an acceptance of same-sex love by defending the validity of the "secondary path." In this story, Yoshiya addresses the issue of sexual orientation as not a choice but an intrinsic part of individual identity; by actively engaging with contemporary sexological discourse, she argues for the legitimacy of adult same-sex love and enables it to become a part of modern love ideology. Rather than illustrating this love as a bizarre phenomenon, she suggests that it is just as positive and "real" as heterosexual love.

Even more than *Two Virgins in the Attic*, this story takes risks in articulating such a position. By introducing the concept of "abnormality" in a teacher-student love relationship, it disturbs the common trope of the innocent female bond. Thus, even in a private publication, the story carefully suppresses the two taboo factors associated with adult same-sex love: sex and masculinity. Akiko denies the possibility of sexuality in female-female love, commenting that "of course, it is impossible to have any 'Sexual connection' between those of the same sex," and she argues that love can exist without any physicality (1:22).[68] At the same time, however, Akiko uses words such as "lust" (*jōyoku*) and "illicit desire" (*hikage no aiyoku*) to describe her suppressed emotions, hinting that there are real sexual feelings but they can be expressed only in negative, derogatory terms (2:22, 28).

Masculinity is also hidden: unlike Stephen Gordon, the female protagonist in *The Well of Loneliness*, Akiko does not exhibit masculine features or dress in male clothes. Ellis, who developed theories about the concept of inversion, suggests that masculinity is a key characteristic, a "part of an organic instinct" that the invert "by no means always wishes to accentuate." It can be understood as a kind of internal reality that may or may not be overtly accompanied by outer accoutrements, such as dress and demeanor.[69] Akiko is not depicted visually as a "Mannish Lesbian," a "new medico-sexual category" developed by sexologist Richard von Krafft-Ebing in *Psychopathia*

Sexualis, but she does exhibit internal signs of masculinity by using masculine speech in her inner dialogue.[70] Indeed, "A Tale of a Certain Foolish Person" subtly employs gender difference in Japanese language to show how Akiko performs normative gender and sexuality.

In challenging the misogynistic school principal's authority, for example, Akiko speaks in a very feminine manner, using "schoolgirl speech" (*jogakusei kotoba*).[71] While strategically disarming him through her outward innocence and femininity, Akiko speaks roughly in her own mind, using aggressive words associated with male speech, such as "you fool" (*baka me*) and "what the hell" (*nandai*) (1:17). This could of course be interpreted as one way that women co-opt the power of male language because femininity precludes the possibility of being assertive and rebellious. Akiko never says these thoughts aloud but only articulates them silently in her mind, underscoring the inappropriateness of such language for a woman of her age, class, and educational status while at the same time showing an internal rebellion that can be presented on the page, if not in actual speech.[72]

The simultaneous use and suppression (nonvocalization) of masculine language also connotes a part of Akiko's identity: an inverted nature that must be kept hidden. I do not mean to suggest this as evidence of Yoshiya's own beliefs, that she accepted the idea of the invert as being essentially masculine. Rather, what she does here should be read as a tactical borrowing of sexological "truths" about the "abnormal" woman; Akiko's "abnormality" is expressed not through cross-dressing or demeanor but through language, which supposedly reflects an individual's true self. The masculine language that is suppressed in the text thus becomes a kind of code to alert readers familiar with the notion of inversion to Akiko's erased difference.

By highlighting masculinity and femininity in language, the text does not essentialize the gender divide but problematizes it, showing how gender performance is made possible by language and suggesting that, as Judith Butler has famously pointed out, "there is no gender identity behind the expressions of gender."[73] The use here of gender code-switching through linguistic-textual performance gestures toward a revolutionary rereading of female identity, even as it reminds the audience of the constant masquerade that Akiko must keep up in order to hide her "abnormality." Ultimately what this calls into question is the stability of sex and gender differences, a basic premise for determining "normal" and "abnormal" types of love.[74]

In the end, Kazuko's father insinuates that Akiko has made Kazuko "love sick" (*koi wazurai*) and he sarcastically calls Akiko a "female hero" (*onna no gōketsu*), perhaps a subtle inference that she is an invert (8:45). Although she and Kazuko share "a feeling impossible to be articulated . . . akin to love" (8:57), Akiko realizes that her relationship with Kazuko cannot continue. She decides to leave town forever, especially because Kazuko's parents are already in the process of arranging their daughter's marriage. Instead of a melancholic, romantic separation in the vein of *Flower Tales*, however, the women's relationship is severed in an extremely violent, shocking manner. A few days after graduation, Kazuko is found raped and murdered on a nearby road, apparently victimized by a passing carriage driver.[75] On hearing this news, Akiko faints, and as she falls, she hears a burst of laughter and a voice calling, "Thou foolish one!" (*Nanji orokashiki mono yo!* 8:64). This condemning voice, the closing line of the story, seems to be the voice of God—the "thou" (*nanji*) indicative of biblical language.

Is "A Tale of a Certain Foolish Person" suggesting that Akiko and Kazuko are punished by God for desiring the "second path"? Although Akiko expresses herself internally through the power associated with masculine forms of speech, in the end she is defeated by both male authority (the Father) and male violence. Yet the ending can also be read as a critique of a society that allows such a tragedy to occur. On that fatal evening, Kazuko intimates that she will visit Akiko's home, and the two walk from school together. At the last moment, however, Kazuko changes her mind, because her family has forbidden her to visit her teacher; Akiko lets her go, and as a result, Kazuko meets her death walking home alone. From this perspective, the story can be interpreted as an indictment of social prejudices against same-sex love. The ending silences Akiko, the "foolish person" of the title, for loving another female, but at the same time the voice can also be heard as a chastisement of Akiko for not insisting that she will walk with Kazuko on the symbolic "secondary path." Could this be Akiko's voice criticizing her own "foolishness," the persistent masquerade of normative sexuality? With its eloquently ambivalent ending, this story speaks of the need to challenge discrimination and censure. Ultimately, "A Tale of a Certain Foolish Person" presents a poignant depiction of adult same-sex love as legitimate, permanent, and deserving of acceptance, but still severely censored in mainstream society.

With the cancellation of *Black Rose*, Yoshiya ceased to explore "abnormal" same-sex love in her writing. A number of other stories published in *Black Rose* feature a protagonist named Akiko, and judging from their comments, many readers seem to have viewed these works as reflecting Yoshiya's own experiences (6:55). In interpreting characters named Akiko as Yoshiya herself, these fans read such texts as I-novels in which the author writes about "his or her personal life in a thin guise of fiction."[76] Even the term *abnormal* becomes a descriptive for Yoshiya: one *Black Rose* fan called Yoshiya "abnormal, yet completely pure and innocent" (*abunōmaru na, daga akumademo junketsu muku*); another identified Yoshiya's "praise of 'same-sex love' and denunciation of normal love—particularly marriage" as a result of her "abnormal feelings" (*abunōmaru na okokoromochi*), "a characteristic [she] was born with" (4:52; 7:59). As an unmarried writer who would begin to live with her female partner the following year, it was probably necessary for Yoshiya to stop writing about adult "abnormal" love in order to protect her social position.

Although innocent love in girlhood could be articulated as a positive, necessary part of female growth, championing adult same-sex love, especially through the sexological notion of "abnormality," proved to be a difficult task. Yoshiya was able to publish this story without negative repercussions because of the liberal trends of the early to mid-1920s and because she chose to publish it in her own private magazine. After *Black Rose*, however, she shifted gears: abandoning the "pure literature" (*junbungaku*) style used in her adult fiction, she embraced the more widely acceptable (and lucrative) "popular fiction" genre. She cultivated a female adult audience by writing fiction for popular women's magazines.[77] This move enabled her to establish a literary niche (apart from girls' fiction) and to secure a solid, broad readership amid the shifting political and social landscape of the late 1920s and 1930s.

Instead of overtly exploring same-sex sexuality in her popular fiction, Yoshiya reverted to a tactic reminiscent of *Flower Tales* in writing for women's magazines. This time she represented adult same-sex love not as an *alternative* to heterosexuality but as a kind of sisterhood, an integral part of female identity that *complements* heterosexuality. Here the love between women is a pure and permanent bond that can be sustained throughout the female life cycle. Just as male-male love in literature is often articulated through homosociality, female same-sex love can be expressed as an intense friendship that endures despite (or because of) experiences of marriage and motherhood.[78]

In works such as *Arashi no bara* (The rose in the storm, 1930–1931), the extremely successful *Onna no yūjō* (Female friendship, 1933–1934), and *Zoku onna no yūjō* (Female friendship continued, 1935), female protagonists experience personal growth through marriage, childbirth, divorce, and other domestic matters. Hardships and disappointments are overcome by female friendships; for all these women, sisterhood is the central sustenance in their lives. By rewriting same-sex love in this way, Yoshiya posits a new model of development for female identity. She rejects the common prejudice that female friendships do not last, and she reconfigures pure same-sex love as an admirable characteristic of the adult female. In the heterosexual world of her popular adult fiction, the notion of abnormality is erased even as the novels underscore the primacy of the love between women.

The Rose in the Storm, a work serialized in the widely circulated magazine *Friend of the Housewife*, provides such an example. Mioko, who is suffering from an unhappy marriage and the death of an infant daughter, goes to live with Fujiko and her family; Fujiko is her closest friend from higher girls' school. While Mioko lives with them, she and Fujiko's husband fall in love with each other. Mioko, however, ultimately rejects the husband to be true to Fujiko, who is "like a younger sister [*imōto*]." Recalling their happy schoolgirl days, Mioko pledges faith to their friendship and vows that she will never betray Fujiko: "If I ever betray you—my kind, only friend in the whole world that I love so dearly—if such a time should ever come, I will kill myself."[79] In the final scene of the novel, Mioko leaves Fujiko and her family in order to remain true to her promise; the husband is set off to the side while the narrative focuses on the two women bidding each other farewell. As Fujiko runs along the platform in the snow, Mioko leans out from the departing train to hold her hand tightly; the narrator comments that although they will not see each other again in this world, they will be together again in heaven.

Although this work superficially reinforces the primacy of heterosexuality and marriage by relegating Fujiko and Mioko's love to the heavens, it also suggests that female-female love supercedes any other type of romance and is in fact the most important aspect of female self-identity. Certainly happiness is not attained through the consummation of heterosexual love. This point is brought home not only by the ending but also by the fact that Mioko's own love-based marriage has been nothing but a source of pain and suffering. Although Mioko's marriage to her artist husband who lives abroad remains intact and Fujiko's family ties are strengthened, these women, like other protagonists in Yoshiya's adult popular fiction, attain true love through sisterhood, originally nurtured in "those pure days of being a virgin—unsullied and ignorant of sin."[80] By revisiting their shared preheterosexual past,

Mioko and Fujiko regain purity and innocence, values that bolster and sustain what Adrienne Rich calls the "lesbian continuum."[81] The "pure" wives in these stories present an acceptable form of female same-sex love that can be experienced by all women.

As a popular fiction writer, Yoshiya ultimately focused on female-female friendships that function, at least on the surface, to strengthen heterosexual ties and "family values." Just as Rich's idea of the lesbian continuum can be criticized for overly expanding the notion of the lesbian, Yoshiya's writing in this genre may be interpreted in a negative light, not only for its reinscription of accepted social structures, but also for diffusing the meaning of same-sex love. Yet her tactic of popularizing this love as female friendship was not simply a silencing but an effective political maneuver that allowed her to continue to explore various aspects of and possibilities for same-sex love and female identity in her writing. Throughout the 1930s she was able to disseminate widely the idea that same-sex love is of primary importance for girls and women of all ages, and that this love is a powerful force that resolves the problems of a male-centered world.

By rewriting the "truths" of same-sex love, Yoshiya's prewar works revisit modern love ideology, interrogating the connection between female self-discovery and the promise of heterosexual romance. Despite (or because of) the silences in these texts, Yoshiya is able to champion eloquently the importance of female-female love. The women and girls she portrays are "sisters" who challenge society, overcome life's difficulties, and even reform men as they articulate modern female identity. In the end, Yoshiya arrives at a socially acceptable yet politically resistant presentation of same-sex love as a force that develops and completes female selves while redirecting society in a better direction.

PART TWO

The Wife's Progress

FOUR

Love Marriage Ideology

Introduction

A love marriage (*ren'ai kekkon*) is a marriage based on mutual love and initiated by the partners themselves. The term is still used in present-day Japan to contrast this form of union with the so-called arranged marriage (*miai*), in which photographs and vitae are exchanged and the couple is formally introduced through an intermediary. With the development of dating services, marriage agencies, Internet sites, and manifold possibilities for quasi-formal introductions, however, the distinction in contemporary Japanese society between love marriages and arranged marriages has become increasingly murky. In the first half of the twentieth century, though, this distinction was clear; marrying for love was rare in practice and considered a bold departure from tradition. During the 1920s the notion of love as a prerequisite for marriage, and the concomitant idea that marriage was the ultimate goal of love, became part of the broader cultural discussion and an important theme in the popular media. The discourses that coalesced during this time led to the wide dissemination of *love marriage ideology*, a set of values that promoted love marriage as the ideal form of marriage. For women, love marriage became the perfect means of achieving several modern objectives—the development of a higher self and the achievement of an egalitarian male-female relationship.

Before focusing on the emergence of love marriage ideology and its popular dissemination during the 1920s, it is important to review briefly the relationship between love and marriage during the Meiji period. As discussed in Chapter One, love between husband and wife was considered a critical element of Japan's enlightenment; with this "modern" foundation at the heart of the family, the nation and its people could advance accordingly. By the 1880s, the ideal of love within marriage had been promulgated by Christian educators such as Iwamoto Yoshiharu, particularly through his promotion of *katei* (home). *Katei* ideology stressed the importance of creating an ideal home shaped by Christian love; it especially espoused spiritual love as the foundation for the husband-wife relationship.[1] In 1888, Iwamoto wrote in *Journal of Female Learning* that a marriage based on mutual love and respect leads to "great progress in terms of happiness and morality in the human world." In "Kon'in ron" (Theories of marriage, 1891), Iwamoto objects to marriages that are forced on women by their family without a chance for them to meet their future husbands; he also writes negatively about cases in which the prospective groom is known to be promiscuous or immoral, or in which marriages are entered into without much thought.[2] Iwamoto, however, does not seem to be opposed to arranged marriages *per se*; he is concerned, rather, with the presence of love between the marriage partners. Love could be expected to emerge between husband and wife even if they were united in a traditional arranged marriage. Iwamoto's stance reflects the reality that most marriages were arranged by families and not based on individual choice or mutual love.

However, as indicated by the term "marriage by threat" (*kyōhaku kekkon*), used in the Meiji period, the arranged marriage was considered less enlightened than the love-based marriage or "marriage by free choice" (*jiyū kekkon*).[3] The ideal for the Meiji intellectual was for romantic love (*ren'ai*) to lead to the goal of marital love (*kekkon ai*), and in this sense, all marriages initiated through arrangements and based on considerations such as class, family relationships, and finances were less desirable. In actuality, however, the practice of marrying for love was still not common even among the intelligentsia, a situation that created considerable anguish for the progressive modern man who aspired to experience new forms of courtship and wedlock.[4]

In works of Meiji literature we find many instances of such anguish when love and marriage are in opposition. The intellectual praises love but ultimately is unable to break out of tradition and fails to marry for love; or he carries out his goal, only to realize later that the act of marriage has erased love. In these texts, love marriage is recognized as the ideal, but serious doubt is raised about the possibility of realizing it in everyday practice, as well as about its viability for Japanese society.

In his seminal 1892 essay "Disillusioned Poets and Women," writer Kitamura Tōkoku presents love as a new ideal. At the same time, however, he also paints a pessimistic picture of marriage, ultimately rejecting the possibility of love being sustained between husband and wife. Kitamura was one of the rare early practitioners of love marriage; he married Ishizaka Minako after a passionate courtship in 1888. Although both were Christians, they had to battle the disapproval of their families because of the difference in their social status. Despite their hard-won state as husband and wife, the marriage was not a success. Kitamura's suicide in 1894 is often attributed to the despair he felt over the gap between his romanticism and reality.[5]

In "Disillusioned Poets and Women," Kitamura clearly marks the difference between the ideal of love and the reality of marriage. He asserts that love and marriage are irreconcilable opposites: love is an ideal whereas marriage is a social responsibility that belongs to the mundane, unromantic world. He also suggests that due to the innate nature of women, love cannot survive marriage. "Women," Kitamura claims, "are creatures of emotion, and thus *tend to love because they are loved, rather than love actively.* . . . Like a vine wrapped around the trunk of a tree, the woman clings to the man."[6] His viewpoint is echoed in many works of Meiji literature in which the male protagonist holds great hopes for love but is dragged down by the unenlightened Japanese woman, an unequal partner whose backwardness makes it impossible for the relationship to be sustained. Marriage thus becomes an onerous everyday condition that destroys love.

Starting in the Meiji period, then, we see both the idealization of love marriage and doubt about the possibility of its success in the real world. In the Taishō and early Shōwa periods, this tension between ideal concept and actual practice remained; love marriage did not suddenly become a common phenomenon or eclipse the normative arranged marriage. Historian Harald Fuess notes that during these periods, in fact, love marriage was still "a rare occurrence" in contrast to the traditional arranged marriage, which took either of two forms: a marriage arranged without the parties ever seeing each other, or *miai*, in which the parties met at least once before betrothal. Fuess explains that in the Taishō period, only 3 percent of marriages were love marriages while 38 percent were *miai* and 40 percent were marriages "contracted sight unseen."[7]

Although actual practice may have remained a rarity, during the 1910s and 1920s love marriages were reframed and celebrated in a new way as the perfect male-female relationship, not only in intellectual and Christian circles but also in popular culture. Cultural critics and historians often refer to this veneration and promotion of love-based marriage as "love marriage ideology" (*ren'ai kekkon ideorogii*).[8] This ideology was an intrinsic part of liberal humanist thought and a prominent feature of the Taishō and early Shōwa cultural landscape. Love marriage ideology emerged from feminist discussions of love and marriage, particularly those of Hiratsuka and Key. Their ideas were later popularized on a national scale by Kuriyagawa Hakuson, whose bestselling love treatise *Views of Love in the Modern Era* (1921) made love and love marriage part of everyday knowledge. Kuriyagawa's theoretical explanations were widely read, particularly in light of a famous love scandal, the 1921 Byakuren incident, in which a cousin of the emperor ran away from her husband to be with her lover. This scandal, as well as the serialization of *Views of Love in the Modern Era*, played out in the pages of *Tokyo Asahi shinbun* and *Osaka Asahi shinbun*, two of the most influential newspapers of the day. During the 1920s, these media "events" shaped the popular understanding of love marriage and its role in society.

Love Marriage Ideology: Hiratsuka Raichō and Ellen Key

Meiji concepts such as *katei* laid the groundwork for love marriage ideology by promoting the desirability of marital love and advocating the idea that the husband and wife both play an important role in the family. The idealization of love marriage during the Taishō to early Shōwa periods was, however, different from Meiji *katei* discourse in several key respects. First, because love marriage ideology grew out of the broader modern love ideology as articulated by Ellen Key and Hiratsuka Raichō, love marriage was valued first and foremost as an expression of selfhood. Love-based unions were seen as sites for self-development and completion; because the man and woman could choose their own spouse, they would both be able to realize their individual potential and attain their true selves. This emphasis on the individual and insistence on equality between husband and wife are clearly different from

Iwamoto Yoshiharu's view of the wife as a helpmate to her husband.[9] Second, instead of promoting spiritual love in the home, love marriage ideology stressed the importance of the fusion of spiritual and sexual love (*rei-niku itchi*). Marriage was seen as an ideal locus for the practice of love, as a microcosm of an advanced egalitarian society in which husbands and wives could mutually progress and complete their characters or personalities (*jinkaku*).

Although love marriage was promoted as a crucial vehicle of progress for both sexes, it became a particularly important ideal for women, who hoped to achieve a modern self through this expression of agency, equality, and self-cultivation. Initially, Hiratsuka Raichō viewed love and marriage as separate concepts; she was highly suspicious of the institution of marriage, although for reasons entirely different from the conflict expressed in Kitamura Tōkoku's "Disillusioned Poets and Women." She advocated love while criticizing marriage as part of a system that perpetuated male-female inequality. In an essay titled "Yo no fujintachi e" ("To the Women of the World," 1913), she explained to her readers that Bluestocking women "are not against marriage per se, but cannot at all submit to the present-day concept of marriage or the current practice of the system of marriage."[10] Also, in starting her life with Okumura Hiroshi, in 1914 she wrote in a letter to her parents, published in *Bluestocking*, "I am not satisfied with marriage as an institution in its present form, and so do not want to get married by following such a system or being recognized under such a law. . . . There is nothing more natural than for a man and a woman who are in love to live under one roof, and as long as they have an understanding, I think the formality of marriage is of little consequence."[11] Here we see Hiratsuka rebelling against the institution of marriage and rejecting society's control of female sexuality.

Soon afterward, however, she abandons such explicit attacks on marriage and instead focuses on the importance of love between the couple, particularly emphasizing its value for the maturation of female identity. This shift stems from her personal life with Okumura as well as from the influence of Key's *Love and Marriage*. In Key's thought, the ideal trajectory of love is the evolution from romantic male-female love to the experience of maternal love, which is considered the highest form of love. Key rejects the idea that the legally or religiously sanctioned marriage is more important than the experience of love, and she does not consider marriage an absolute necessity. If, however, one is to marry, the ideal form of marriage is the love marriage; because it is founded on love, it enables women to develop themselves through the natural progression from romantic love to maternal love.[12]

Hiratsuka herself did not legalize her union with Okumura until 1941, when wartime considerations made such legalization advisable for the sake of her son.[13] Although she remained technically unmarried during the prewar period, critiquing the institution of marriage never became the focal point of her politics. Rather, after beginning her life with Okumura, she began to champion love marriage as the ideal husband-wife relationship; this stance is reflected in essays she wrote for *Bluestocking* as well as in her post-*Bluestocking* works. Regardless of the fact that she was not legally married while promoting the practice, it is clear that she saw herself as a legitimate practitioner of love marriage. The relative flexibility of what was considered real marriage during this period certainly must have contributed to this view.[14]

In 1916, Hiratsuka defined the "new morality" as one that requires "love to be at the center of marriage" and explained "the purpose of marriage as a mutual completion of character and improvement of the race through the practice of love."[15] In 1918, she expressed disappointment that "the old-fashioned savagery, a kind of loveless marriage called go-between marriage [*baishaku kekkon*] or arranged marriage [*miai kekkon*]" was still being practiced in Japan. She noted, however, that the young people of the "so-called intellectual class" were no longer happy with this practice, and she expressed satisfaction that among the well-educated, "even the middle-aged and the elderly . . . have finally begun to accept the importance of love in marital life."[16] Although Hiratsuka combines ideas about the importance of good genes and the need for financial stability, her basic view of marriage is that it should be based on love, in order to allow for the full realization of both male and female selves.

Kuriyagawa Hakuson and the Byakuren Incident

Hiratsuka's discussions of love marriage may not have immediately reached a popular readership, but with the publication of Kuriyagawa Hakuson's *Views of Love in the Modern Era* and in the wake of the sensational 1921 Byakuren incident, love marriage ideology was disseminated to a broad spectrum of society. Kuriyagawa's highly influential love treatise was serialized in *Tokyo Asahi shinbun* and *Osaka Asahi shinbun* in 1921; at that time both venues were nationally circulating newspapers printing approximately 291,000 and 483,000 copies per day, respectively.[17] In 1922 *Views of Love in the Modern Era* became a bestselling book; it was later published with other writings about love in Kuriyagawa's 1929 collected works, *Kuriyagawa Hakuson zenshū*, published by Kaizōsha. Historian Kano Masanao has stressed the widespread influence of *Views of Love in the Modern Era*, noting that with its publication, ideas about love became systematized and popularized as part of everyday common knowledge.[18] Kuriyagawa, an English literature professor at Kyoto University, includes many of the ideas of Ellen Key and Hiratsuka Raichō in this treatise, reintroducing them for a general audience.

As a proponent of Western democracy, Kuriyagawa argues that a marriage entered into without love is akin to rape or prostitution. The love match, on the other hand, is the most evolved and advanced form of marriage, and therefore the most befitting for the twentieth century. Kuriyagawa historicizes the development of love marriage, claiming that the "ancient period" was a time of carnal instincts when the woman was treated as an object existing to fulfill male sexual desires and procreative needs. This period was followed by the "middle ages," a time of spiritual and religious female worship in which the woman was seen as something higher than merely human. After these two periods in which the body and the soul were separated, the "modern period" finally enabled the body and soul to be united and the woman to be treated as fully human. During this period, Kuriyagawa explains, love marriage emerged as the ultimate relationship in which men and women could come together in a union both sexual and spiritual. Acknowledging that Ellen Key's and Edward Carpenter's theories of love are representative of this view, Kuriyagawa asserts that love is "nothing other than a symphony created by the union of two individuals of different sexes, a symphony in which both sexes can fulfill and complete each other's selfhood as 'humans.'"

Kuriyagawa's work popularized several important ideas about the concept of love marriage. First, love is not destroyed by marriage but deepened through it; love "evolves and changes," turning into a more lasting relationship in which "flighty love is grounded . . . the flower fades away to bear fruit." Second, conjugal love is both sexual and spiritual. Third, love marriage is based on the idea that both the husband and the wife are individuals with agency and hence are equals. Fourth, this kind of relationship mirrors national advancement and allows individual progress:

> The union of a man and woman who are both free individuals, as well as a life that enables the completion of the self [*jiko*] through this union and that creates new spirit—these things can be attained only through mutual love. Marriage without love will not only make the individual's existence as a human being meaningless, but it will also be a great impediment to the development of a people [*minzoku*] and the evolution of humanity.[19]

Kuriyagawa's text opened the gates for other publications that reframed the idea of love as a primary consideration for marriage. Love treatises published in intellectual and popular magazines as well as newspapers and books came to be an integral aspect of the culturalism (*kyōyō shugi*) movement; the understanding of such modern concepts as love became a part of everyday life.[20] The value placed on individual progress seen in such ideas as culture (*kyōyō*), self-cultivation (*shūyō*), and character (*jinkaku*) particularly encouraged a view of love marriage as a site for mutual self-improvement and personal growth for both husband and wife.[21]

Yoshiya Nobuko comments in her private magazine, *Black Rose* (1925), that Kuriyagawa's treatise was read by "a great many people" but to someone such as herself who had studied Key's *Love and Marriage* with other Bluestocking women, his ideas about love seem no more than "common knowledge." Certainly Kuriyagawa's basic ideas about love derive from Key and Hiratsuka's writings. Love is part of the "evolution" manifested in human history and society; it also "evolves" over the course of an individual's life. Love is important because it enables self-completion and the attainment of male-female equality. Although Yoshiya describes Kuriyagawa's work as being only a "basic primer about love," she does recognize its value as an "explanatory work" to enlighten those who remain ignorant about the subject.[22] As a bridging text between intellectual feminist discourse and the popular reading public, *Views of Love in the Modern Era* was instrumental in disseminating love marriage ideology to a wide audience.[23]

The year 1921 saw not only the serialization of Kuriyagawa's treatise but also a highly publicized media event that dramatized issues at the heart of love marriage ideology. This was the Byakuren incident, a love scandal involving poet Yanagihara Akiko (1885–1967), also known by her writing name Yanagihara Byakuren.[24] This scandal coincided with the serialization of *Views of Love in the Modern Era* and underscored the ideal of love marriage in the popular imagination. Byakuren was already a celebrity prior to the love scandal; she was a renowned beauty, a cousin of the Taishō emperor, the illegitimate child of a peer, a writer of dramatic love poems, and a divorcee who had remarried Itō Den'emon, a Kyūshū coal-mine millionaire, in 1911. She fulfilled all the requirements for a media star—a tragic, beautiful poet of noble blood forced by her family to marry Itō, a rich, illiterate man with many lovers. Her first poetry collection, *Fumie* (Icon, 1915), was well received, but she became nationally famous after *Osaka Asahi shinbun* published a gossip-filled ten-part series on her life titled "Tsukushi no joō

Akiko" (Akiko, Queen of Tsukushi) in 1918. This dramatic "real-life" feature included photographs and excerpts of her writing, and much was made of the mysterious contrast between her passionate love poems and her love-less marriage to Itō. After the serialization of "Akiko, Queen of Tsukushi," Byakuren received fan mail from all over Japan.[25]

Byakuren's story of domestic unhappiness even inspired professional writers. One of Yoshiya Nobuko's *Flower Tales* stories, "Moyuru hana" (Burning flowers), appears to be modeled on Byakuren's relationship with her husband. In the fictional resolution, the Byakuren character successfully runs away from her husband and escapes to a Catholic school; there she chooses to die with a young girl in a fire, showing a "pure" expression of sisterhood.[26] A work clearly associated with Byakuren was *Shinju fujin* (Madame Pearl, 1920), a bestseller by popular author Kikuchi Kan (Hiroshi, 1888–1948) that was serialized in *Osaka Mainichi shinbun* and *Tokyo Nichi Nichi shinbun*.[27] Readers at the time assumed that the protagonist of *Madame Pearl*, a young girl of noble birth forced to marry a nouveau riche man, was modeled on Byakuren.[28] Indeed, Byakuren herself thought she was the model for the heroine and sent a letter of inquiry to Kikuchi about it when the advertisement for the work was first published in the newspapers. Although Kikuchi denied using Byakuren as a model, parts of *Madame Pearl* do bear an uncanny resemblance to episodes from "Akiko, Queen of Tsukushi."[29] Famous for having created a new type of heroine in the popular domestic fiction genre, *Madame Pearl* flourished in part because of readers' fascination with Byakuren.[30]

By 1921, Byakuren was already a national celebrity and very much cognizant of the power of the media and popular opinion. On October 20, 1921, she ran away with a younger lover—Miyazaki Ryūsuke (1893–1971), a socialist activist and the son of Miyazaki Tōten (1870–1922), a well-known revolutionary—creating one of the biggest scandals of the day. This affair, which would come to be known as the Byakuren incident, was distinct from numerous other love incidents that occurred during the period, because on October 23 Byakuren published in *Tokyo Asahi shinbun* and *Osaka Asahi shinbun* a letter to her husband, Itō, explaining her reasons for leaving him and berating him for the lack of love in their marriage. Given that female infidelity was punishable by law at the time, this was a bold use of the media by the lovers to gain support for their actions. Byakuren writes in this letter that her marriage to Itō was forced on her by relatives, and "love and understanding between the two of us were completely lacking from the very beginning." Despite this fact, she goes on to explain, she had tried to nurture "true love and understanding" but had failed because of the many lovers Itō kept and because of the lack of morality and order in the household. She is now determined to "resurrect herself through the love that has been given to her" by Miyazaki and has run away "in order to protect her free individuality and self-worth."[31]

A look at the coverage of this affair in *Tokyo Asahi shinbun* and *Osaka Asahi shinbun* reveals an almost obsessive interest in the scandal. The October 22 full-page spread explains that Byakuren disappeared two days earlier while traveling in Tokyo with her husband. It includes photographs as well as interviews with her lover, Miyazaki, and with servants and relatives; it even gives the train schedule for Itō's trip and when he is due back in Fukuoka. Itō, who learned of the incident from the newspapers, was shocked to see her letter to him in the October 23 issue; this edition also featured a photograph of Byakuren taken while she was in hiding, and a reproduction of a postcard from Byakuren to Miyazaki. For the next several weeks, newspapers covered the Byakuren incident extensively, not only reporting on the latest developments but also publishing numerous editorials and letters from readers that discussed the scandal.[32]

While this incident was playing out in the pages of *Tokyo Asahi shinbun* and *Osaka Asahi shinbun*, Kuriyagawa Hakuson was still serializing *Views of Love in the Modern Era* in the same venues. A reader's comment published on October 25 illustrates that the Byakuren incident became a kind of case study for understanding love and love marriage. Well-versed in Kuriyagawa's ideas, the reader asserts that Byakuren's relationship with her husband was not real love because it did not entail "a coming together of two characters [*jinkaku*] . . . a coming together of two souls."[33] After the month-long serialization of *Views of Love in the Modern Era* was completed, Kuriyagawa himself wrote a much-awaited commentary on the Byakuren incident in the October 30 edition of *Tokyo Asahi shinbun* and *Osaka Asahi shinbun*. He supported Byakuren's actions as correct and "unavoidable from the perspective of the highest human morality." Her actions, he argues, were necessary in order for her "to escape from the animalistic lifestyle of prostitution marriage [*baiin kekkon*] or slave marriage [*dorei kekkon*] . . . to complete the self as a human being and to hold onto her character."[34]

Hiratsuka Raichō's comments about this incident also support Byakuren's choice to leave Itō.[35] Both Hiratsuka and Kuriyagawa suggest that this incident is a prime example of the tragedy brought on by unenlightened arranged marriages. Kuriyagawa entreats people not to enter into such marriages "conducted not for love but for reasons such as fortune, family name, and other needs," denouncing them as "uncivilized indecency."[36] Hiratsuka admonishes society to remember that "marriage is the character-based [*jinkakuteki*] union of a man and a woman through mutual love." She expresses hope that Miyazaki will be a true partner to Byakuren, one who will help "complete [her] character" (*jinkaku no kansei*).[37] Unlike the couples in many scandals that ended in love suicide, Byakuren and Miyazaki stayed together and were finally allowed to legalize their marriage in 1924. Due to the incident, Byakuren's name was taken off the peers' list, but she remained very much in the public eye as an active writer who supported her family financially. This was a unique love incident, not only for its strategic use of love marriage discourse, but also for its inspirational message of idealism. Byakuren and Miyazaki remained happily married until her death in 1967.

By the early 1920s, love marriage became established as an important ideal, but this did not mean that it suddenly became a common practice. Even Kuriyagawa, in his treatise, notes an actual case in which two school teachers who fell in love and married had to resign from their respective jobs because of their "immoral" behavior.[38] In the case of the Byakuren incident as well, public opinion was not entirely in favor of Byakuren and Miyazaki. After Itō published a rejoinder letter to his wife in *Osaka Mainichi shinbun* and *Tokyo Nichi Nichi shinbun*, many readers took his side.[39] For people who sympathized with Itō, the idea of realizing the self through love marriage was an undesirable, nonconformist notion. In the October 31, 1921, issue of *Tokyo Asahi shinbun*, there was an analysis of the public's responses to the incident based on 412 letters that the newspaper had received. It showed that those who were completely in favor of Byakuren's actions were not in the majority. At the same time, many of the letter writers located the original problem in the arranged marriage, viewing the institution as having created the undesirable situation in the first place.[40] Despite the still prevalent "traditional" ideas about women's need to be obedient and chaste in marriage, love marriage was becoming a recognized ideal for the "modern" advancement of Japanese society.

Love Marriage Ideology, Women Writers, and Miyamoto Yuriko

Love marriage appears in a number of prewar works by women writers, especially in I-novels in which the author relates her own experiences. Unlike the majority of upper- and middle-class women, many writers married for love, often more than once, in both legal and common-law unions. These authors wrote about their relationships in a variety of ways. Critics often read these narratives only for biographical interest, but in many texts the exploration of female identity and love marriage (whether fictional or not) is actually part of a larger cultural conversation. These stories reveal the ways in which women writers were processing, articulating, and / or rejecting then-contemporary ideas about love marriage.

Although she did not specifically focus on love marriage per se, Uno Chiyo (1897–1996) immediately comes to mind as an author who wrote about male-female love; she is famous for having had different liaisons, marrying for love several times, and emphasizing the importance of such passionate relationships in her life.[41] Overall, however, works by women about the experience of love marriage often express disappointment; despite its promise, the union fails to advance the male or the female self. Such stories frequently underscore the particular difficulties for a woman writer whose identity is tied to the act of writing; marriage hinders her progress, because she often has additional responsibilities to carry out, such as domestic duties and child care. We see this dynamic in stories throughout the prewar period, from Tamura Toshiko's "Kanojo no seikatsu" (Her life, 1915) to Sata Ineko's late 1930s I-novel, *Kurenai* (Crimson, 1936–1938). In the former tale, the protagonist, who marries for love, ends up relinquishing her writing career for her husband and child; *Crimson* features an intellectual proletarian couple who constantly battle each other over time and resources to write.[42]

Women's hopes for an ideal love marriage and their questions about personal and social change are particularly complicated in proletarian literature. As I suggest in the next chapter, views about female completion and advancement shifted in the mid- to late 1920s with the influx of new discourses about love and the rise of socialist ideology. Often a conflict between love and politics is expressed: Was love marriage compatible with socialism and Marxism or was it simply part of bourgeois values? At the same time, we also find women who desire to be fulfilled through both the marital relationship and activist politics. In the short I-novel "Nagesuteyo!" (Throw them away! 1927) by Marxist Hirabayashi Taiko (1905–1972), the protagonist's husband becomes dispirited about radicalism, claiming that he is only a "proponent of love's supremacy-ism" (*ren'ai shijōshugisha*), not a "social activist." Invoking a term associated with Kuriyagawa's ideology, the husband characterizes love as a less problematic means of transforming individuals and society, and rues his endeavors to bring about a socialist revolution. For the protagonist, who becomes disenchanted by her husband, love and politics are fused as one ideal. She comes to the conclusion that their marriage is not based on "true proletarian love" (*hontō no musansha no ai*) and rejects their life together as based on "blind lust," an attachment that must be "thrown away."[43]

Machiko (1928–1930) by Nogami Yaeko (1885–1985) is famous as a critique of the extremism within the proletarian movement and is thought to have been inspired by Miyamoto Yuriko's *Nobuko*. Machiko, the eponymous protagonist, is depicted as an idealist who believes in both love and class struggle; she rejects arranged marriages as well as the bourgeois lifestyle. She is ready to run off and marry a radical activist, but she discovers that he has made her friend pregnant. Horrified by his lack of personal responsibility, Machiko realizes that she was not really in love with him but only enamored of the idea of social change. She finds the perfect middle ground with another suitor, a wealthy intellectual who is genuinely sympathetic to workers' suffering; by the end of the story it is intimated that Machiko will make a successful love marriage with this man. Nogami, who chose of her own volition a husband supportive of her writing career, published stories and translations in *Bluestocking*. We can see how *Machiko* reflects certain elements of love marriage ideology; the modern woman is to be fulfilled through a love-based union, one that will allow the couple to progress as equal partners and contribute to social improvement.[44]

It is impossible to generalize about love marriage narratives written by women during the prewar period, but we can say that whether they express disillusionment or happiness about a love-based union, and whether or not they are based on real experiences, many of them were influenced by the love marriage ideology disseminated during the 1910s and 1920s. The husband-wife relationship in its most ideal form was the love marriage, a practice that was supposed to elevate and advance the couple and aid in the transformation of both individual and society.

Of the many women writers of this period, Miyamoto Yuriko was recognized as a practitioner of love marriage. She became famous in 1916 when, at age seventeen, she published her first story in a major pure literature magazine. By 1921, when the Byakuren incident occurred, she was well known in Japan as a successful woman writer who herself had married for love. Not surprisingly, the media solicited Miyamoto's opinions about the Byakuren incident. Four days after the scandal, *Yomiuri shinbun* published an interview in which Miyamoto expresses sympathy for the desperate choice

Byakuren had to make in order to be with her true love: "All women who are married want only one thing, which is to be loved by their husbands. But it is clear . . . that there was no pure love [between Itō and Byakuren]. This [Byakuren's running away with Miyazaki] is not a simple issue that can be easily discussed as . . . being either good or bad."[45] Her statement here is all the more poignant considering Miyamoto's own situation in 1921; her love marriage to Araki Shigeru was beginning to unravel at this time.

Miyamoto's personal life certainly provides an important key to her writing, and critics have traditionally read her stories from such a perspective. Yet it is also crucial to consider her writing in context. Miyamoto's diary entries reveal that she was very much aware of the publications, discussions, and incidents associated with love marriage. In the entries from 1921 to 1923, for example, she analyzes her failing marriage by referring to love marriage discourse and related contemporary issues. Her desire to progress and complete the self is combined with discussions on spiritual and sexual love, equality, and the question of true love and true marriage. She also writes about Byakuren, mentions Kuriyagawa, and provides lengthy commentary on Ellen Key's *Bosei no fukkō* (*The Renaissance of Motherhood*; English edition 1914), translated by Hiratsuka Raichō in 1919.[46] Deeply aware of such discourses, Miyamoto incorporates these ideas into her fictional works.

Miyamoto Yuriko's *Nobuko* is a key vanguard text that encapsulates a range of critical issues about love marriage. The various concerns found in prewar women's writing, such as the woman's efforts to make intellectual progress within the home, the question of love's authenticity, and the relationship between notions of personal and social betterment, are all explored in the different editions of *Nobuko*. Furthermore, this is a work that fully engages with love marriage ideology and shows various shifts in intellectual thought during the 1920s. Rather than using *Nobuko* as an I-novel that reveals the "real" story of Miyamoto's marriage, I examine this text and its sequels within the discursive framework of the prewar period, revealing their profound engagement with the ideal of love marriage and the meaning of its dissolution.

FIVE

Miyamoto Yuriko
and the Nobuko Narratives

Introduction

Miyamoto Yuriko startled the literary establishment when at age seventeen she made her debut in the prestigious magazine *Chūō kōron* (Central review). "Mazushiki hitobito no mure" (The flocks of the poor, 1916), a powerful tale about poverty in a rural village, propelled her to national fame as a "girl genius" and an important intellectual writer. She would go on to become one of the most recognized names in literature until her death in 1951. Her most famous work is *Nobuko* (1924–1926), considered a feminist I-novel; she is also viewed as one of Japan's leading proletarian writers. Miyamoto lived in Moscow from 1927 to 1930, and in 1931 she joined the then illegal Japan Communist Party. Unlike many of her contemporaries, she remained committed to her politics despite imprisonment and persecution. Her second husband, Miyamoto Kenji (1908–2007), who shared her politics, remained a prominent party leader until the 1990s; both Miyamoto Yuriko and Kenji are still venerated by the Japanese Left as visionaries who remained true to their convictions during the Fifteen-Year War and refused to recant despite mistreatment by the authorities.

Viewed as Miyamoto's "pre-proletarian" novel, *Nobuko* tells how the eponymous heroine discovers herself through the disappointments of the husband-and-wife relationship and decides to seek divorce. The novel was serialized in the journal *Kaizō* (Re-creation) from September 1924 to September 1926, and was later considerably revised as a book published in 1928 by Kaizōsha.[1] *Nobuko* is a semiautobiographical work based on Miyamoto's first marriage to Araki Shigeru, a scholar of ancient languages whom she met during a trip to New York City (1918–1919). The union between the twenty-year-old Miyamoto (then Chūjō Yuriko) and the thirty-five-year-old Araki was a love marriage carried out on their own initiative without any input from parents or relatives. After they returned to Japan, however, the marriage unraveled and ended in divorce in 1925. *Nobuko* is the first of Miyamoto's three-part I-novel series. *Futatsu no niwa* (The two gardens, 1947) and *Dōhyō* (Signpost, 1947–1950) continue the story of Nobuko after her divorce. Because these stories closely follow Miyamoto's own life, literary critics often focus on Nobuko as Miyamoto, examining the tales through the lens of Miyamoto's relationships.

It is often assumed that *Nobuko* was an immediate success when it was first published during the 1920s. Yet surprisingly the novel did not make a great impact on the literary scene when it first appeared. During the 1920s and 1930s it influenced neither the proletarian literature movement nor the pure literature genre. It was during the immediate postwar years, from the mid- to late 1940s, that the novel enjoyed a significant revival and was reissued by a number of publishers.[2] As Japan rebuilt itself as a democratic state, *Nobuko*'s message of liberation from marriage and desire for equality resonated powerfully with the reading public.

In a 1948 commentary written for a new edition of her selected works, Miyamoto underscored this aspect of *Nobuko*:

> Now that Japan finally has a Constitution that includes the words *people's rights*, and human equality between men and women has become recognized, what does it mean for *Nobuko*, a work written more than a quarter of a century ago, to have become so popular and be read by such a broad spectrum of readers? Does this not say that *Nobuko* examines social issues yet to be completely resolved in the lives of young Japanese women today?[3]

The "social issues," we can infer, are women's struggles within the family system, equality between men and women in marriage, and women's desire for self-realization in both the public and private spheres. Although this view of *Nobuko* as a feminist work is widely accepted, we should also recognize that such a reading of the novel (even as it is offered by the author herself) is very much shaped by its postwar rediscovery. While acknowledging the significance of *Nobuko* as an I-novel, a number of critics have interpreted the work in new ways, moving away from purely autobiographical approaches that consider Nobuko *only* as an authentic reproduction of Miyamoto herself. Yet there has been almost no questioning of the postwar reinvention of *Nobuko*; in other words, despite the fact that Miyamoto is clearly engaged with then contemporary concerns in her diaries as well as in her fiction, the novel has not been fully examined in its original prewar discursive context. *Nobuko* certainly grapples with "social issues" pertaining to women, but it does so as a work profoundly shaped by 1920s discourses on such topics as love marriage, self-cultivation, and individual and national health. By understanding prewar views of love, marriage, family, and divorce, we can access the significance of Nobuko's desire to achieve her own "identity" (*"watashi" to iu mono*).[4] In this chapter I revisit *Nobuko*, both the 1924–1926 serialization and the 1928 revised text, as well as the other Nobuko narratives. Modern love ideology and love marriage discourse are keys to understanding Nobuko's yearning for individual development and the attainment of a modern female selfhood.

Nobuko*'s Progress and Love Marriage Discourse*

Nobuko opens in New York City, where Sassa Nobuko, a twenty-year-old writer is staying with her father. It is 1918, the year that will see hostilities cease between countries engaged in World War I. Nobuko meets Tsukuda Ichirō, a thirty-five-year-old man who works at the YMCA and studies comparative linguistics at C University, specializing in ancient Indian and Iranian languages.[5] Nobuko falls in love, boldly proposes to Tsukuda, and marries him despite his lower-class status, poverty, and dubious reputation within the expatriate Japanese community. After returning to Japan, Nobuko soon comes to realize that the love marriage was a mistake. Tsukuda has problems with Nobuko's family and friends, and although he manages to become a university professor, he has no ambitions to "progress" in terms of culture and learning. Nobuko finds him inadequate as a partner and becomes stifled as a writer; her domestic duties as a wife and her unhappiness in the relationship make it impossible for her to focus productively on her own literary work. In 1924 she meets Yoshimi Motoko, a single woman who is a magazine editor and a student of Russian literature.[6] They become fast friends, and Nobuko realizes that she is more fulfilled by this friendship than by her marriage. The novel closes a few months later, with Nobuko and Tsukuda agreeing to separate.

In reading *Nobuko* as a novel of self-discovery, we can identify Nobuko's disillusionment as the catalyst for growth. Once she frees herself from the idealized image of heterosexual love and marriage and questions the position of a wife, she is able to realize her true identity. Yet such a reading from our contemporary perspective is misleading without fully understanding what love and marriage (and love marriage) meant for an upper-class, educated woman like Nobuko during the 1910s and 1920s. Here I reread the novel through its conversation with prewar love marriage discourse.[7] *Nobuko* does not present a clear-cut criticism of marriage as a myth that fails to bring about true happiness. Rather, it explores what love marriage really means for women in the modern world, questioning what determines its legitimacy (as a "real" love marriage), asking when divorce can be considered a valid solution, and probing what it means for a wife to attain equality and progress. In other words, this novel is not simply about Nobuko's disillusionment with her marriage; it also illustrates, in painstaking detail, that the Nobuko-Tsukuda relationship is lacking as a true love marriage because it fails to provide satisfactory female development and self-completion.

The standard, widely read 1928 version of *Nobuko* is awkwardly constructed and at times extremely disjointed. This is because it is an edited, shortened version of the original 1924–1926 serialization.[8] Of particular note is the way in which the later text obscures Nobuko's use of love marriage discourse. Although many critics do not discuss the earlier text, I believe it is important to look at both the 1924–1926 and the 1928 versions for a full understanding of *Nobuko* and its relation to contemporary notions of love and marriage. The general plot itself is the same in both versions, but the difference in details—particularly what is erased from the earlier text—is quite revealing. As mentioned earlier, *Nobuko* is often read as part of a trilogy that includes two postwar sequels, *The Two Gardens* and *Signpost*, and critics comment on Nobuko's development throughout the three works. In contrast, however, the changes in *Nobuko* from one version to the other have largely been ignored. By exploring the erased narrative of the Nobuko-Tsukuda courtship and the textual alterations regarding love and marriage, we are able to arrive at a much more complex picture of Nobuko's "liberation" and self-discovery. In this chapter I discuss both versions of *Nobuko*. The quotes specific to the 1924–1926 version are cited in endnotes; when the textual differences are limited or unremarkable, or when I specifically discuss the later version, I use quotes from the 1928 work, noting them parenthetically in the text.[9]

Although Nobuko seems to enjoy all the accoutrements of a modern, well-to-do lifestyle, traveling abroad to cultivate herself in the West, she is desperate to establish her own identity separate from her family. In the 1924–1926 version in particular, this is made very clear; it is explained that Nobuko is eager to "touch life directly with her own bare hands," and that she is seeking her own "path" in order to escape being only "an observer" while life passes her by.[10] It is under these circumstances that Tsukuda enters the scene as a mysterious expatriate who stimulates Nobuko's curiosity and makes himself indispensable as an aide to her father. Nobuko becomes close to Tsukuda, and their romance begins abruptly during her illness with influenza. Tsukuda kisses the delirious Nobuko as she lies in a hospital bed; she responds by kissing back and embracing him even as she falls unconscious. Already from the start their courtship is problematic, because it is based not on mutuality or even self-awareness but on a one-way expression of male desire that is answered by a barely conscious sick girl. The romance begins, as it were, in the context of Nobuko's diseased hallucinations; but despite this flaw, the kiss makes Nobuko see herself as a lover who can change and save the unhappy Tsukuda.

This unlikely prince's kiss is described as "awakening all of her senses" (52), as thrilling Nobuko in her sexual awakening even as she loses consciousness.[11] Although the courtship thus begins without any sense of balance between sexual and spiritual love, Nobuko interprets the relationship in ideal terms from the start. In the 1928 version, much of the early part of the story depicting Nobuko's thoughts about Tsukuda and their courtship process are deleted, making her eventual marriage proposal to him seem sudden, jarring, and without context. When we revisit the original 1924–1926 text, however, it becomes clear that Nobuko consistently interprets the relationship through the filter of love marriage discourse.

Tsukuda's kiss, in Nobuko's reading, is an expression of his "true feelings" (chūshin): "Call me what you will, a child or a baby. I understand everything—a thirty-five-year-old man kissing the lips of a twenty-year-old girl whom he formally addresses with her last name? He does this with only fatherly sentiment? What an absurd idea!" She supplements the passionate kiss with spiritual concerns about transformation of character, particularly the chance for Tsukuda to change into a positive individual. She comes to believe that she can provide what (she thinks) he wants: "a bright, straightforward life, brimming with courage and love."[12] Eventually, however, Nobuko experiences problems with Tsukuda's jealous and uncommunicative nature, and after their engagement a number of people try to persuade her to break off the relationship. Yet she remains steadfast in her choice, saying she has "faith" that "love changes people" (94).

She also sees this relationship as a way to claim her own identity and assert her will; she tells Miss Pratt, her concerned tutor, "I am the one who loves him. I am the one who believes in him" (84). Love is seen as combining the spiritual element of self-transformation and betterment with a sexually charged attraction. Love also enables her to claim a unique individual identity separate from her family and friends.

In the 1924–1926 text there is a telling sequence that is entirely edited out of the later book version. After marrying Tsukuda, Nobuko returns to Japan and explains to her angry mother the reason for her marriage: "I wanted for once to be able to love without being told by anyone what to do." Her mother seems sympathetic to this sentiment and becomes less critical of her daughter, but Nobuko is disturbed by her own explanation:

> Thinking deeply about those words that slipped out, that she wanted to be able to love at least once according to her own will, she wondered if this suggested an uncanny, fateful outcome. . . . "Did I come to love Tsukuda by chance, simply controlled by fateful circumstance? If that was the case, it could have been any man who had appeared in front of me under the same conditions!" Nobuko wept, hating her thoughts. "Such ideas are demeaning and painful. It doesn't matter if I lost or won against fate. I loved him because I loved him!"[13]

This question—whether her decision to marry for love was based on a desire for individual choice and will (and thus could have been carried out with any man) or was a result of genuine "true love" that required Tsukuda—sets the tone for her marriage. The narrative suggests that Nobuko may have been in love with the ideal of love marriage but not necessarily with her partner; misreading the situation, she projected love marriage ideology onto a problematic relationship.

The 1924–1926 version clearly illustrates Nobuko's desire for self-identity, agency, and transformation through love. Reading this edition, then, enables us to understand fully why she is so moved when Tsukuda responds to her marriage proposal with the same idealistic language about love and marriage. This famous scene shows Nobuko proposing to Tsukuda in a roundabout way as they walk along the Hudson River. She says that if she were to marry, she would not want to marry anyone but him. She then asks how he would feel about a wife who wanted to keep working even after marriage. Nobuko explains what she desires from a marital relationship:

> "I want to make our love blossom [*yoku ikashitai*]. . . . I want to take what we have nurtured in our hearts and make it grow straight, into some-

thing admirable [*rippa na mono*]. I don't want just to create a husband and wife."

"I understand that."

"I want us both to be at ease and attain a deeper, broader self through this love. . . . I really love you. This is the truth. But I also love my work. Just as much as you! . . . If I had to give up my work······it would be really—painful, but······I wouldn't have any choice but to hold on to my work and······say goodbye······to you." Nobuko bit her lip and just barely managed to hold back her tears. . . .

"That is the last thing you should worry about.—I know that there is something that is important to you. Someone who loves you would never do such a thing, to tell you to give it up! I think this far—even if this meant throwing myself away, I want to help in completing you [*anata o kansei sasete agetai*]. I am not looking for a housekeeper······I have always wanted to assist a woman who has her own work, to make her into something admirable [*rippa na mono ni shite mitai*]······but I am sorry to say that I am lacking in power."

Nobuko was so happy that she stopped short and stood there stiffly.

"Really? Do you really think this? . . . —Thank you so much! Do you know how happy you've made me? Thank you! Oh really! Thank you!"

This sequence is almost identical in both the 1924–1926 and the 1928 versions, although the repeated references to the word "love" (*ai*) seen here are edited out in the later edition. Nobuko believes in the ideals of love marriage and self-cultivation: that the husband and wife should mutually help each other grow. She is thus ecstatic not only to be able to express her own will in choosing her husband, but also to find in Tsukuda the ideal modern man, committed to the progress of his wife in terms of her art and humanity. Nobuko's desire to change Tsukuda's character, to build his "confidence" and "dignity," is perfectly matched with his desire to complete her into "something admirable." Yet Tsukuda's response can actually be interpreted in different ways. To Nobuko, his words echo her own sentiments and beliefs about the ideal form of love and marriage. However, the phrases "I think this far" (*omotteiru hodo desu*) and "I am sorry to say that I am lacking in power" (*chikara no tarinai no ga ikan desu*) can also suggest that Tsukuda only contemplates such ideas but ultimately feels unable to carry them out (78).[14]

Although the scene seems uplifting and empowering for Nobuko—she is the one who proposes and dictates the decisions about their marriage—the text also ominously suggests that the union being formed here is fatally flawed, that it is *not* the ideal model presented by advocates of love marriage such as Hiratsuka Raichō and Kuriyagawa Hakuson. Indeed, the fundamental difference between Nobuko and Tsukuda is already encoded in their names. Although the *kanji* characters for their names are visually similar, Nobuko (伸子) is one who can progress, as symbolized by the vertical stroke in the *kanji* "to grow" (*nobiru*), while Tsukuda (佃) cannot develop and is unable to break out of his rigid shell, as signified in the contained look of the *ta* radical in his surname.[15]

While love marriage discourse flourished during the 1910s and 1920s, there was simultaneously an awareness of the problems inherent in making a quick decision to wed or in blindly worshipping the ideal of love marriage. Poet and *Bluestocking* contributor Yosano Akiko, one of the prominent early practitioners of love marriage, who wed poet Yosano Hiroshi (Tekkan, 1873–1935) in 1901, warned in 1917 that because love marriage is a "democratization of love," both parties are held responsible for their choice of spouse. Selection must be made with the utmost care, because one common danger is to mistake something for love that is not really love: "despite lacking the necessary background to arrive at true love, one decides swiftly that the relationship is love, based on a momentary feeling of curiosity, impulse, sexual desire, powerful emotion, erotic adventure." Yosano stresses that she advocates "love marriage as the ideal marriage," but recognizes that at times it can be "no less dangerous than a go-between marriage."[16]

An example of a popular work that parodies such a problematic desire for love marriage is Tanizaki Jun'ichirō's *Chijin no ai* (A fool's love, 1924–1925), a bestseller published at the same time as *Nobuko*. The protagonist, Jōji, an upwardly mobile engineer enjoying a carefree life in Tokyo, rejects the traditional arranged marriage and instead chooses a life of mutual progress with Naomi, a child-bride he has selected of his own volition. Like Tsukuda, he professes to be committed to the development of his wife, an uneducated, poor café waitress, so that she can become an "admirable" (*rippa*), "great" (*erai*) woman; and when they consummate their marriage, they both weep and promise to work hard to please each other. Yet rather than working toward a heightening of their character and cultivating knowledge, this couple "progresses" through a sadomasochistic love, honing their skills for mutual satisfaction in a radical rewriting of the love marriage ideal.[17]

Although Tanizaki makes fun of this husband-wife dynamic that supposedly mirrors the advancement of Japanese society, *Nobuko*, especially in the original 1924–1926 version, depicts the female protagonist's sincerest hopes for love marriage. Because Nobuko's interpretation of Tsukuda and their relationship is colored by the lens of love marriage ideology, she idealizes their love, misreading a problematic relationship doomed to fail from the start.

Nobuko "grows up" in this novel, not through a simple disillusionment with regard to love and marriage, but through an intense struggle to understand herself as someone who has actively chosen Tsukuda as a spouse.

The real-life issues for women discussed within love marriage discourse are synonymous with the very concerns that Nobuko faces in her marriage. At the time, for example, birth control was a much debated issue. In 1922, birth control activist Margaret Sanger (1883–1966) visited Japan at the invitation of the publishing house Kaizōsha (the same company that published both *Nobuko* and *A Fool's Love*), but the government forbade her to speak publicly about birth control methods. To families overburdened with children, information about birth control was coveted knowledge for both financial and health reasons, but from the government's point of view birth control was a subversive act that would limit the growth and expansion of the nation and empire.[18]

Birth control was a negative practice from the perspective of modern love ideology as well, although for reasons other than the government's desire to increase Japanese subjects. After becoming pregnant for the first time in 1915, Hiratsuka Raichō admits that she had practiced birth control before and understands its value and necessity. However, she says she now believes that, in accordance with Ellen Key's thought, "great love" should lead from love marriage to procreation and the discovery of maternal love; taking "precautions" to prevent pregnancy now fills her with a "severe feeling of disgust" because it "dirties and debases the couple's love." Although Hiratsuka admits to still being fearful about becoming a mother (because of economic responsibility and the demands on her own time for self-development), the growth of her identity that began with love marriage, she is convinced, will be completed through childbirth.[19] Key and Hiratsuka are both very much aware of the conflict between childrearing and pursuing one's own career, but they stress that love as part of female identity progresses from egotism to altruism, with love marriage opening the doors to maternal love.[20]

In discussing her feelings about children with Tsukuda, Nobuko echoes the same ideas. On the one hand, she does not want to have children (for economic and career reasons) and has deep anxiety about childbirth, but on the other hand, she cannot treat birth control in a "purely scientific manner" and feels "guilt" toward the "natural, beautiful, higher" mystery of conception. Tsukuda responds that she should not worry about this issue, because he knows "something of these matters" and "her feelings might change in the future" (80). Nobuko's desire not to have children has been highlighted by critics as an expression of her reproductive freedom and commitment to her work, but the implications of this choice have not been discussed with regard to love marriage discourse.[21]

At one point in their marriage, Nobuko's period is late by two weeks and she is forced to face the fact that she may be pregnant. She looks back on her initial decision not to have children and remembers that it was based on her career; she wonders, however, if this "loathing and fear" she feels toward motherhood is more of an instinctive reaction, that "the woman inside her figured out that he [Tsukuda] is an unacceptable man for a father." The text suggests that Nobuko has made a mistake in her selection of a mate: "Isn't that why she felt such wariness then? She had not wanted that man's child, but chose him as a husband" (209–210). In the original 1924–1926 version, this point is even more explicit:

> Nobuko did not hate or dislike her yet unborn child. The child was sweet. Sacred as a jewel and lovable, the child was of the utmost importance, a source of the highest dreams. Her own child must not be defiled by anyone! Ah, yes. Wasn't it the case that she hated imagining . . . that she would, that she had to, bring this precious, precious child into such an environment with such a man for a father? . . . She did not want this man's child. This man is her husband, a husband she loved and became attracted to—is it ever possible to love someone without wanting a child by him?

To Nobuko's mind it is unclear if her aversion to having children only proves that she has a "strange nature" and a "twisted personality," or if this is a sign that her love for Tsukuda is not legitimate. The installment ends with Nobuko "trying to understand her real self" as she sits alone in a dark, cold room.[22] Although Nobuko's desire to eschew motherhood can be understood as a part of the working woman's dilemma, her ambivalence toward this supposed pregnancy also symbolizes the inadequacy of her marriage, a relationship that is not based on genuine love.

Her late period, it turns out, is only a false alarm. In the logic of love marriage discourse, Nobuko and Tsukuda's love should have blossomed through reproduction, adding to their mutual development; but the marriage is sterile, deficient, and unable to complete Nobuko in this manner. This lack, in fact, turns Nobuko herself into a childlike figure ultimately under Tsukuda's control. Nobuko initially appeared to have agency in the relationship, in actively proposing to him and setting the rules for their marriage; she had bought him a toy duck during their courtship and watched him play with it like a child (73–75). Once married, however, Tsukuda holds the power, treating her like a wayward child and calling her "baby" (275). Nobuko's mother correctly assesses the situation, noting that Tsukuda knows very well how to manipulate Nobuko for his own ends (266).

A true love marriage is a union of two equal selves. Yet throughout the novel we see Nobuko and Tsukuda fighting over the issue of power in the relationship. In Tanizaki's *A Fool's Love*, Jōji and Naomi, who also choose to be childless, engage in a struggle for dominance. The initial status of Naomi as "Baby san" and of Jōji as "Papa san" or "Professor Kawai" is reversed once Naomi begins to have control of her patron. Jōji is eventually humored as "a very good child"; but as the emblematic scenes of their "horseplay" suggest, Jōji only *seems* to have regressed into the subhuman "horse" ordered about by the "rider," Naomi. In actuality he is in full control of their play as the father figure and demanding masochist. The complexity of the power politics within their sadomasochistic relationship playfully problematizes the simplistic notion of equality between husband and wife, questioning this much-idealized notion within love marriage discourse.[23]

Although Nobuko and Tsukuda's struggle is depicted in a much more serious vein, like Tanizaki's characters their interaction also prompts a reexamination of what it means to give "equally" in a marriage. Kuriyagawa Hakuson explains in *Views of Love in the Modern Era* that love marriage completes one's "true self" by, paradoxically, an erasure of the "self." One can achieve a higher self by fulfilling the other's (not one's own) desire, by being completely focused on the other's needs. To illustrate this point, he criticizes Nora, the heroine in *A Doll's House* (1879) by Henrik Ibsen (1828–1906), as an example of failure in this respect. Nora, of course, was an important representation of the New Woman who leaves her husband and children to find her real self; the first Japanese performance of *A Doll's House* in 1911 prompted much discussion, most notably by the Bluestocking women.[24] Instead of praising Nora, Kuriyagawa calls her a foolish "Old Woman" (*furui onna*) for leaving the home:

> Throwing away the Nora-type selfhood [*jiga*] is actually the way to fulfill the true self and enable selfhood to emerge. The New Woman has become the New Wife, and the New Mother. . . . For the man too, if he can offer up his body and soul to the woman that he loves, this is actually the only way to satisfy his real selfhood. The pain of a person who cannot love despite wanting to love, the loneliness of a life when love is gone—all this happens because true, deep selfhood is not satisfied.

Kuriyagawa stresses that this ideal is different from the selflessness expected of women within the "traditional and backward Good Wife, Wise Mother ideology."[25] Both husband and wife must practice self-sacrifice; by relinquishing their egos, the couple can find their better selves, be truly satisfied as individuals, and attain real equality. It is no coincidence that Tsukuda consistently uses the language of self-sacrifice to justify his relationship with Nobuko. He proclaims repeatedly that he will do anything for her; he is prepared to "sacrifice himself" (137), he is "nothing but a sacrificed being" (150), he will "do anything if it will lead to Nobuko's happiness" (223). In his initial promise to Nobuko he says he is prepared to help "complete" her even if it means "throwing" himself "away" (78).

Although Tsukuda's words perfectly echo Kuriyagawa's ideas, he uses such language only to self-identify as a martyr and to maintain a sense of superiority in the relationship. Literary critic Mizuta Noriko suggests that for Tsukuda, "self-sacrifice" means avoiding direct confrontation with Nobuko's "self."[26] Another way to view this is that Tsukuda knows he can manipulate Nobuko; by professing his selflessness, he makes her feel obligated to reciprocate. Nobuko is frustrated by his hypocrisy: "What an unusual person you are, always determined to do something just for the other's sake" (225). Tsukuda does not make Nobuko happy, and they are in a constant battle with each other. He vows that he loves her and that she does not fully appreciate his love; she responds by saying that he is only pretending to be in "an ideal marriage" while being perfectly aware that they are "fighting each other in our hearts" (238).

Ironically, in contrast, Tanizaki's Jōji and Naomi fight, break every moral code, and shatter all lofty concepts invoked by the love marriage ideal, but actually do manage to grow and attain their "true selves" as husband and wife. By the end of *A Fool's Love*, Jōji does everything to fulfill Naomi's desires; he has moved into a Westernized mansion and given up half of his property for her use, enabling Naomi to live as she pleases. For her part, Naomi recreates herself into Jōji's ideal as a *femme fatale*; her skill surpasses even the Hollywood actresses of the silver screen. Tanizaki's couple ultimately become perfect companions, each unable to function without the other. In a parodic reinscription of Kuriyagawa's ideals, they are the inseparable egalitarian couple who fulfill their own desire by fulfilling the other's desire, successfully progressing in their marriage—albeit through sadomasochistic love.

Although Naomi thrives in her marriage, Nobuko is stymied by her relationship, unable to move forward in terms of love, career, or self-cultivation. Tsukuda, who no longer reads much, cannot be a stimulating partner for the intellectually curious Nobuko. Pained by the "lack of an artistic atmosphere" (172) in the home, Nobuko can write only when she is away from him. Although she finds restful moments in their marriage, they are times of complete inertia and inactivity:

> Nobuko felt most at peace when the two of them were not talking or laughing about anything in particular and were sitting dully on the veranda, looking at something, perhaps trees. They were just like two dogs sitting in the sunshine, chins placed on top of outstretched front legs, dozing off. But this sleeplike peace did not last for long. It was always the case that Nobuko began to feel an inexpressible sense that something was lacking. (174)

In both textual versions Nobuko is sad to be sitting still like a dog and fears becoming a "domesticated beast" that grows "used to any environment" (172).[27] Her marriage not only stops Nobuko from developing as a human being, it also reduces her into a dumb animal that stays inert. It is clear that any effort to progress in the marriage is ultimately futile; in order to rouse herself from this stagnancy, there is no other solution for Nobuko but to escape from her marriage. The love marriage discourse that she uses to try to understand this relationship becomes a list of criteria that are not fulfilled; it is only by accepting that her marriage has been a failure that Nobuko can reclaim her own identity.

Marriage as Disease, Divorce as Cure

During the 1910s and 1920s, as love became closely scrutinized as an idealized practice, the question of its legitimacy and morality played an important part in the discussion. Because love could not be scientifically gauged, the pursuit of its "truth" raised many unanswered questions. Was love something that happened only once in a lifetime? Or could it be "real" more than once? If love marriage was based on true love, what did it mean for it to fail? And when was divorce justified? In negotiating these questions, *Nobuko* uses the metaphor of disease to legitimate the dissolution of the Nobuko-Tsukuda union. Without rejecting the love marriage ideal *itself* as a myth, the novel uses love marriage discourse to endorse the separation of Nobuko and Tsukuda as necessary and entirely appropriate.

Since the 1910s, those promoting love marriages were already grappling with questions about the truth of love, particularly in relation to the notion of "free love" (*jiyū ren'ai*). This idea interpreted love as legitimate and genuine no matter how many times or with however many partners it occurred.[28] Used as an excuse, the pursuit of love became an easy justification for casual or multiple relationships. The dangers of practicing such free love were illustrated to the Japanese by the notorious 1916 Hikagejaya incident, a love scandal involving anarchist Ōsugi Sakae (1885–1923) and several prominent Bluestocking women. An advocate of free love, Ōsugi stipulated that men and women should be economically independent, live separately, and have absolute freedom, even with regard to sex. He was married to Hori Yasuko (ca. 1883–1924) and simultaneously involved with two lovers: Itō Noe (1895–1923), editor and publisher of *Bluestocking*; and journalist Kamichika Ichiko (1888–1981). Clearly unhappy with this arrangement, Kamichika stabbed and wounded Ōsugi in 1916.[29]

Because all of these women were associated with *Bluestocking*, Hiratsuka Raichō saw this incident as the unfortunate "swan song" of the Bluestocking Society.[30] In a 1917 *Osaka Asahi shinbun* article, Hiratsuka criticizes free love, citing the Hikagejaya incident as a negative example. She stresses that free love lacks responsibility and is immoral and contrary to the true ideals of love because it puts women in an extremely weak position. Such a misinterpretation of "love," she says, contributes to further corruption of the nation, which is still in a state of "noncivilization" because it holds on to "polygamy" (*ippu tasai shugi*), a "relic . . . of barbaric times." She recognizes, however, that this logic poses a dilemma for love marriage because free love is connected to the issue of "free divorce" (*jiyū rikon*). If love is considered the moral foundation of a male-female relationship (as love marriage discourse argued), it would follow that it would be immoral for the union to continue once the love was gone. Although Hiratsuka believes in free divorce, that is, the right to divorce freely once the love has faded from a marriage, she also comments awkwardly that "this truth, when put in practice, must also have various limitations put upon it, under various terms."[31] Her concern was that the practice of free divorce would lead to multiple love marriages easily begun and terminated, in the same manner as free love.

With the development of love marriage discourse it became important not only to define "real" love as the basis for marriage, but also to determine correctly when love had died and divorce was acceptable. Ellen Key, who was a strong proponent of free divorce, cautioned in *Love and Marriage* that

> only he who, after unceasing effort and patient self-examination, can say that he has used all his resources of goodness and understanding; put into his married life all his desire of happiness and all his vigilance; tried every possibility of enlarging the other's nature, and yet has been unsuccessful,— only he can with an easy conscience give up his married life.[32]

In 1925, writer and dramatist Kurata Hyakuzō (1891–1943), also famous for his love treatises, published a very long and detailed analysis of when it is acceptable to divorce. He argues that "correct marriages" should never be torn asunder, but "false marriages" should always be terminated. This principle obtains in cases of arranged marriages as well as in marriages undertaken for any reason other than love (such as "profit," "lust," "pity"); divorce should also be undertaken when, after marriage, it is discovered that one spouse has mistaken the other spouse's "character" and "value." Because marriage is a project in which one completes and heightens the self through the spouse, marriages that lower one's character must come to an end.[33]

By marrying for love, Nobuko had aimed to complete her self and progress as an individual. The implicit assumption here is one of moral betterment, of advancement in terms of male-female relations. Love marriage, with its emphasis on equality and a higher self, was often perceived to be a preventative for divorce, which was considered the result of lack of choice and unenlightened practices. Many commentators during this period considered love marriage "essentially more enduring."[34] In *Views of Love in the Modern Era*, for example, Kuriyagawa Hakuson suggests that couples who choose their own spouses make more effort in their marital life compared to couples in traditional arranged marriages when problems arise. There is a higher probability of divorce in arranged marriages because the couple makes little attempt to salvage the relationship.[35] The struggle that Nobuko faces with regard to divorce is not over the issue of financial survival, a serious problem, as noted by Hiratsuka in 1923: "the disappearance of love as leading to divorce also means the woman's loss of her livelihood."[36] Nobuko has a career of her own, and her wealthy family would help her financially if necessary. For her, a woman searching for a modern identity, the decision to divorce must be legitimated as an essential need and not considered a regression back to an unenlightened past. Divorce must stem from the lack of love and must function as a corrective to the erosion of her selfhood.

Although postwar feminists have embraced the ending of *Nobuko* and her decision to divorce as a triumphant, liberating moment, the meaning of divorce within love marriage discourse and in the context of prewar Japan is actually quite ambivalent. As historian Harald Fuess points out, during the early twentieth century, divorce increasingly was seen as a "national disgrace." Articles in mainstream and specialized venues discussed divorce statistics, noting that Japan's divorce rates were embarrassingly high for a so-called "modern" nation. Headlines such as "'Japan Leads the World in Divorce' (1916); 'Most Divorces in the World' (1917); and 'Japan's Divorce [Rate] the First in the World' (1921)," indicate society's concern about Japan's image as a backward nation where marriage is not considered sacrosanct. There was also an increased sense of shame about divorce, particularly for women, related to changing notions of virginity, chastity, and sexuality. Fuess suggests that such new attitudes toward divorce contributed to the decline in the number of divorces from the 1900s to the 1930s.[37]

Divorce was thus seen as barbaric and "premodern," as a libertine practice that enabled couples to unite and separate with little hindrance; it was also commonly interpreted as a sign of female disempowerment because of the wife's inability to protest against unwarranted separation or abandonment. At the same time, however, divorce could also be perceived as a "modern" phenomenon in which women gained agency by leaving unsatisfying marriages, thus creating a new morality that emphasized love, equality, and individual will.[38] For Nobuko, it is vital that her choice to separate from Tsukuda be not a backward step but a step in keeping with the ideals of love marriage discourse, that is, a justifiable moral imperative for finding her true self.

In addition to portraying the marriage in terms of lack, *Nobuko* presents the relationship as "diseased," as threatening the health of Nobuko's self. The marriage is configured not as a progression toward a higher state but as a regression and deterioration through illness. Although this aspect of the novel has been overlooked by critics, the theme of disease running throughout the work is an important component for understanding Nobuko's attainment of a modern identity. The failure to "improve" despite treatment and the need to be free from the threat of contamination and contagion legitimate her divorce as cure; the erasure of her identity as a wife becomes an absolute necessity for her self-discovery.

In both the 1924–1926 and the 1928 versions of the story, disease is a prevalent motif from the beginning of the narrative. Nobuko and her father both fall victim to the influenza epidemic in New York and almost lose their lives;

much of Nobuko's early courtship with Tsukuda takes place in the hospital; and immediately after her marriage she rushes back to Japan due to the possibility that her diabetic mother might die giving birth. Once Nobuko begins to feel trapped in their marriage, Tsukuda tries to comfort her, saying, "It will become better.—You will get used to it" (*Ima ni yokunaru.—Ima ni naremasu*) (172). Tsukuda promises improvement in terms of the relationship and Nobuko's state of mind; the word *yokunaru* (become better) also suggests healing or recovery from illness. Perhaps what he is actually suggesting, however, is that Nobuko will get used to the present state of things (*nareru*), a prospect that fills her with fear. The 1924–1926 text emphasizes the illness metaphor somewhat more strongly. In the 1928 version, Nobuko and Tsukuda's courtship in the hospital has been almost completely cut out, but the original installment, titled "Tōmin" (Hibernation, 1924), elaborately depicts their romance in the context of disease. This depiction sets the tone for the "sick" marriage, making dubious Tsukuda's later promise of recovery. He suggests that their relationship will heal because of their love: "It will become completely better [*Ima ni sukkari yokunarimasu*]. We love each other so much."[39]

As a relationship nurtured in illness, however, the marriage has little chance of becoming better; Nobuko does not see any improvement or progression toward health. She tries to convince Tsukuda that they should try living separately and explains, "But when we become sick, we seek another climate or go stay in the hospital, don't we? For us, our marital life is in a state of sickness" (237). Although Nobuko spends a great deal of time away from her husband, illness is a constant presence in the text as a reminder of their relationship. When Tsukuda goes away on a business trip, Nobuko develops a foot injury, made worse by her initial attempt at treating it herself. She still has this injury when he returns, and they travel together to a hot spring, a vacation that Nobuko hopes will cure their marital problems. Yet even on a hike they take during this trip, Tsukuda shows no consideration for Nobuko's bad leg. He does not allow her to rest during a thunderstorm but hustles her along, arm in arm; when she trips and falls on the muddy road, he avoids slipping himself by leaping over her back, almost kicking her in the process. The vacation ends with a fight and they leave for separate destinations. Although hot springs are considered restorative spaces that treat a variety of ailments, their marriage is incurable.[40]

The most significant illness in this work is Tsukuda's lung disease, made manifest as blood in his sputum, a warning usually interpreted as tuberculosis (TB). Although it never develops into full-blown TB and Tsukuda ultimately recovers his health, this disease becomes an important metaphor for the sickness of their marriage. As Susan Sontag has noted, TB (and related lung diseases) is associated with a range of metaphorical meanings due to its mysterious and often deadly nature. Tsukuda, who has always interpreted illness as connected to his emotions and feelings, understands his ailment as "a psychological event."[41] Early on in the novel, for example, he mentions that one can avoid catching the flu by having a strong mental state ("*kokoro no mochiyō*," 22). The fact that he now has lung disease is for him a confirmation of his unhappiness, and proof that Nobuko is making him "suffer" (294). In both traditional Japanese and Western belief systems, lung disease has sometimes been seen as a result of emotional suffering, often a longing for love (*koi wazurai*), and thus is potentially curable through the power of love.[42]

The most influential love story associated with lung disease in the prewar Japanese context is Tokutomi Roka's (1868–1927) *Hototogisu* (The cuckoo, 1898–1899), a bestselling work serialized in *Kokumin shinbun* (People's newspaper) and later turned into plays, film, popular song, and even poetry.[43] By the time Miyamoto was writing *Nobuko*, the story of Namiko, who falls ill with TB and is cruelly forced to divorce her husband, had been widely known for several decades. Namiko is a tragic figure, mistreated by both her stepmother and her mother-in-law. Her disease may be inherited (her mother died from TB), but it is clearly exacerbated by the harsh treatment she receives as a daughter-in-law and by the enforced separation from Takeo, her beloved husband. Although theirs is an arranged marriage, this couple is so much in love that they continue to correspond and long for each other even after the divorce; in the end, Namiko wastes away and dies from the disease.

Although Takeo cannot save Namiko despite his love, Nobuko is able to nurse Tsukuda back to health. Nobuko realizes, however, that she takes care of her husband only to satisfy herself, to see herself as a virtuous person who stays in the marriage even when threatened with the possibility of contagion. In the 1928 edition, this is made explicit when Nobuko says that she is not taking care of him for love but for self-satisfaction (294). Tsukuda, who dramatically suggests that Nobuko divorce him for her own health, insists on reading the Bible, a book Namiko in *The Cuckoo* also reads for comfort. Although Nobuko and Tsukuda remain married, their relationship is not at all like the romantic Namiko-Takeo union; if anything, it is a battle to see who will win in attaining a higher self. Is it the selfless wife who devotes herself to a sick husband, or the selfless husband who prepares for death by reading the Bible and offering his wife her "freedom" (280)?

Tsukuda's disease confirms his reputation as a "hypocrite" with an "empty character" (90, 96), an unworthy husband for Nobuko. Looking at the blood in his sputum, Tsukuda sighs, "It has finally come" (280). He tells Nobuko that he had always expected to die, because for many years he had not taken care of his health. When Nobuko's mother finds out about Tsukuda's disease, she comments, "If it is the case that Tsukuda had tuberculosis and knew about it, how could he marry you and keep it a secret? How sinful and evil of him" (291). In addition to its romantic associations, TB could also signify "sin" or "moral transgression."[44] Not only was it a metaphor for corruption or immorality, it was also a disease that required a moral response on the part of the carrier to "contain" himself—not only through physical quarantine, but also by refraining from marriage and reproduction. By this time, the tubercle bacillus had already been recognized as the cause of the disease, but heredity was also considered an important risk factor.[45] As a sickness that "corrupts" others in proximity and can even be passed on to the next generation, TB was deeply feared. If Tsukuda had suspected such a weakness, his love should have kept him from approaching Nobuko.

Nobuko's mother's words are harsh, echoing the perspective of the unrelenting mother-in-law in *The Cuckoo*, who demands that Namiko be cut off from her son for the sake of the family line and its health. Nobuko's mother tells her daughter, "You must really be very careful. If you end up catching something terrible like that, we don't want it in our house / family [*uchi ja okotowari dayo*]" (291). Yet this desire to cut off disease and demand quarantine is also present in the love marriage discourse promoted by Ellen Key and Hiratsuka Raichō. Even though love is the most important factor in a marriage, those who have hereditary diseases and could potentially pass them on to their children should not marry; the possibility of harming the spouse through infectious disease should also be a deterrent.[46] Ultimately, in Key's view, the free selection of one's partner ("love's selection") would lead not only to the "highest enhancement" of "individual personality" but also to the improvement of the race as a whole; love marriages, in other words, were meant to make "every man and woman well fitted to reproduce the race."[47]

In the beginning of the novel, we see Nobuko claiming to be "a good nurse" (43, 47) who can cure her father's influenza, but she ends up catching it herself and becoming seriously ill. In the 1924–1926 text, Tsukuda gives Nobuko a doll wearing a Red Cross nurse's uniform, as if to provide

Nobuko with a suitable feminine identity as a caregiver who will look after Tsukuda, the diseased patient. This is an ominous foreshadowing in that it becomes clear that Nobuko cannot become his "nurse" without becoming sick herself and succumbing to his twisted character.[48] By presenting Tsukuda as pollutant and Nobuko as victim, the novel underscores the legitimacy of their divorce, not only in terms of the traditional obligation to preserve the family line but also within the logic of love marriage ideology.

The need to maintain Nobuko's health is also a part of the larger project of national progress. The mortality rate from TB was considered a gauge of social conditions. From 1919 to 1933, Japan experienced a decline in TB deaths—a sign of its advancement; yet in 1938 a Western epidemiologist still commented that Japan's mortality rate from the disease was unexpectedly high for an industrialized nation.[49] As Michael Bourdaghs notes, "the binary of health / unhealth, purity / impurity" became a way to understand the health of a society; the individual and the nation were "placed in a new relationship, wherein the purity / health of each was dependent upon that of the other."[50] Tsukuda is a germ that threatens Nobuko, the marriage, the family, and the nation. Although she does not actually catch lung disease from her husband, Nobuko is so influenced by him that she begins to see illness as the norm. Even after Tsukuda recovers from lung disease, he is described as "a kind of sick man in terms of his mental state" (312), and Nobuko feels embarrassed that she is healthy; it takes a friend to reassure her that "the natural state for all that lives is health [*genki*]" (300).[51]

Throughout the novel, Nobuko is drawn to "nature" (*shizen*) and everything "natural," from uncalculated actions to thriving vegetation.[52] We also see the natural cycle of the seasons unfolding as a backdrop to this unnatural, "sick" marriage. Nobuko is in constant spatial movement—going from the United States to Japan, changing her residence several times, vacationing in various places, shuttling back and forth between the Sassa and Tsukuda homes—but her movement does not reflect progress or growth in terms of her marriage. Instead, this insistence on geographical change is reminiscent of a common treatment for TB that moves the patient to a better climate (*tenchi ryōhō*). In Nobuko's case, the sick marriage does not improve despite such efforts. Nobuko continues to work in cramped spaces, trying to write with "a sick perseverance" (317). This oppressive sense is replicated in the relationship, culminating in Tsukuda's threats and demands for her to remain in the marriage. In the end he asks in English, "Do you still love me?" (353), interrogating her for two straight days in a hot, stifling room, closed off from the outside world. Nobuko can only free herself from her "exhausted nerves" and escape "becoming insane" (356) by leaving her husband for good.

In the famous final scene, Tsukuda dramatically frees their pet birds by cutting open the birdcage. Although one flies back into the broken cage, Nobuko refuses to emulate this bird. The ending suggests that she will fly away from this marriage to regain her natural state of freedom. By presenting this marriage as disease, with divorce as the only cure, the novel meticulously legitimates the marital breakdown, portraying it not as immoral or unenlightened but as healthful and progressive. Although Nobuko's love marriage has failed, her liberation from wifehood can be fully understood through love marriage discourse and related ideals. Marriage and divorce in *Nobuko* are not clear-cut opposites; both are part of modern love ideology and interrelated with the values of self-completion and the search for the true self.

Erasing Love Marriage: The Bolshevik Wife

Compared to the 1928 revised edition, the original 1924–1926 serialization of *Nobuko* presents a more complete picture of the Nobuko-Tsukuda relationship, particularly with regard to the concepts of ideal marriage and love. The earlier version clearly shows the ideals that motivate Nobuko and also justify her divorce. Through Nobuko's marriage and its dissolution, the novel explores issues that are at the heart of love marriage ideology. Although the criteria for "real" love marriage were rigidly determined, advocates never fully resolved the questions about its practice in 1920s Japan. *Nobuko* probes such questions, asking what it means for a woman to achieve self-realization through marriage, and examining the relationships between love, marriage, and divorce.

If the 1924–1926 edition does this so clearly, then why did Miyamoto find it necessary to transform the novel for publication in book form, to cut out numerous parts of the text relating to the ideal of love marriage as well as the early depictions of courtship? This editing process, I would suggest, reflects two developments: a shift in the broader discourses on love and marriage, and Miyamoto's increasing dissatisfaction with bourgeois society and its concerns. Miyamoto began revising for book publication toward the end of 1926, saying that "the beginning part [of the serialization] is especially not good." Yet the omissions cannot be explained simply as the need for concision or a change in her "emotions."[53] It is more likely that by the time Miyamoto began rewriting the text, Nobuko's fundamental belief in love marriage ideology and her insistence on marrying of her own volition had begun to seem overly naive. The mid- to late 1920s saw counternarratives to the idealization of love marriage; in 1927, for example, Soviet politician and feminist Alexandra Kollontai's fictional love stories were translated into Japanese, sparking a "Kollontai boom." The short story "The Loves of Three Generations" (1923; trans. 1927 as "Sandai no koi"), was particularly influential; it not only started a series of debates between male and female intellectuals but also underscored the sense that love marriage was becoming old-fashioned as an ideal. In this work, Genia, a young woman who represents the new generation, is unlike her grandmother, who has married twice for love. Genia has no need or desire to feel love and prefers sex without any emotional attachment. Her self-fulfillment comes not from heterosexual relationships but from love for her mother, for Lenin, and for political work. Female writers including Hiratsuka Raichō and Takamure Itsue later criticized Genia's cavalier attitude, objecting to her view that sex is nothing more than a purely physical experience. They were also critical toward male critics who celebrated Genia's "liberated" attitude. In addition to such discussions of the morality of free sex, however, these debates reflect in different ways the growing recognition that love marriage alone could not provide a radical solution to female disempowerment and inequality within Japanese society.[54]

During this period there was also a shift in emphasis within love marriage discourse itself. In the works of popular writer Kikuchi Kan, for example, love marriage becomes less of a sacred ideal and increasingly associated with pragmatic issues. In his extremely popular love treatises published in women's magazines, Kikuchi rejects Kuriyagawa Hakuson's perspective that love is more important than anything else. In *Ren'ai to kekkon no sho* (Writings about love and marriage, 1935), for example, Kikuchi explains that love is a means to an end; it is "a kind of a disease," "a transported state of excitement" that enables one to marry—"a frightening action that cannot be carried out in a normal state of mind." In Kikuchi's view, love marriage is not a marker of national progress or a nurturing site for individual advancement. It is simply one form of marriage that can be more desirable than others, because the partners choose to marry of their own accord and thus have fewer regrets. Kikuchi's down-to-earth treatises, covering issues such as infidelity, sexual diseases, and relationships with one's in-laws, stress that even those who marry for love do not escape everyday concerns and must expend a great deal of effort to maintain the marital relationship.[55] He also makes a point of satirizing the way love marriage has been overly idealized by women. For example, in one of Kikuchi's short stories, "Ren'ai kekkon seido" (The institution of love marriage, 1930), an obsession with love marriage almost destroys the female protagonist's chances of finding a suitable husband.[56] Kikuchi's cynical approach represents a less idealized, more qualified perspective on love marriage that developed from the mid- to late 1920s.

In the 1928 edition of *Nobuko*, the multiple references to love marriage discourse have been erased, muting Nobuko's optimistic belief in the ideal of love marriage. Even more striking, Nobuko questions the institution of marriage itself—an element in the plot that does not exist at all in the 1924–1926 version: "For a man and a woman in love, was marriage the only thing there was?" (67). Nobuko suggests that the identity of "wife" can threaten to erase a woman's individual sense of "identity" (230). Also different from the original version is Nobuko's explanation to her mother about why she married Tsukuda. Instead of discussing her need to love as an expression of self-identity, Nobuko says only that she would not have been happy with a match made "within the same class, with a family with the same traditions or under the condition that one would advance [socially], a little or a lot, as much as fate would allow." In response, her mother tells her, "Your thinking is like a Bolshevik" (115)—presumably the sharpest criticism she can think to direct toward her daughter.

This suggestion of Bolshevism is quite significant in understanding the changed direction of *Nobuko*, which originally focused on the crisis of the love marriage ideal and on questions about modern female identity. The later *Nobuko* tries to incorporate a critique of social institutions and bourgeois society. From the mid- to the late 1920s, the Japanese intelligentsia were increasingly influenced by ideas such as socialism and Marxism, and attracted to the notion of class struggle. As I discussed briefly in the previous chapter, many female proletarian authors expressed desire for an ideal male-female love that supported their commitment to political activism and social change. Yet there was also a growing sense of doubt that love marriage could successfully reorganize social and gender relations—certainly not on its own—and love marriage became further associated with "bourgeois" individualism.

Looking back after the war, Miyamoto commented in 1946 that when she was writing *Nobuko* in 1924 to 1926, she did not fully understand "the new development of history" in which people were beginning to rebel against the traditional class system.[57] In her 1947 history of women's literature, *Fujin to bungaku* (Women and literature), Miyamoto also says that at that time she had no knowledge of the proletarian movement or its literature, and was not aware of class as a concept.[58] However, the effort made in erasing love marriage discourse and including references to social issues in the 1928 edition foreshadows the direction of Nobuko's search for her true self, continued in the postwar sequels that follow her life from after the divorce to about 1930.

Although we never see Nobuko's explicit moment of awakening in the Nobuko trilogy, formerly idealized notions of love marriage, self-cultivation, and progress in the private sphere disintegrate through the course of the three novels. In *The Two Gardens*, Takeyo, Nobuko's mother, falls in love with her son's tutor, an insincere younger man, and seriously considers divorce in order to marry for love. The mother, who wed Nobuko's father in an arranged marriage, overly idealizes love as something on which she has missed out. Nobuko feels sympathy for Takeyo's pure sentiments and adoration of love marriage as a union of spiritual and sexual love, but at the same time she is extremely critical of the way her mother blindly idolizes the tutor. In this 1947 work, Nobuko is able to articulate a clear criticism of love marriage ideology while recognizing why women project their dreams onto this practice; she fears that her mother might make the same mistake as she did in desiring self-completion through love and a marriage made through one's own will.

Yoshiya Nobuko's protagonists are able to find themselves through same-sex love, but for Nobuko the "secondary path" is just as unfulfilling as love marriage. Toward the end of *Nobuko* she befriends Motoko, described as a soulmate; but once they begin to live together, in *The Two Gardens* and *Signpost*, their relationship becomes full of squabbles and miscommunication. Unlike Motoko, a woman who smokes a pipe, uses male styles of speech, and "sees her life through the way her feelings lean toward women," Nobuko interprets their cohabitation as only "mimicking" the traditional husband-wife relationship. Throughout both novels, Nobuko and Motoko are presented as having a platonic relationship; the texts stress that they are not "sexually abnormal people" (*seiteki ijōsha*). It is clear, however, that Motoko's identity is based on the fact that she "loves women the way men love women." In *Signpost*, the two women are taken to a lesbian "café" in Berlin, where Nobuko realizes with a shock that the female couples are composed of one woman wearing a suit and the other wearing a dress, just like Motoko and herself. For Motoko, the everyday aspects of domestic life with Nobuko are a source of contentment, and she revels in her economic independence and work. Nobuko, however, is dissatisfied in the relationship and still yearns for greater meaning in life. In addition to hinting at a difference in their sexual identities, the novel depicts Motoko as an individual focused on achieving personal progress and happiness while Nobuko is the one who desires broader changes that will lead to growth for both individual and society.[59]

By reading Nobuko's development—from the 1924–1926 version highlighting love marriage discourse and the meaning of divorce to the 1928 version that incorporates institutional and class critique, as well as through the two postwar sequels—we can trace her transformation as part of a broader ideological shift in society. The process begins with a focus on the self as a means to attain a modern identity through love, and it is suggested by the end of *Signpost* that Nobuko will turn toward "the group of people who are persevering in their fight against authority."[60] Already in 1937 we find Miyamoto criticizing *Nobuko* in a detached manner: "the ending of *Nobuko* clearly shows that the author was not yet at all aware of what true development meant for the intelligentsia in terms of historicity."[61] In other words, real progress and self-realization can occur only through Marxism and the proletarian movement.

In another 1937 essay, "Wakaki sedai e no ren'ai ron" (Theories on love for the young generation), Miyamoto encourages Japanese youth to look at love and marriage in a new light. She claims that the focus on "freedom of choice and autonomy" for women that was advocated by the Bluestocking Society was historically revolutionary but is now inadequate. Marxist ideology and the establishment of the Soviet Union had transformed the way "progressive men and women of the world" thought about love and marriage. No longer was the understanding based on the perspective of "female liberation or male-female equality" and "abstract ideas about the value of character [*jinkaku*] and freedom in terms of love." The new view emphasized "the relationship between economic power and the individual that fundamentally controls our experiences of love, the class-based differences in love that this creates, and the connection between the possibility for love to flower naturally and the progress of social conditions."[62]

Like many women writers of the period, Miyamoto started with a commitment to selfhood. In a 1915 essay, written in a style reminiscent of Hiratsuka Raichō's famous *Bluestocking* manifesto, "Genshi josei wa taiyō de atta: *Seitō* hakkan ni saishite" (In the beginning, woman was the sun:

On the occasion of *Bluestocking's* inaugural publication, 1911), Miyamoto stresses that the most important thing in life is the "completion of self" (*jiko kansei*): "There is nothing superior to the flower of individualism blossoming on the tree of truth, and its fruit of self-completion can replenish the thirst of the countless many."[63] The original story of *Nobuko* is about a woman who aims to achieve this goal through love marriage but realizes that the relationship is flawed. She arrives at the decision to divorce by thoroughly examining the lack in her marriage and by understanding that the union is a "disease" that threatens her identity. This story is very much shaped by modern love ideology and love marriage discourse, yet through textual revisions and postwar critical re-presentation, *Nobuko* is reconceptualized as a work that promotes woman's liberation from male oppression and attacks "the middle-class environment" and "established conventions of society."[64] Like Nobuko herself, this novel can be best understood as a process that reflects a series of shifts in understanding notions of female completion and self-discovery.

Hiratsuka Raichō turned to maternal love as a way to complete and validate female identity, eventually becoming complicit with the war effort; Miyamoto, on the other hand, embraced Marxism as the answer to the search for the true self. This divergent trajectory for exploring female self-completion guaranteed, to an extent, Miyamoto's postwar success with *Nobuko* as a socially conscious political text. Hiratsuka and other pro-motherhood feminists were required to reinvent their identities and ideologies after the war, downplaying their wartime writing while highlighting their endeavors in early feminism, such as participation in the Bluestocking Society, and actively becoming involved in the postwar peace movement. Unlike these feminists, Miyamoto remained "untarnished" and was able to assert her position easily as a prominent writer on democracy and women's rights in the immediate postwar years. Despite such differences, for many women during the 1920s modern love ideology was a critical starting point for exploring the relationship between individual betterment and social advancement as well as the interrelationship between women and nation. *Nobuko* scrutinizes love marriage and its legitimacy as a space of self-completion; in this tale of a wife's progress, we recognize the desire and conflict in realizing a modern female identity through love.

PART THREE

Reinventing Motherhood

SIX

Maternal Love

Introduction

Perhaps more than any other human emotion, maternal love is considered universal and timeless. Maternal feelings in general, as well as the specific love of a mother for her child, are often seen as inherent and instinctual components at the heart of female identity. Without devaluing the importance of maternal identity, however, I would suggest that the idea that it is a natural and definitive part of womanhood has led to a certain level of oversight. That is to say, historical specificity and the social construction of notions of maternal love are quite frequently ignored. In regard to France, for example, Elisabeth Badinter famously argues against such an essentializing view, pointing out that this "timeless" love emerged as a result of changes in childrearing practices during the eighteenth century. Before this time, upper-class female identity was not based on motherhood, and wealthy women were discouraged from bringing up their own children, despite the well-known fact that infants sent away from home soon after birth often died of inadequate care. During the eighteenth century in France, participation in court and salon culture was deemphasized and the home rose to prominence as an important sphere of activity for upper-class women. It thus became admirable for these women to raise children in their own homes and to pay attention to their children's growth. Badinter suggests that it was only after such social and cultural changes that maternal love became an important aspect of female identity.[1] In Japan, the idea that *maternal love* (*boseiai*) is the defining core of womanhood can also be traced to particular historical developments and discourses. A term created in the twentieth century, its connotation and associated mystique emerged from the development of modern love ideology.

The term *motherhood* (*bosei*) was introduced into the Japanese lexicon during the early twentieth century as a concept translated from the West.[2] Until *bosei* became standardized, words such as *boshin* (maternal heart / feeling) and *botai* (maternal state / body) were used.[3] *Bosei* has a wide range of connotations, referring to the state or nature of being a mother, to motherliness, to the sex that is or becomes a mother, and even to a mother's love for her child. Ellen Key's use of *motherhood* in her writings seems to have played a role in determining the nuance of the word in Japan. Historian Kanō Mikiyo suggests that *bosei* became a standard, everyday term as a result of the famous 1918–1919 Motherhood Protection Debates (*bosei hogo ronsō*), in which Hiratsuka Raichō, Yamada Waka, Yosano Akiko, and Yamakawa Kikue discussed the issue of the state's financial assistance to mothers and the meaning of motherhood for female identity.[4]

Maternal love (*boseiai*), the compound term made up of *bosei* and *ai* and specifically emphasizing love, was not commonly invoked during the 1910s and, according to Kanō, has been widely used only since the late 1920s.[5] The 1930s in particular saw the development of a broad, essentialist view of maternal love, not only as a specific mother's love for her child, but also as an emotion existing *a priori* in all women. The emergence of the idea that this love is a dominant aspect of female identity can be considered a result of nationalistic discourse as well as of modern love ideology. Maternal love is praised as the goal for heterosexual love, but it is also transformed into an essentialist value that revises the paradigm of progress for both individual and nation.

Hiratsuka Raichō and Takamure Itsue

Hiratsuka Raichō was influential in popularizing the idea of the importance of maternal love for the female self, but her ideas about this love changed during the course of the 1910s through the 1930s. In 1915, while expecting her first child, she wrote in *Bluestocking* that although she was not aware of it at the time, the "desire for a child and the desire to become a mother" had already been embedded in the love she initially felt toward her partner, Okumura. In learning of her pregnancy, she at first felt only "anxiety and fear," but these feelings disappeared once she understood that children were a positive result of love. Once pregnant, Hiratsuka fully embraced the viewpoint put forth by Ellen Key in *Love and Marriage* that the female self is realized through heterosexual love. This trajectory leads ultimately and naturally to maternal love, considered of the utmost importance for female completion as well as for the overall health of society. Hiratsuka agrees with Key's point that the "momentous conflict" of present-day life for women is between the "life of the soul" (*sōru raifu*) and the "life of the family" (*famirii raifu*), that is, the choice between individual work that sustains one's own soul, and childrearing that sustains family life. Although she acknowledges this conflict, Hiratsuka accepts her pregnancy, enthusiastically repeating a line from Robert Browning quoted in Key's *The Renaissance of Motherhood:* "Womanliness Means [sic] only Motherhood; all love begins and ends there."[6]

The influence of Key's works and Hiratsuka's own experience of motherhood shaped the course of Hiratsuka's post-*Bluestocking* feminism. Although she was involved to some extent with the "women's rights" (*joken*) movement, which focused on obtaining suffrage and other equal rights, she is usually considered a leader in the "mothers' rights" (*boken*) or "motherhood" (*bosei*) movement, the mainstream form of feminism during the 1930s.[7] Motherhood feminism placed value on sexual difference, stressing various rights for women as mothers or future mothers. Although Hiratsuka accepted the importance of maternal love, during the mid-1910s through the 1920s she did not see maternal identity and "a mother's love" (*haha no ai*) as natural, inherent parts of the female self. Rather, such identity and love emerged through the growth of the child and in the course of the mother-child relationship. The mother's love that develops is a new step in the self-discovery process. Hiratsuka explained in 1917 that she had embraced "romantic love" (*ren'ai*) as the "affirmation of selfhood [*jiga*] and its development" but now understands that it is also a "door that leads to an altruistic life based on love for others [*ta'aiteki seikatsu*]."[8] This love for others is made possible through the experience of maternal love—the highest form of love for a woman and the ultimate goal of female progress.

The notion of maternal love as a sign of love's maturity had already been suggested by Kuriyagawa Hakuson. While promoting the completion of the self through the unification of spiritual and sexual love, he also emphasized the "evolution" of love in *Views of Love in the Modern Era*:

> Romantic love leads to a spirit of mutual support between man and wife, becoming a highest kind of closeness, then progresses even further, changing to parental love for their children. Particularly maternal love [*boseiai*], the most hallowed love that women possess, is in this way rooted in sexual, romantic love and is its manifestation in an altered form. This love is eventually reciprocated by the child through his or her love for the parent. With further evolution and expansion of the spirit of love, this feeling is extended not only to one's family, but also to neighbors, one's own race [*minzoku*], society, and ultimately to all of humanity on earth.[9]

The attainment of maternal love enables women to love beyond the narrow confines of kinship or the individual self. Hiratsuka notes in 1920 that the Bluestocking Society's focus on "the establishment of selfhood" and the proclamation that "women are also human" marked the beginning of the women's movement. With the movement's progression, the aim has now become "the evolution and betterment of the race" through women's identity as mothers, to garner "love's freedom" and "mothers' rights" in order to "re-create" (*kaizō*) society through "romantic love, marriage, re-production, childrearing, and education." The search for true self through romantic love leads to fruition in the discovery of "mothers' love" (*bo ai, haha no ai*), a powerful source of personal and social change.[10]

The progress of the Japanese feminist movement is thus mapped here as a shift away from the notion of selfhood and toward motherhood. Later, Hiratsuka's ideas changed further, and she came to view maternal love as an essential, preexisting aspect of female identity rather than as an outcome of personal experience. This change in her ideas can be understood in part through her relationship with poet, writer, feminist, and (later) historian Takamure Itsue. Takamure's revisions of modern love ideology and her re-writing of motherhood were influential in shaping feminist thought during the 1930s and profoundly contributed to the promotion of a mythologized notion of maternal love.

Takamure was a schoolteacher and journalist in Kumamoto Prefecture during the 1910s and moved to Tokyo in 1920. In the early 1920s she became known for her poetry and other writings.[11] She was not a Bluestocking Society member, but in a 1926 letter to Hiratsuka she presents herself as Hiratsuka's "faithful daughter," born from her "maternal body" and "love" (*ai*).[12] Hiratsuka in turn calls her "my favorite woman living in Japan today," "the true Modern Girl," and "my spiritual daughter" (*seishinteki musume*).[13] At this point, the two women seem to have had similar perspectives on politics and feminism. In 1930, Takamure and Hiratsuka, with twelve others, established Musan fujin geijutsu renmei (Proletarian Women Artists' League) and Takamure began publishing its journal, *Fujin sensen* (Women's battlefront, 1930–1931).[14] Hiratsuka dubbed *Women's Battlefront*, which was strongly influenced by anarchism, "the second *Bluestocking*."[15] Although Hiratsuka's own interest in anarchist ideology was short-lived, her ideas about motherhood and maternal love shifted profoundly in conjunction with Takamure's discourse on love and female identity.

Ren'ai sōsei (Creation of love, 1926), a lengthy essayistic love tract, established Takamure's feminist thought and determined the direction of her future historical research. In this work, Takamure argues for the re-creation of modern love ideology and a new view of love for women. She categorizes different feminist ideologies and the historical understanding of love, explaining that Ellen Key's works promote "*josei shugi*" (womanism), that is, feminism founded on the idea of sexual difference, as well as "*rei-niku itchi shugi*" (ideology of the unification of spiritual and sexual love). Takamure offers in their place a new alternative, what she calls "*shin josei shugi*" (new womanism) and "*ittai shugi*" (becoming-one ideology). She claims these as her own ideas, and that Japanese women will lead a new feminist movement based on these notions.[16]

"New womanism" promotes the idea of sexual difference, but it is different from "womanism" in that it is based on anarchism and calls for the abolishment of all social structures, most importantly the institution of marriage and the educational system. "Becoming-one ideology" dismisses as a "mirage" the idea promoted by Kuriyagawa Hakuson and others that the merging of spiritual and sexual love leads to male-female equality. Takamure suggests instead that love is a desire to be completely at one with the other, a longing impossible to achieve either by a merging of minds or the act of sex. This desire is manifest in reproduction, which at the level of the sperm and ovum entails perfect unification, a becoming-one. In a mystical interpretation of history, Takamure views this notion of becoming-one as a movement toward the future in which sexual difference gradually disappears and humanity ultimately dies out as a result. Love is an impulse toward this "oneness" and is thus at once productive and destructive.[17]

On the surface, *Creation of Love* seems to be a rambling, often illogical "work of negation" in which Takamure attacks a broad range of philosophies and ideologies.[18] Its argument and free-flowing, unstructured form, however, suggest an important challenge to the understanding of progress in relation to love and female identity. *Creation of Love* rejects the notion of advancement, considered the project of modernity, and reveals disappointment with the modern love ideal, seeing it as an inadequate means for a woman to find her true self. Takamure critiques Key's faith in "evolution and betterment" and asserts that human history leads to an end rather than to endless progress.[19] This rejection of the trajectory of development expresses a desire to return (*kaiki*) to a transcendent past. It is no accident that the text ends with a discussion of romantic relationships in the ancient period, citing examples from the poetry collection *Man'yōshū* (*Ten Thousand Leaves*, eighth century) and the mytho-historical *Kojiki* (*Records of Ancient Matters*, 712) as exemplary instances of male-female love.[20]

By rejecting the forward/upward direction of history and promoting a return to a premodern, pre-Westernized Japan, Takamure revises modern love ideology. She suggests that the essence of female identity—the "instinct" (*honnō*), "naturalness" (*shizen*), and "authority" (*ken'i*) in love and reproduction that can be seen in ancient Japanese women and goddesses—already exists within the Japanese woman. Thus, women can reclaim love (*ren'ai*) and maternal love (*boseiai*) as essential, natural parts of womanhood by returning to the collective past, which offers a timeless, eternal sense of identity.

This work by Takamure creates a new way for women to affirm themselves through love. Maternal love, on a continuum with romantic love, is praised as an "instinctive," "pure love" (*junshin na ai*), a "love of the great earth" (*daichi no ai*).[21] Kanō Mikiyo suggests that Takamure "established the mythic, metaphoric notion of motherhood as the pillar of feminism." *Creation of Love* was instrumental in making "motherhood" (*bosei*) a part of female "nature" and "instinct," and the notion of maternal love further expanded mythic associations.[22] Hiratsuka highly praises *Creation of Love*: "In this book, we can observe the original, unsoiled, true soul of womanhood, unable to be found in the intellectual contemporary woman. Here is instinct, passion, imagination, wisdom."[23]

This validation of maternal love as the originary source of female power was certainly not the only feminist viewpoint at the time. Marxian socialist Yamakawa Kikue, for example, still valued the notion of progress and claimed that women needed to advance further. In 1928, Yamakawa commented that "women have awakened to the value of selfhood" and "achieved great progress" in accepting love marriage as a basis for male-female equality, but they have not come far enough in the fight for economic independence necessary to experience the "true love" of equals.[24] It was the feminism advocated by Takamure and Hiratsuka, however, that became dominant during the 1930s. Rather than seeking love between men and women that mirrored equality between the sexes, these women turned to motherhood and maternal love as the ultimate source of empowerment. Discovering "true love" at the core of female identity meant that no further betterment was needed; the "modern" trajectory of progress is abandoned and a return to "premodern" origins is promoted. By 1930, Hiratsuka's views on maternal love have completely changed. No longer is this love a part of the development of modern female identity and based on personal experiences of childbirth and childrearing. Instead, Hiratsuka praises maternal love and motherhood as a mystical "instinct" that exists *a priori* in all females, "more powerful and larger" than she can now comprehend.[25]

Nationalism and Feminism

The endpoint of modern love ideology, the idea that women could complete their selves through love, is a return to maternal love as a mythic, essential force unique to women. This "return" can be seen as a revisionist alternative to the quest for true selfhood that focuses on male-female love, but it is also the expected outcome of an ideology that equates the progress of women with the so-called evolution of love. Maternal love in this sense is limiting because it erases other possibilities for female identity, but as a love specifically associated with women, it also creates a space of difference, allowing the construction of a unique (and even superior) identity vis-à-vis men.

Certainly this validation of maternal love is part of broader social changes from the mid- to late 1920s that question the idea of progress and highlight the importance of motherhood. Historian Kano Masanao notes that with the destabilization of the traditional family structure and the loss of patriarchal authority, maternal love was increasingly touted as an enduring, forgiving love, able to hold the family together. As the idea of romantic love and love marriage became more widespread, maternal love came to be considered a more "solemn" love than heterosexual love and an "unchanging" love that united the family through its focus on the parent-child relationship.[26] The rise of nationalistic discourse and the beginning of the Fifteen-Year War also fueled the promotion of maternal love, not only as an actual virtue for mothers, who were expected to protect the homeland and produce imperial subjects, but also as a powerful symbolic ideal that guaranteed the integrity of the family-state. The Greater Japan National Defense Women's Association (Dai Nihon kokubō fujinkai), a federation of "common women" established in 1932, for example, placed the greatest importance on expressing "maternal love" to soldiers and their families. This group's activities expanded especially after the 1937 start of the China War and the National Spiritual Mobilization (*kokumin seishin sōdōin*) campaign; the women helped families of the war dead, retrieved soldiers' remains, and assisted wounded soldiers. It was one of the largest women's groups in Japanese history; one of every two adult females became a member.[27] Particularly from the late 1930s to the end of the war, images and discussions of maternal love proliferated within all levels of culture, profoundly shaping both female and national identities.[28]

Both Hiratsuka and Takamure, like most feminists during wartime, ultimately became complicit with the state. The feminist agenda and the nationalist cause merged in lionizing women as valuable subjects able to participate in both the private and public spheres, reproducing and raising children but also working while men were at war.[29] This validation allowed all women to be elevated by the concept of maternal love, regardless of their actual biological experience.[30] The term "*josei*" (woman or female) became increasingly interchangeable with "*bosei*" (motherhood) after the beginning of the China War.[31] Also, newly created vocabulary such as *boseiga* (maternal self)—used in place of *jiga* (selfhood)—and the notorious "*kokkateki bosei*" ("motherhood-in-the-interest-of-the-state") inextricably bound individual female identity to the needs of the nation.[32] Such convergence of female and maternal identities, as well as the erasure of self and the promotion of the state, constricted women; at the same time, however, it also enabled the articulation of a gendered Japanese identity that appeared powerful and unique. We see this expressed, for example, in a 1940 campaign ad from the popular women's magazine *Friend of the Housewife* that called for entries in the "Moving Tales of Maternal Love Fiction Contest": "Of all the love in humans, there is no love as pure and unsullied as a mother's love. There is no love as noble and great. Furthermore, it is known that the Japanese have the strongest feelings of maternal love of all peoples in the world."[33] By 1943, selfless maternal love was considered the "invincible weapon" of the nation: stoic mothers encouraged their sons' sacrifice for the war, and sons returned their mothers' love with obedience. As *Nihon no haha* (The Japanese mother, 1943), by Yamaguchi Aisen, suggests, this love is a mystical bond that makes both mother and son immortal and part of the greater national body: "When soldiers are dying on the battlefield, they praise the name of the emperor by calling out 'Banzai' while they are still conscious. But once they begin to lose consciousness, it is said that they call out, 'Mother.' When human beings lose consciousness completely, they become gods, and they return [*kangen*] to become reincorporated as one with the god Mother [*haha naru kami*]. This does not occur with foreigners, because they do not have the same kind of parent-child relationship." This frightening love that binds together mother, child, and emperor extends beyond personal or biological ties, and functions as a mark of an unparalleled and distinct Japanese identity. The author stresses that in order to be a "true Japanese mother," one must love all Japanese as one's own, as "treasures of the nation."[34] This love, at once private and public, powerful and self-denying, became not only the central aspect of Japanese female selfhood, but also an essential signifier of the Japanese nation itself.

In short, during the mid- to late 1920s, the notion of maternal love began to change; no longer a specific mother's love for her child, it ultimately became an essential part of female identity and a mythic power that continuously validated her true self. During the Fifteen-Year War, the return to an authentic nativist identity and the goal of "overcoming" the West became further tied to the worship of motherhood and maternal love. Such a "discovery" of maternal love, the result of modern love ideology and the search for female identity, was thus distinctly determined by nationalist propaganda and changes in feminist thought.

Maternal Love, Women Writers, and Okamoto Kanoko

Discourses about motherhood and maternal love became particularly important during the 1930s. After the China War began in 1937, mother and nation were increasingly fused, and with the start of the Pacific War, the ideas represented in *The Japanese Mother* became well established. It is important to remember, however, that a wide variety of literature was being published throughout the 1930s; and we should not assume that all writers, even during the late 1930s, suddenly focused *only* on motherhood and mothers. To be sure, as novelist Sata Ineko observed in 1937, there was a publishing boom for books theorizing about motherhood; but in general fiction and women's literature, not all works discussed motherhood, and when they did explore the topic, they treated maternal love from a variety of perspectives.[35]

Motherhood was often illustrated in day-to-day terms in I-novels by women writers; rather than presenting an idealized image, these texts pointed out the social and biological realities of reproduction and childrearing. Although in modern love ideology maternal love may have been the fruition of romantic love, many women were raising stepchildren as well as children from former marriages or liaisons. This often caused conflict within the household and led to questions about husband-wife and parent-child relationships. In Sata's I-novel *Kigi shinryoku* (The new green of the trees, 1938), the protagonist is torn between love for her child (from a former marriage) and a budding relationship with her future husband, who jealously objects to her identity as a mother.[36] Motherhood is not presented as an all-encompassing identity here; despite experiencing strong feelings of love for her infant, the protagonist also recognizes how these emotions complicate work and romance.

In general, it is in popular literature (by both men and women) rather than pure literature that we find the idealistic praise of maternal love. In Yoshiya Nobuko's bestseller *Otto no teisō* (The husband's chastity, 1936–1937), for example, maternal love is the linchpin that solves all conflict for both family and nation.[37] Although this work is famous for questioning the sexual double standard regarding chastity and fidelity, the narrative is very much focused on the redemptive qualities of motherhood. The childless protagonist, on discovering her husband's affair, becomes determined to think of herself not as his wife but as his mother who will patiently correct his wayward behavior. She ultimately adopts her husband's child by another woman and develops an intense bond with this mother and child through "maternal love." It is through such a pure, superior love that the husband is reformed, family bonds are reestablished, and the female lover is even able to marry another man. With such selfless love uniting these characters and their families, the future of the Japanese empire is secured. Although this work contains many elements of rebellion, such as the overly passionate sisterhood of the two women and the critique of patriarchy, *The Husband's Chastity* presents a pro-motherhood message suitable for the times. Maternal love is an all-important virtue for both woman and nation, and an essential part of female identity regardless of actual biological experience.

Although popular literature played a valuable role in promoting motherhood, the most recognized name in 1930s fiction featuring motherhood and maternal love is the pure literature writer Okamoto Kanoko. Okamoto was involved in the feminist literary movement from its early years; she met

Hiratsuka Raichō in 1907 and joined the Bluestocking Society in 1911. She became a regular contributor to the journal, and her first *tanka* poetry collection was published as a book by the Society in 1912. Her writing career started with poetry, particularly poems focusing on heterosexual love; but during the late 1930s Okamoto prolifically published fiction that explored maternal love in relation to female identity.

Many of these works, read as semiautobiographies, are interpreted as celebrations of her own identity as a mother. Contrasted with I-novels by women that question or criticize motherhood in some way, Okamoto's works are seen as rapturously endorsing maternal love. Her stories are also often viewed as being complicit with nationalist-imperialist politics. Instead of simply reading these texts as translations of personal experience or expressions of nationalism, however, we should recognize their engagement with broader discourses about love. Okamoto wrote these works using modern love ideology and the changing meanings of maternal love, incorporating ideas that were of crucial importance during the 1930s.

To an extent, such use of the theme of maternal love may have been a strategic decision. Okamoto was, after all, a woman writer trying to create her own niche when national and maternal identities were becoming closely intertwined in the cultural imagination. This was not, however, just a superficial strategy. I suggest that by focusing on maternal love, Okamoto was able to contemplate fruitfully the relationships between woman, nation, and the project of progress in modernity. In the next chapter I turn to Okamoto's late 1930s fiction—works that articulate the contradictions and problems associated with the emergence of a transcendent maternal identity and its complex relationship to modern Japan.

SEVEN

Okamoto Kanoko
and the Mythic Mother

Introduction

Okamoto Kanoko once described herself as a "camel" with "three humps"—
"poetry, novels, and religion"—three areas of literary production intrinsic
to her identity.[1] Despite her untimely death in 1939 at the age of fifty, she
enjoyed considerable success in all three genres. Okamoto began publishing
tanka poetry in 1906 in *Myōjō* (Morning star), and her debut poetry collection, *Karoki netami* (Light jealousy, 1912) was the first book to be published
by the Bluestocking Society. From 1912 to 1915, Okamoto published approximately two hundred *tanka* poems in *Bluestocking*.[2] Starting in the late
1920s, she wrote plays, essays, and poetry related to Mahāyāna Buddhism
and became famous as a Buddhist philosopher-writer. After returning from
a sojourn in Europe (1929–1932), she began to publish fiction; the 1936
short story "Tsuru wa yamiki" (The crane is sick), about novelist Akutagawa
Ryūnosuke (1892–1927), launched her career as a prominent fiction writer
and secured her association with the highbrow journal *Bungakkai* (Literary world). During the last four years of her life (1936–1939) she published
prolifically, and even after her death, until 1941, a number of posthumous
novels appeared, stoking a "Kanoko boom."[3]

Okamoto is known for her affluent lifestyle, her mysterious love affairs, and the dramatic relationship she had with husband Okamoto Ippei (1886–1948) and son Okamoto Tarō. Ippei is famous as an early political cartoonist; avant-garde artist Tarō is recognized for works such as "Taiyō no tō" ("Tower of the Sun"), the symbolic monument of the 1970 Japan World Exposition (*Nihon bankoku hakurankai*). Critics have tended to rely on autobiography to read Okamoto's texts, perhaps because her life was so unconventional. Buddhist nun and writer Setouchi Harumi (Jakuchō, 1922–), for example, helped boost Okamoto's fame with her engaging and well-researched biographies *Kanoko ryōran* (Kanoko in bloom, 1962–1964) and *Kanoko ryōran sonogo* (After Kanoko in bloom, 1978). These books renewed critical interest in Okamoto and inspired subsequent feminist criticism, but they also strengthened the view that Okamoto's fiction was very much tied to her personal experiences.[4] It can be said that Okamoto's writings have been overshadowed by her life; it is important to take biographical details into consideration, but at the same time it is limiting to interpret all of her fiction as I-novels or as reflections of her religious beliefs.

The works written in the late 1930s, especially those that explore motherhood, are particularly prone to be read from such a standpoint, as reflections of Okamoto's love for her son or as a narcissistic self-identification with the all-forgiving Kannon, the maternal Goddess of Mercy.[5] These works have additional "baggage" as well: they were highly praised by writers who held strong pro-imperialist, nationalistic beliefs, such as Kamei Katsuichirō (1907–1966) and Hayashi Fusao (1903–1975). Although Okamoto died in 1939, before the start of the Pacific War in 1941, her posthumous validation was spearheaded by men who belonged to the Japan Romantic School and advocated a "return to Japan" (*Nihon e no kaiki*). This group is widely remembered for its participation in the 1942 Overcoming Modernity (*Kindai no chōkoku*) symposium documented in *Literary World*.[6] In other words, Okamoto's later works are usually read from a biographical perspective, or seen as endorsing wartime ideologies associated with her right-wing admirers.[7]

In this chapter I take a different approach, exploring Okamoto's "Boshi jojō" (Mother and child, 1937) and *Shōjō ruten* (Wheel of life, 1939) to show the complexities and subtle nuances in her presentation of maternal love and motherhood.[8] By engaging with the notion of love's progress and using a range of important discourses from feminist thought, native ethnology, and women's history, Okamoto questions what it means for women to arrive at maternal love as the fruition of their true self. These works cannot simply be reduced to autobiography or religion, nor are they straightforward nationalistic texts promoting the mother as the ideal image of womanhood. Rather, they produce alternative narratives for understanding the relationships between modernity, national identity, and the Japanese woman. The maternal love in these works is multivalent, simultaneously endorsing and questioning the trajectory of female completion and the meaning of modern female identity in 1930s Japan.

From "Mother and Child" to Wheel of Life

When Okamoto joined the Bluestocking Society in 1911, she was a wife, already married in a love match to Okamoto Ippei, and a mother, having given birth to son Tarō earlier that year. The *tanka* poems she contributed to the journal do not focus on motherhood or maternal love, however, but are primarily about romantic love. Ironically, the most notable reference to motherhood found in her *Bluestocking* writing is in a letter that describes "*sango no gyakketsu*" (blood rushing to the head after childbirth), a condition that seems to be the equivalent of postpartum depression. This illness apparently caused Okamoto to have a serious mental breakdown in 1913.[9] Although Okamoto is remembered as a writer who focused on motherhood, most of her works on this topic were written during the 1930s, only after maternal love became prominent in the cultural imaginary as an ideal for female self-completion.

Okamoto's most famous work on maternal love is the semiautobiographical "Mother and Child," published to great acclaim in the March 1937 issue of *Literary World*. Critic Kobayashi Hideo (1902–1983), who praised this story in a newspaper review, highlights its "unique interpretation of maternal love [*boseiai*]."[10] The protagonist of the story is a married writer referred to as "she" (*kanojo*) whose son Ichirō lives in Paris. Although "she" did not want to be separated from her son, she allowed him to stay abroad to study art while she and her husband returned to Tokyo. This woman's love for her son is so profound that she begins to experience strong emotions toward a young man named Kikuo, who reminds her of Ichirō. They are on the verge of having an affair, but she resists the temptation because her "maternal instinct" prompts her to break off the relationship. The ending of the story, however, is ambivalent; she imagines the "motherhood" within her welcoming Kikuo's mirage with open arms, and it is suggested that her understanding husband may allow her to consummate the affair with Kikuo, who remains unmarried for her sake. Published several months before the start of the China War, this work complicates the association of motherhood with self-sacrifice and asexuality. The protagonist's "maternal instinct" forces her to remain chaste because she feels that her love for Kikuo "defiles" her son, but at the same time her continued fascination with Kikuo suggests the presence of incestuous desire, a taboo maternal love.[11]

The writer in this story identifies herself solely through the love she has for her son. Yet the text does not promote a simplistic self-fulfillment through maternal identity in the vein of the Good Wife, Wise Mother, that is, through selfless service to the family. Indeed, the traditional mother is criticized through the figure of Kyōko, Kikuo's mother, whose name is written with the *kanji* character for "mirror." Kyōko "mirrors" the protagonist as a kind of doppelganger who embodies what "she" is not. Although they are both mothers who love their sons, Kyōko is concerned with the mundane values of society; she is eager for Kikuo to finish college, marry, and get a good job. Although she is a widow, she continues to be ruled by patriarchal authority and remains enclosed within the stifling space of the home, a structure covered by creeping vines. As critic Kōra Rumiko points out, Kyōko's entrapment is further emphasized by the vine-leaf pattern on her kimono. A plant that needs to wrap itself around something in order to grow, the vine can be read as both patriarchy and the family that lives off the mother's sacrifice.[12] The writer, "she," in contrast, wants Ichirō (and by extension Kikuo) to fulfill his dreams and realize his true self. The gates and lock of her property are also covered by vine, but she herself moves about freely outside, at home in the public spaces of Paris and Tokyo.

The title of this story, "Boshi jojō," translated literally would be "Mother and Child, a Lyric." The word *jojō* suggests that the story is "lyrical," that is, a poetic presentation of a mother and child relationship, but it also means an "explication of one's thoughts and emotions." In this sense, the story can be seen as a manifesto that endorses a love that extends beyond a narrow understanding of maternal feeling. The motherly love that "she" feels toward Kikuo is an all-consuming obsession, stronger than the emotion she has for her husband. Her love is a desire to protect this young man from his own mother and from filial obligations, but it is also a highly romantic and erotically charged feeling. This unconventional love is disconcerting because it subverts the idea of a pure, asexual mother's love and exposes her incestuous desire. The protagonist's maternal love also opens the way for absolute self-affirmation, offering her the possibility of both romantic and maternal fulfillment that do not require any self-sacrifice.

In writing about motherhood during the late 1930s, Okamoto rides the wave of pro-motherhood sentiment in society. In March 1937, for example, the Mother-Child Protection Act (*Boshi hogo hō*) was passed, giving financial assistance to poverty-stricken mothers and caregivers of children under age thirteen. The passage of this law was considered a triumph for Ichikawa Fusae's feminist movement, which had given up lobbying for suffrage in 1934 and chosen instead to advocate for motherhood protection.[13] It is significant, in this context, to note that "Mother and Child" presents taboo elements but they are never actually practiced. That is to say, despite the ambivalence of the ending, "she" remains a chaste wife and mother, faithful to her family; the affair with Kikuo remains only a *possibility*. By taking this strategy, the story cultivates both aspects of maternal love: on the one hand, it is a radical and transgressive exploration of a mother's love that defies social convention; on the other hand, it reinforces the purity and nobility associated with maternal love. This approach allows the story to thrive in the cultural context of the late 1930s, a time in which motherhood was a central aspect of female identity. By presenting this story as an I-novel that describes her own deep love for her son, Tarō, and the unconventional relationship she has with her husband, Ippei, Okamoto markets herself as an author who embodies a "unique interpretation" of maternal love.

The love that "she" (*kanojo*, echoing the name Kanoko) has for Ichirō (a combination of Ippei and Tarō) certainly functions to heighten the intrigue about Okamoto just as she is establishing her name as a pure literature writer, but it is inadequate to read this work only in the light of biographical facts or as a marketing strategy for a female writer. It is also unconvincing to say that it is a straightforward complicit text that endorses nationalistic ideas about motherhood. Although "Mother and Child" is the most famous of Okamoto's motherhood stories, it needs to be understood within the broader context of her late 1930s writing, as the starting point for Okamoto's reexamination of maternal love as a goal for female development and self-completion.

The ambivalent ending of "Mother and Child" suggests the multiple meanings of maternal love as well as its radical potential, but it is in *Wheel of Life*, published in *Literary World* several months after Okamoto's death in 1939, that the exploration of this love is taken even further. Serialized from April to December 1939 and published by Kaizōsha as a book in 1940,

Wheel of Life revises both modern love ideology (and its schema of creating a modern female self) and the broader framework of modernity.[14] It presents maternal love not in any actual terms of motherhood but as a symbolic, ultimate self-love that fulfills the individual. This love also becomes a way to transcend the linear trajectory of progress in terms of gender and modernity; in essence, it enables a reordering of traditional power dynamics between the sexes and between advanced and developing nations.

More than four hundred pages in length, written in a dense, baroque language, the novel relates the story of a girl named Chōko, "butterfly-child," who grows up and searches for her true self. The first-person narrative is told in her voice, but it is by no means a straightforward tale, because it features a series of bizarre occurrences and complicated twists and turns of events. The work can be divided roughly into three parts. First, we see Chōko's childhood and schoolgirl years in Tokyo; she is caught up in a series of love triangles and in a lengthy adventure involving her schoolteacher, Miss Ataka. Second, after the death of Chōko's mother, her only kin, Chōko leaves home to wander around the countryside, pretending to be a mad, mute beggar. Here Chōko narrates the stories of the various characters she meets and provides commentary; these tales often focus on the meaning of love. Third, Chōko's real identity is discovered and she settles down, becoming a prosperous businesswoman; in the end, however, she leaves town with a mentally disabled beggar named Bunkichi, a kind of symbolic son figure, to embark on a new journey.

The style of the text can be described as modernist, involving shifts in time, perspectives, and identities; multiple embedded stories; and mixtures of narrative genres, including legends and myths from various cultures and religions. With Chōko's maturity, the narrative becomes increasingly fantastic, shifting from a realistic story to one with supernatural elements. Maryellen Toman Mori suggests that this work combines the features of a *bildungsroman* and a "novel of rebirth and transformation."[15] Ultimately, Chōko discovers her true self, not as a real mother but as an asexual mythic mother figure called the "*Ur Mutter*" (*Ūru Muttaa no onna*), the "root mother" (*ne no haha*), full of "maternal universal love" (*boseiteki no hakuai*).[16]

Although this work has few autobiographical elements, critics tend to call it Okamoto's "spiritual autobiography," a narrative in which the author celebrates her own life through the powerful protagonist; others read the story as a Mahāyāna Buddhist parable that replicates the course of enlightenment.[17] In general, this work has not been given the critical attention it deserves, despite the fact that it continued to be read in the immediate post-war years as a significant, representative work of modern Japanese litera-ture. Novelist Dazai Osamu (1909–1948), for example, considered this novel "one of the three great full-length novels of modern Japanese literature," along with Miyamoto Yuriko's *Nobuko* and Shimazaki Tōson's (1872–1943) *Yoakemae* (*Before the Dawn*, 1929–1935).[18] Although it is a strange and puz-zling text in terms of both content and style, *Wheel of Life* is an important work that revises modern love ideology and reconsiders the relationship be-tween woman and nation. The complex possibilities for maternal love that Okamoto began to probe in "Mother and Child" find full expression in this later full-length novel. Indeed, it is through this work that we can un-derstand issues of modernity, gender, and national identity during the late 1930s as Japan tried to overcome the trajectory of modernity. In the follow-ing sections I read *Wheel of Life* through its conversation with contemporary discourses on maternal love as well as national history and identity.

Becoming a Female Marebito

As she grows up, in the first part of the novel, Chōko, an illegitimate daugh-ter of a wealthy professor and a *geisha*, encounters various kinds of love. As a sixteen-year-old enrolled in a progressive, coed school, she begins to feel the desire to experience "that something called romantic love" (*koi toka ai toka iu mono*, 41).[19] At the same time, however, she does not feel this will fulfill her deeper yearning for an eternal love, something she can only call "eternal father, eternal mother" (*eien no chichi, eien no haha*, 78) or "root parents" (*nemoto no fubo*, 30). Having observed the problems between her real parents, Chōko suspects that all male-female relationships only create disappointment, and she seeks a transcendent love. Men are drawn to her, but she already knows they will not provide her with what she is looking for. Nor does Chōko turn to same-sex love as an alternative. An important character, Miss Ataka, Chōko's physical education teacher and a proponent of "puritanism" (*pūritanizumu*, 66; celibacy), makes sentimental overtures to her, but Chōko rejects outright the role of younger "sister."

Chōko's progress is unusual in that it entails turning away from various forms of love. In the beginning she seems to be an idealistic girl, unsatisfied with relationships, but it quickly becomes clear that Chōko is no ordinary character; she shows a godlike nature with supernatural abilities. For Chōko, earthly love and sex have little meaning; although she eventually has a relationship with one of the male characters and loses her virginity, it is the result not of "love or passion" but of a "weary languorousness" and a rejection of society's overemphasis on female purity. The relationship ends with little ado and she remains unattached throughout the rest of the novel. Because sex for her is of little consequence in light of "the pain in this world of impermanence [*shogyō mujō*]" (229–230), her transcendence of sexual desire can be read as a Buddhist message about the mutability of human existence and relationships. At the same time, however, Chōko's journey and quest for a higher love is not simply an allegory of enlightenment; it is also a mythologization of the modern female search for self-completion through love. Instead of finding fulfillment through same-sex love, romantic love, or a love marriage, she will complete her identity by finding eternal love within her own self.[20]

Interpreting Chōko is a difficult task because she is a realistic character in a coming-of-age narrative but simultaneously a woman endowed with symbolic meaning. I would suggest, however, that rather than discount the supernatural elements in the story as outlandish embellishments that disrupt the realistic narrative, it is important to recognize that myths, legends, and religious symbolism are central parts of the text and play a key role in creating a kind of mythic narrative. This larger-than-life aspect of the novel produces a sense of timelessness, which in turn highlights Chōko as an everywoman searching for true self through love while interrogating the linear trajectory of modernity.[21]

In this quest for self-discovery, Chōko looks for her roots. Returning to her origins means accepting her father's real lineage; although her father, Chōzō, had been adopted into a professor's family, he is actually the son of a beggar (*kojiki*). In her own search for self Chōko adopts this identity, disguising herself as a beggar to travel away from Tokyo. Chōko's wanderings are associated with the Buddha's archetypal spiritual quest; her travels may also imply the transmigration of the soul progressing toward enlightenment.[22] The fact that Chōko pretends to be a crazy mute who can say only "*Ah*" and "*Un*" also suggests that she symbolizes eternal space and time as encapsulated in the Sanskrit *a-hūm*—the alpha and the omega, the beginning and the end, the entire cosmos embodied between two points.

In addition to such religious allegory, Chōko's itinerancy can also be interpreted vis-à-vis the figure of the vagabond, a prominent female identity in the literature of the time. In Hayashi Fumiko's (1903–1951) *Hōrōki (Diary of a Vagabond*, 1928–1930), a hugely successful novel reprinted throughout the 1930s, the female wanderer is a medium of modern language, moving fluidly through different spaces, identities, and jobs, as well as through different literary genres and styles. In *Diary of a Vagabond*, the narrator often disappears into the overwhelming flood of text while at the same time asserting a powerful corporeal self that desires and is desired, encountering different lovers. As Seiji M. Lippit and William O. Gardner both point out, Hayashi's work rejects the notion of woman as a passive object of male desire, emphasizing instead her independent agency and sexual presence. At the same time, the narrator is also a disembodied vessel for different texts and voices, moving easily in and out of various perspectives.[23]

Okamoto's wanderer in *Wheel of Life* resembles Hayashi's narrator in *Diary of a Vagabond* in this respect: she is an unobtrusive, yet omnipresent medium for the multiple voices that construct the novel. Chōko is both insider and outsider in the communities she haunts; her status as a harmless beggar allows her to be a part of the landscape and to experience other characters' life stories as an extension of her own journey. It is through her voice that other characters' stories are told; all of these people are, in their different ways, searching to complete themselves through love. In particular, Chōko's voice melds with that of a woman named Ohide, who cannot hope for a good marriage or a position as mistress and considers seeking fulfillment by adopting a child. Despite the suggestion that Ohide will ultimately pursue this path, however, Chōko does not develop any desire to be a mother herself. As we will see, the narrow, specific sense of maternal love—a mother's love for her child—is not what completes Chōko in her search for her true identity.

According to critic Arai Tomiyo, "wandering tales" were in vogue during this time. *Wheel of Life* comes out of this context in which works such as *Diary of a Vagabond*, as well as Takamure Itsue's *Ohenro* (Pilgrim, 1938), were widely read.[24] Chōko's depiction may have been influenced by the works of Takamure Itsue, in which the female wanderer is an important motif in both poetry and prose. In *Hōrōsha no shi* (Wanderer's poems, 1921) and "Iede no shi" (Poem of running away, 1925), for example, wandering is often an exploration of self-identity and of the meaning of love.[25] Takamure, who herself undertook the *ohenro* or *junrei* pilgrimage in Shikoku, wrote a number of works about such forms of travel; in *Pilgrim*, for example, she describes "pilgrim's love" (*ohenro ai*) as an exalted, universal love.[26] Arai suggests that Okamoto would have been aware of this work in particular, because the afterword was written by Hiratsuka Raichō and the cover was illustrated by Hiratsuka's partner, Okumura Hiroshi, people she knew from her *Bluestocking* days.[27]

Chōko as beggar in *Wheel of Life* is simultaneously human and divine—
a woman searching for truth through her wandering and an omniscient
presence that merges various narratives into one. Her transformation into
a beggar, rather than into a vagabond or a pilgrim, is actually an important
distinction. Although they all move from place to place, Hayashi's vagabond
is a working girl who changes occupations and locales; her movement is
erratic, but she is rooted in everyday experience and far from the supernatural. The pilgrims of Shikoku circumambulate the island, going from
temple to temple to pray; although they have a certain unearthly quality to
them, they travel with a distinct direction and purpose as mortals who aim
to free themselves from the sins of this world. The beggar, however, is part
of the mundane everyday and also a liminal, divine visitor; such a traveler's
path is unmappable and unpredictable, not only traversing village boundaries and public and private spaces, but also moving between this world and
an Otherworld.[28]

This identity is a "return" to Chōko's roots in more ways than one; not
only does it refer to her personal genealogy, but it also gestures toward the
rediscovery of a national identity shaped by a folkloric cosmology. Beggars
are associated with *marebito*, "visiting gods," a term developed by *minzokugaku* (native ethnology / folklore) and literature scholar Orikuchi Shinobu
(1887–1953) during the 1920s. *Marebito* is an opaque concept that is still debated today, but one aspect of Orikuchi's theory links beggars with divinity,
as visiting gods, liminal figures that come into the village to confer blessings
on households in exchange for food.[29] The rise of *minzokugaku* during the
1920s and 1930s contributed to the return to nativism—the recovery of "authentic Japaneseness" found not only in the stories and practices of the folk
but also in the cosmology of native deities, and recreated through daily practices such as festivals and giving alms. Both Orikuchi and the "father" of the
field, Yanagita Kunio (1875–1962), published widely at this time; ideas relating to *minzokugaku* would have been in broad circulation by the late 1930s.

Marebito has a special significance in that it is a god who comes from
tokoyo, an Otherworld, often considered a foreign space of abundance or a
dwelling place of gods and ancestors. This deity's visitations can be read in
a myriad of ways: as a symbol of change, a link with the past, or a reminder
to villagers of cyclical ritualistic time—based on seasons, customs, harvests—
that supercedes the linear progression of modern time.[30] Becoming a *female
marebito* suggests a "return" to the past in which women were considered
godly. *Minzokugaku* played an important role in vesting the female sex with

native authority, even though this also meant a reinscription of women into the space of traditional premodernity. An example of such simultaneous validation and devaluation can be seen in Yanagita's famous work "Imo no chikara" (Power of women), first published in 1925 and then compiled into a volume with the same title in 1940. Yanagita argues here that the taboos and negativity associated with women are actually residual signs from earlier belief systems in which women were feared for their shamanic powers and connection to divinity. This argument makes a strong case for the divine roots of womanhood while also reifying women's negative associations in contemporary society.[31]

By taking on the supernatural identity of a wandering beggar, Chōko not only undertakes a rite of passage for her self-search, but she also strengthens her connection with the past and with the eternal mythic world. This transformation into a beggar is a necessary step for her to find her originary identity in both personal and national terms; she accesses her personal family history and, as an everywoman, searches for the true identity of the nation, one that transcends the direction of modernity's progress.

In 1935 Okamoto Kanoko wrote that when Ibsen's Nora left the "doll's house" to search for her "self" (*jiga*), such a goal was seen as the "new continent" for women. Now, however, selfhood has become an old cliché and nothing more than a focus on one's ego. The times now demand an "escape from" and "discarding of" the self; people are "searching for its replacement." Rather than seeking Nora, Okamoto looks to the female protagonist of D. H. Lawrence's short story "The Woman Who Rode Away" (1928), about an American woman who leaves her husband and children and goes into the mountains of Mexico in search of a local Native American tribe. The tribe captures her and in the end she willingly becomes a human sacrifice.[32] Okamoto says that this protagonist finds what she was looking for in "self-erasure" and in a "return to the natural root" (*shizengen e no kimei*). She dies, but is elevated from an ordinary individual to an integral character in a sacred myth, fulfilling an important prophesy. This story, Okamoto comments, "hints at the decline of white man's civilization" and is suggestive of the "spirit of the times." Okamoto feels that the "modern women of today have already moved beyond Nora" and are looking for a new ideal in "a space transcending both self and other."[33]

In *Wheel of Life*, such a "return" is ultimately tied to maternal love, reinforcing the natural, innate divinity of womanhood. It is no accident that in her reading of Lawrence, Okamoto highlights the importance of myth as a means to access the elusive new ideal. In her novel, the quest for true female identity leads to the discovery of an originary mythic self, a transcendent national identity created through mythic narrative. Because of the length and complexity of *Wheel of Life*, I am unable to discuss all of the episodes that pertain to this issue, but in the next section I focus on one specific example of this process of female becoming / overcoming: the story of Miss Ataka, the teacher who functions as a reflection of and a foil for Chōko. Ataka's narrative rewrites and mythologizes the female search for identity through love, reframing it in the context of modern Japanese history.

National Mythopoesis: Ataka's Tale

In *Wheel of Life*, a long story-within-a-story is recounted before Chōko begins her travels as a beggar. In this episode, Chōko goes on a journey to Mt. Akagi in Gunma Prefecture, to seek Ataka, who, as it turns out, has resigned from school due to her love for Chōko. She finds Ataka living in a hut near her native village on the mountain and spends three nights listening to Ataka's life story. Although Ataka and this episode are overlooked in most discussions of the novel, her story that is like a "tale from old legends" (211) is the key to understanding Chōko's process of development. Incorporating various myths, legends, and religious motifs, Ataka's tale rewrites the modern women's search for self-realization through love, and reexamines by extension the trajectory of Japan's progress since the Meiji period. In Ataka's narrative, maternal love is mythologized not as a simple virtue that services and fulfills the desires of others, but as the ultimate love that reflexively completes the female self.

The episode on the mountain is full of myths (narratives that occur outside historical time) and legends (tales of events within historical time) both foreign and Japanese. Ataka is associated with Ryūnyo (Dragon Girl), a girl in a local legend who became a dragon deity and is also described as "*yamahime*," a mountain goddess.[34] An important story that Ataka tells is taken from the *Kalevala*, the Finnish national epic, shaped by Teutonic and Scandinavian myths as well as by Christian symbolism. At the end of the sequence, Ataka emblematically reenacts the birth of Venus, the goddess of love. Ataka tells her life story in tripartite form, over a period of three nights. The tales are respectively entitled, "the night of confession" (201), "the night of prayer" (208), and "the night of ascension" (212); they are followed by Ataka's symbolic rebirth or resurrection.

Against the backdrop of the development of *minzokugaku* and the rise of interest in national myths, epics, and legends, *Wheel of Life* creates a new mythic narrative. By mythic narrative I mean not only a story that incorporates myths but also one that enables the creation of a transcendent national identity. In Ataka's tale, the personal struggle to find her true self becomes a larger-than-life story, inextricably linked to the nation's own search for identity. Her narrative combines various myths and rewrites them to create new meaning in a process similar to the production of "critical mythopoesis," the revisionist rewriting of myth to challenge dominant discourse and structure.[35] Ataka's story enables female identity to be rewritten as something positive, and revises the modern quest for self-completion as ending in a timeless, self-sufficient space that is maternal. By producing a new narrative of modernity and the search for identity through love, Ataka makes the female self a crucial part of national history.

Ataka, an unmarried woman, had in her youth been engaged to a man she loved, but this engagement was broken off because of spiteful rumors that she was the reincarnation of Ryūnyo, "a girl with scales" (*uroko musume*) who "could not have sexual relations with a man" (202). After this disappointment in love, Ataka decided to erase her negative identity by escaping from the backward village of her birth, professing celibacy, and overcoming what she considered *female* weaknesses. She went to Tokyo, became a physical education teacher, and even traveled to Finland to study the latest sports theories. She was successful in the male drive to "establish the self, rise in the world" (*risshin shusse*), and in the modern project of "re-creation" (*kaizō*), which physically transformed her sickly body into a healthy and resilient one.

Although the virtue of *risshin shusse* can be read as a representation of Meiji-period values, *kaizō* was a Taishō / early Shōwa concern. The concept of *kaizō* in relation to the female body became very popular during the 1920s; it emerged from notions of Social Darwinism, eugenics, and racial hygiene that marked bodies as "premodern" (inferior) or "modern" (superior).[36] Athletics and sports education were a particularly important regimen of *kaizō* in order for women to have a modern, healthy body.[37] In an educational treatise from the mid-1920s, for example, we see discussion of the necessity to surpass the West by creating active, healthy female bodies through athletics, so they can reproduce and transform the Japanese into a "superior people."[38] The female body, already perceived as inferior in comparison to the standard (male) body, becomes an extension and representation of the nation, something to be modernized, strengthened, made beautiful, and imbued with health in order to be a perfect vessel for reproduction.

Ataka, who dresses in a masculine fashion and smokes a Western pipe, views her "femaleness" as akin to caries, the destruction of bones caused by tuberculosis. In her case, the goal in recreating the self is not to become a beautiful and healthy (productive) female but to erase all female aspects in order to become "male." She describes her re-creation process as a painful removal of rotting bones, a task undertaken with the "dagger of intellect [*richi*] and the arrow of self [*jiga*]" (203–204). Ataka achieves this new identity through a Social Darwinist model, in which one must continually evolve and become superior in order to survive. In this framework, *superior* can be defined only as male (not female), center (not periphery), advanced (not primitive), and Western (not Japanese).

Ataka's efforts to recreate herself through athletics, education, and focus on selfhood profoundly echo the nation's drive to transform itself since the Meiji period. In this context, Japan is caught in the paradoxical trajectory of modernity as a non-Western nation, always striving toward (but never reaching) the West. Although she attains a superior, "male" identity associated with the West, Ataka reveals to Chōko that ultimately she found this identity to be unsatisfactory. Her disappointment with this approach to self-construction is also reflected in the story of her father, who had been let down by "progressive" Meiji ideals. As a village headman during the Meiji period, he had advocated new, puritanical Western morals that prohibited youth from having premarital sex, and he had praised values stated in Samuel Smiles' *Self-Help* (1859), a bestseller in Japan, translated as *Saikoku risshi hen* (Success stories of the West, 1871). As a result of such efforts to modernize the village, however, his family was ostracized. Ironically, it was her father's fanatical belief in advancement that brought about Ataka's unhappiness in the first place; because he zealously persecuted those who did not follow his orders, villagers burned his house and later victimized Ataka by making use of local backward beliefs, spreading rumors that she was the reincarnation of the monstrous dragon girl. Her father eventually emigrated to the United States, but died without achieving any form of success.

Like her father, Ataka strove for betterment through "Western" means, but she explains that this identity built on "intellect" and "self" did not provide fulfillment. She then turned to what she calls an "Eastern" (*tōyōfū*) view of the world as a timeless space of nothingness and chaos. Yet in this space too she felt confused and uncertain; as she explains, the West had become an integral part of her identity, so much so that its opposite could no longer be satisfactory: "Our minds have been nurtured since the Meiji period by a Western culture that saw itself as understanding all things through precise dissection and solid perception. How could we be at rest in an Eastern world?" (205). She says she felt like "a monkey that had fallen out of a tree" (206), a proverbial reference to having made an unexpected error. This comment also echoes the ideas of Social Darwinism, suggesting that she has lost her place in the evolutionary path and has become confused as to how to proceed.

In this state of uncertainty, Ataka sensed her "femaleness" reawakening due to the love she felt toward Chōko: "I thought I had been successful in surgically removing the female [*onna*] within me by changing the bones, taking away the womb. . . . I had fancied myself a surgeon able to change my character [*jinkaku*], but I had overlooked a place that still needed to be cut away" (206). This weakness that still required removal is identified as "*bosei*" (motherhood):

> Chōko, I am embittered by my longing for you [*natsukashikumo urameshii*]. I created this body of steel by wringing out my blood, but from this body you easily draw out the motherhood within me. Sitting alone by the window in the dark of the evening, combing my hair, I think of you as my daughter. Or on the other hand, I think of myself as your innocent daughter, wanting to be suckled with your milk. . . . (208)

Using *longing*, a key concept often used in same-sex love, Ataka describes her love for Chōko in terms of a mother-daughter relationship. Ataka fought against this emotion, fearing it would lead to defeat, but once she had transformed her feelings for Chōko into hatred, Ataka's entire body and soul became dismembered and burst apart:

> Looking around, I saw that the Western-style intellect and selfhood, as well as the Eastern-style primeval chaos, had all disappeared. What was left was my own spirit that had fragmented and scattered. . . . But wait, it would be jumping to the wrong conclusion to think of this as my self-destruction. Because the bones I now acknowledged as my body and soul, that is, the scattered, fragmented skull, backbone, ribs, hipbone, bones of the hand and feet, they were all scattered everywhere, yet all were transparent like crystal, different from the remains of the dead exposed to wind and rain. (210–211)

Ataka must start again from the beginning to re-create herself, but this time she knows that her bones are beautiful, not diseased. The acceptance of "femaleness" or "motherhood" can occur only if Ataka is able to love, not others but her own self; furthermore, she must look inward rather than turning to the West or to the East.

The final discovery of Ataka's true identity is articulated on the third and last night of her storytelling, through a reinterpretation of a tale from the *Kalevala*, known for its instrumental role in the construction of Finland's national identity. This particular episode describes the hero Lemminkainen's death and resurrection; his body is torn apart by an enemy, but his mother collects his remains and knits them back together through her love and determination, bringing him back to life using a special salve. In Ataka's narrative, the Finns are described as a unique race that embodies the convergence of West and East. They look like Westerners, yet they were originally "Asian" (*tōyōjin*), with "an Eastern simplicity and single-minded passion" (212).

Ataka explains that this tale from the *Kalevala* is about her. Like Lemminkainen's mother, she wants to put life back into the scattered bones:

> I was wrong to have thought that this story was just a beautiful, made-up tale, born under the snowy skies of the north. Looking back, it was a tale that had been made for me. Because I am unmarried and have never given birth, I myself am simultaneously a mother and child. The mother within me looks at the child, the crystal bones scattered everywhere, and feels such painful suffering. Yet I never give up. . . . I am determined to put the bones back together. . . . The mother within me is now thinking very hard. This salve that resurrects: what is it, and where can it be found? (214)

Maternal love, redefined as love for the self, is the key that will enable Ataka's re-creation in terms of both nation and gender. Ataka's tale suggests that the East-West conflict in modern Japanese identity as well as in the individual search for a higher, complete self through love can both be resolved by a "return" to a mythic notion of maternal love. Instead of transforming the self to become an actual mother fit to produce superior subjects, Ataka ultimately finds self-completion through this radical, reimagined maternal love. Although this affirmation of female identity, a kind of self-love, may seem clichéd to present-day readers, it had a powerful resonance during the 1930s. Read against the backdrop of war, the grief-stricken mother, painstakingly collecting the dead son's limbs, creates an image of self-sacrifice. Rather than promoting service for the greater nation and empire, however, this story depicts a woman who finds female divinity through her own rebirth and resurrection.

The Finnish epic *Kalevala* was put together in its present form in 1849 by doctor and folklorist Elias Lönnrot (1802–1884).[39] There was significant interest in the *Kalevala* in Japan during the 1920s and 1930s, particularly in relation to *minzokugaku*, mythology studies, and nationalism. Several studies on the *Kalevala* were published, and Yanagita includes a discussion on this epic in a 1935 essay about Finland.[40] The first complete Japanese translation of the *Kalevala* was published with the financial assistance of the Finnish government in 1937.[41] An earlier partial translation with commentary was also published in 1929. Because *Wheel of Life* often uses phrases from this particular commentary to explain the story, we can deduce that Okamoto had read this work. The gloss stresses the importance and power of motherhood, describing Lemminkainen's mother as a fundamentally foolish woman who miraculously manages to overcome death through her love for her son: "A woman is weak, but a mother is strong" (*Onna wa yowashi, saredo haha wa tsuyoshi*).[42] Although there are many textual similarities between this commentary and the story told in Ataka's narrative, *Wheel of Life* does not use the familiar trite phrase "a mother is strong." This phrase gives power to mothers and maternal love but at the same time suggests that women in general are weak and show extraordinary strength only when protecting their offspring. The 1929 commentary praises Lemminkainen's mother while inversely denigrating women ("a woman is weak"), but *Wheel of Life* gives new meaning to maternal love, endorsing female identity as a whole.

After the telling of her tale, Ataka disappears in a spectacular and bizarre tableau, reenacting Botticelli's "Birth of Venus." She floats away naked on an ice floe on a lake, into the mica-colored fog, saying, "Don't you think I look just like the figure of Venus, born from a pearl oyster?" (217). Here she literally performs her mythic re-creation as a goddess of love, a woman who can give birth to herself (Venus is commonly interpreted in myth as being born from the foam of the ocean). Furthermore, this lake is where Ryūnyo, the girl of the local legend, had immersed herself and become a dragon deity. By disappearing here, Ataka offers a positive rewriting of the legend that in the past had disempowered her. Through the discovery of maternal love, Ataka is able to accept herself, and enters into an Otherworld as a deity of the mountains.

By merging a woman's search for the self with the nation's struggle to progress and negotiate both Eastern and Western spaces, Ataka's tale offers a critical mythopoesis, situating modern female identity as an integral part of nationhood. The myths and legends in this episode give maternal love a powerful significance as a larger-than-life endpoint for female self-completion, a goal also crucial for the recovery of a re-membered Japan. For Chōko, the listener to Ataka's tale (told over three nights), this is a classic rite of passage involving a separation from daily life, liminal experience in the mountains, then reincorporation back into society.[43] After Ataka disappears, Chōko descends the mountain to continue her search for ultimate love; this story thus provides direction for Chōko's journey. Ataka becomes a mountain goddess, but Chōko will turn to the ocean to find her inner divine nature; the teachings that Chōko receives from her teacher on the mountain help her to complete her own self-search successfully.

Becoming an Ur Mutter

As foreshadowed in the Ataka episode, Chōko erases the negative aspects associated with female identity by rejecting all familiar forms of love. She also leaves Tokyo in order to remain free, running away from those who try to ensnare her into becoming a wife, mistress, or lover. Chōko also rejects her mother's identity as a woman who embodies the disempowerment associated with womanhood. Chōko's mother remains nameless throughout the novel and is identified only through her relationships with men. Due to her lack of a legitimate social identity (she is a former mistress whose patron has died), her ultimate ambition was to make Chōko into "a proper wife of a well-to-do man" (270); she is described as a "tragic woman" (271) who attempted to complete her lack through her child. When she dies, Chōko is finally freed from such negative images of the mother as a self-less person who must rely on others to be made whole. Disguised as a beggar, Chōko leaves Tokyo to search for a new meaning of motherhood and maternal love.

Chōko's wanderings end in the town of Sagi, where she discards her disguise and greets her reflection in a stream as a "girl I meet for the first time" (358). Here Chōko is called an *Ur Mutter*, a woman who cannot be tied down to anyone but seeks to give her "maternal universal love" to all (358, 361). The origins and meaning of this term have never been explained by critics; neither the German term, *Urmutter* (originary mother, primal mother), nor its Japanese gloss, "*ne no haha*" (root mother, 358), were in common parlance at the time in Japan. In the German context, *Urmutter* was originally used to signify the "Ur-mother" or "first mother" such as Eve but later came to be used in a variety of ways as referring to nature, earth, and the like.[44] It is possible that Okamoto learned this word during her seven-month stay in Berlin (1931–1932) or through her reading and decided to ascribe the term with her own definition of an asexual "mother" who cannot be fulfilled by relationships with men. In 1936 Okamoto noted that she had been reading the psychoanalytic works of Freud and Jung.[45] The Jungian archetype of the Great Mother (*die Große Mutter*) may have been a source of inspiration; another likely possibility is that *Ur Mutter* is a rewriting of Freud, who uses terms such as "*Urvaters*" (Ur-fathers) and "*Urmensch*" (Ur-man) to discuss the idea of the primal father or man, the father of human civilization.[46]

Although we can only speculate as to where Okamoto learned the term, the notion of the originary or primal mother, the mother of human civilization, was very much part of the intellectual landscape of the 1930s. During the 1920s, Marxist historiography was already exploring such issues as the emergence of human civilization, class and family systems, and even gender inequalities in terms of specific historical stages. Frederick Engels' (1820–1895) *The Origin of the Family, Private Property, and the State* (1884), which was translated into Japanese in 1922, argues that in the earliest forms of society, "mother right" (matrilineality) was the form of familial descent because "sexual promiscuity" was the norm and there was no means of determining paternity. This mother-centered primitive society was the initial stage in human history, but societal development eventually led to male supremacy through the establishment of monogamy and "father right" (patrilineality).[47]

Engels borrowed ideas about such mother-centered primitive societies from Swiss jurist and legal scholar Johann Jakob Bachofen (1815–1887), whose work *Mutterrecht* (Mother right, 1861) argues that originary communities in human history were characterized by "hetaerism" (sexual promiscuity without marriage) and based on matrilineality. Bachofen states that in early societies, women as mothers were venerated and held in high regard and were not tied to any one man. Such societies were matrilineal, and there were also cases of matriarchy or gyneocracy, that is, rule by women. Bachofen stresses the primacy of "mother love": "The relationship which stands at the origin of all culture, of every virtue, of every nobler aspect of existence, is that between mother and child."[48] In Japan, readers were initially exposed to Bachofen's ideas through Engels' work; later, the introductory chapter of *Mother Right* was translated into Japanese and published in *Bokenron* (The theory of mother right, 1938).[49]

Literary critics eager to find autobiographical references in *Wheel of Life* simply read Okamoto's use of *Ur Mutter* as a reflection of her grandiose view of herself as a larger-than-life maternal figure. In the context of late

1930s Japan and of developments in the feminist movement, however, the concept of an originary mother has a special and broader cultural resonance. In her commentary on Bachofen's *The Theory of Mother Right*, published as the afterword to the 1939 edition, Miyamoto Yuriko writes, "One interesting phenomenon we can observe in contemporary Japan is that the young women [of today] . . . take an active interest in women's history, as an exploration of the path women have taken in the long history of the human race."[50] The idea that the starting point of history is located in matrilineality, matriarchy, and/or the worship of motherhood must have been captivating for women as they fashioned a positive identity around the image of maternal love, an important value that enabled the nation to mobilize women for the war effort. The term *boken* (母権), meaning "mothers' rights" or "motherhood rights," was by this time an important notion for both the feminist and nationalist movements; it suggests motherhood "protection" (*hogo*, government assistance for mothers and caregivers of children) as well as the "right" (*kenri*) and "power" (*kenryoku*) of mothers to be able to give birth, raise children, and be given due respect as mothers of the nation. Such ideas dovetail neatly with the other, now less well-known meaning of *boken*: "mother right" or "matrilineality," an affirmation of female identity as central to the emergence and development of human history, a notion that also allows women to celebrate their sexual difference and uniquely female power of reproduction.

It is no accident, then, that the late 1930s witnessed the recovery of *Japanese* mother right/matrilineality. Takamure Itsue's *Bokeisei no kenkyū* (The study of the matrilineal system, 1938) was the first work of Japanese historiography to reveal systematically the existence of matrilineality in ancient Japan.[51] This work substantiates the symbolic presence of an originary mother of civilization. In 1938, Okamoto wrote a glowing review of the work in *Osaka Asahi shinbun*; she was also a member of Takamure Itsue chosaku kōenkai (Association to Support the Works of Takamure Itsue), a group established by Hiratsuka Raichō and others in 1936 to provide financial support for Takamure's publications.[52] The members of this association included prominent feminists, writers, and artists, which suggests the importance of Takamure's scholarship. Particularly for women, linking the origins of nationhood to a matrilineal system would have had a special resonance at a time when motherhood was becoming a key concept for female validation.

For many Japanese feminists during the late 1930s, the "return" to the *Ur Mutter* and the ancient past in which she held sway expressed a longing for a world in which women are powerful and independent of men. In this imagined pre-patriarchal community, women's sexual and reproductive difference is the source of their authority. Nostalgia for this transcendent space enables women to, in a sense, reclaim and affirm female identity. Significantly, this longing also reflects a powerful desire to "overcome" modernity, to "return" to the origins of human society before the evolutionary progress of history—a linear trajectory that inevitably leads to the consolidation of patriarchal power as well as the supremacy of the West. Yet this return in time is a double-edged sword for women; although it may allow them to escape the linearity of modernity, the reinscription of women into premodernity emphasizes motherhood and maternal love while ignoring other aspects of female identity. This tension, together with the increasing complicity between the feminist movement and nationalistic propaganda, created the discursive context for *Wheel of Life*. Chōko's self-discovery is a return to the "root" that both liberates and constrains the modern female self.

On finding herself as *Ur Mutter*, Chōko emerges as a powerful, influential character who transcends the narrow biological meaning of motherhood (as reflected in her own mother) to become a symbolic mother figure to the entire town. Although her transformation is initially touted as positive, this identity also shows the dangers of maternal love for women, particularly in relation to male/national authority. On the surface, Chōko rejects all male control by refusing to marry and by becoming a businesswoman, the manager of the "public town meeting hall" (*shisetsu no kurabu-shiki kaikan*, 361). However, by becoming a "mother" to this town, by welcoming "each of the men who comes to visit the meeting hall [*kurabu*] with sincere kindness, making them happy and encouraging them" (362), she is dangerously close to replicating her own mother, who ran a private salon out of her house for the men of the neighborhood, a house with "an atmosphere like a strange club [*kurabu*]" (138). Although Chōko's *kurabu* is a respectable and important part of the community, the maternal love she freely gives keeps her in service to others.

Through Chōko's loving influence, the town of Sagi transforms itself from a lonely farmland into a bustling industrial area with "forests of smokestacks" (361); feuding families are reconciled, and all the town beggars are given jobs. The men of the town even begin to develop materials valuable to the nation. They realize that the rocks from a nearby mountain yield cement; they also start studying the possibility of extracting materials from these rocks to produce moisture-proof paper and food substitutes (360).

Here Chōko becomes a "mother" who participates in the empire-building effort; she remains celibate while her work enables men—like children—to grow and prosper for the good of the nation. In narrating this plot twist, however, Chōko makes fun of such "denouement" in "the popular novel" (*tsūzoku shōsetsu*), where all conflicts are resolved and a positive outcome is predicted for everyone. She tells readers that her story does not belong to such a genre, and "unfortunately, despite this resolution in Sagi . . . events spiraled away from this neat conclusion" (362).

As an *Ur Mutter*, Chōko discovers herself as a woman who transcends normal forms of love and sexuality, as well as standard female roles. Although she enjoys the authority and freedom of this identity, she is simultaneously disempowered. That is to say, if she allows herself to be trapped in what she mocks as a simplistic popular novel storyline, she can be nothing more than the sort of inspirational symbol of maternal love promoted by groups such as the Greater Japan National Defense Women's Association. The powerful Chōko belongs at once to everyone and to no one—a re-created identity that takes its cue from Bachofen's sexually independent "mothers" of early primitive societies. In this town (and simplistic resolution), however, her asexual "maternal universal love" is too easily exploited for the purposes of serving men and the nation.

In the final pages of the novel, Chōko escapes from a serious suitor and from other men of the town; she also avoids the superficially happy ending that threatens to tie her down as a symbol of self-less maternal love. She leaves town yet again, this time with Bunkichi, a mentally disabled beggar boy whom she views as her surrogate son. They sail down the river in their boat and reach the ocean, where the novel abruptly ends:

> Why did I do such a thing? It was just to enable Bunkichi to fulfill his wish. He was always saying that he wanted to see the ocean. Whenever I thought of this idiot repeating his wish over and over and never having it come true, my eyes brimmed over with tears without knowing why. I never shed tears for anyone else. Is it because I did not have a child, despite having reached the age in which one could be a young mother? Or was it perhaps because some deeper human desire moved within my female body? The wish to help Bunkichi fulfill his desire became a fresh energy, a new power that bubbled up in my heart. . . .
> Finally, Bunkichi spoke:
> "Are there a lot of living things in there [the ocean]?"
> "That's right, a lot."
> "When they die, where are they buried?"

I was at a loss for words and just said, "Well . . . ," but Bunkichi went on, looking convinced.

"I see. There are no such things as graves in the ocean."

A world without graves—since that time I came to like the ocean more than rivers and I became a female sailor [*onna funanori*]. (403)

The ending of the novel is strange and abrupt, to be sure, leaving a sense of incompleteness and confusion. Indeed, it seems that Chōko has cast off a problematic form of maternal love only to embrace another kind of asexual motherhood by traveling to sea with a son-lover figure. It is possible, however, to interpret this conclusion symbolically, as Chōko's attainment of self-completion and transcendence of linearity. The "maternal universal love" is manifest in her desire to realize Bunkichi's wishes, but this also leads to her own fulfillment. Bunkichi is described as a figure who mirrors Chōko's own desires; his eyes reflect the "constant movement of the waves of the ocean" associated with Chōko (403). Significantly, the ocean symbolizes both the beginning and the end. The ocean is the true *Ur Mutter* from which all life begins, and the final destination to which all rivers flow. By entering the expansive sea, Chōko returns to and becomes part of the originary mother, expressing love toward *herself* as both mother and child.[53]

This reframing of the meaning of *Ur Mutter*—no longer presented as service to men and nation but as a recovery of self-love that affirms female identity—is very much tied to the notion of transcendence. In Buddhist terms, the novel's ending can be read as Chōko's successful overcoming, a representation of Ataka's self-renewal in the mountain lake. Ataka is known as the reincarnation of Ryūnyo, a dragon girl of a local legend; Chōko's entry into the ocean suggests the story of another Ryūnyo, the *nāga*-girl, daughter of Sagara, the Dragon King of the Ocean. Sagara's daughter's tale, found in the Lotus Sutra, is a central motif for understanding the possibility of female salvation. Because the *nāga*-girl transforms first into a man before becoming a buddha, the story has been seen as underscoring the lowly, defiled nature of the female sex. However, many Buddhist commentaries and schools also use this story in a positive fashion, to argue for women's ability to enter into Paradise.[54] If Chōko's disappearance into the ocean is read as transcendence in the sense of enlightenment and salvation, her self-search ends with the discovery of perfection and completion that affirm female identity. As Okamoto explains in an essay on Buddhism, "all people have within themselves the seeds to complete their characters [*jinkaku kansei*] . . . to become perfect human beings."[55]

Rather than choose "maternal universal love" in the everyday world of Sagi, Chōko enters into the Otherworld of myth. Her longing to return to the "root" (*ne*) may have been a reference to "*ne no kuni*" (land of the root), discussed in the mythohistorical work *Nihon shoki* (Chronicles of Japan, 720). In this context, *ne no kuni* is not the underground world of the dead but the Otherworld also sometimes referred to as *tokoyo*, a "distant land across the sea, an eternal world of everlasting life," which is mentioned in both *Records of Ancient Matters* and *Chronicles of Japan*. This place is of course the dwelling place of *marebito*, and it is conflated in some contexts with the undersea "pure land of the dragon palace" (*ryūgū jōdo*).[56] These layered possibilities of meaning all suggest a mythic transcendent space that enables a positive reconstruction of female identity. Instead of a woman associated with defilement or disempowerment, the originary mother whom Chōko discovers has an expansive sense of self that is timeless and self-sufficient. She escapes from the linear notion of progress and history into a mythic space that allows transcendence.

Having said this, this rewriting of the *Ur Mutter* and maternal love remains ambivalent to the end, without a neat resolution or a concrete sense of closure. Although transcendence is achieved through a mystical becoming-one with the ocean, Chōko also tells readers at the very end that she has become a female sailor, taking on yet another identity that allows her to continue her wanderings in the world. Chōko, in other words, refuses to disappear completely into mythic space and changes her identity yet again. Her insistent transformation reminds us of the inevitable wheel of life, the constant cycle of rebirth and death. Even more important, however, it warns against the dangers that originary mythic space holds for women. Although she manifests the power of a transcendent female identity, Chōko also continues to escape, moving in different directions, changing, and resisting definition.

Recreating Maternal Love

Wheel of Life mythologizes motherhood and maternal love as means for female self-completion—not through the fulfillment of biological maternity or the symbolic mothering of men and nation, but through a rewriting of this love as love for oneself and as the endpoint of women's modern search for true identity. This work makes use of the contemporary valorization of maternal love and motherhood while shifting their meaning through revisionary mythopoesis. Chōko's return to the originary mother (the ocean)—or the return of the female *marebito* to the Otherworld—suggests the triumph of mythic space over linear time. As the ending shows, however, there is also discomfort about such transcendence. Chōko refuses to stay still, continuing her travels and speaking with a voice that insists on a tangible, corporeal presence in the real (not mythic) world.

Chōko's unmappable trajectories across the ocean offer a powerful rejection of the simple model of development, progress, and betterment that had shaped both female and national identities in Japan. The fact that her wanderings (and transformations) appear to persist beyond the ending creates fresh notions of modernity and modern female selfhood—as a series of fluid, mutable occurrences that resist clear goals and destinations. Most significant, however, this ending gestures toward the problems that women face in attempting to regain their power by returning to the past, to overcome through myth, and to attain female perfection through maternal love. Although *Wheel of Life* creates a new interpretation of maternal love as a means to empower the female self, this love remains dangerously connected to self-effacement and service to others.

To be sure, the return to origins deifies both Ataka and Chōko, but it harbors the threat of female erasure. Takamure Itsue, who suggests in *Creation of Love* that women should return to the authentic love of the ancient world, discovers in *The Study of the Matrilineal System* a maternal love that is simultaneously powerful and tragic. In *The Study of the Matrilineal System*, which she describes as her "book of love for women and nation,"[57] she argues that the emergence of Japan as a nation was actually made possible through "matrilineal self-sacrifice."[58] In the final chapter, deleted from postwar editions, Takamure explains that "the transition from matrilineality to patrilineality is a given, a recognized course of development." It is in the nature of matrilineality to erase itself (associating mothers with self-sacrifice); thus, by giving way to paternal authority, maternal love enabled the consolidation of central imperial power and the "development of our nation."[59] The idea that self-erasure is definitive of maternal power, even at its place of origin, points to the difficulty of embracing mythic maternal love as the ultimate means for female self-completion.

Okamoto died in 1939 at the height of her career as a novelist, and before the start of the Pacific War. Yoshiya Nobuko, who was inspired to become a professional writer after meeting Okamoto in 1915, remembers Okamoto's insistence on the importance of "creating the self" and aiming for things "higher" than oneself.[60] On the other hand, for Miyamoto Yuriko, who wrote about the dark side of the 1930s "humanist renaissance" in *Women and Literature* (1947), Okamoto's works represent a dangerous affirmation of self-identity that is narcissistic and unaware of its relationship to broader society.[61] Indeed, although I have tried to show how the ending of *Wheel of Life* subtly expresses reservations about the mythologization of maternal love and the *Ur Mutter*, we can also see how this work could easily be co-opted for the promotion of nationalism and imperialism.

Okamoto's stories were enthusiastically embraced by prominent Japan Romantic School writers—men who conveniently ignored the mother-female who challenged taboos and refused to bow to male authority. The woman they discovered in Okamoto's writing was instead the "eternal mother," an embodiment of "great motherhood [*dai bosei*] who gives bountifully without hesitation."[62] By romanticizing maternal love, not as a love that enables female self-affirmation but as a part of the return to the motherland, these critics praised Okamoto as a writer who represented the spirit of the times. Hayashi Fusao wrote in 1938:

> Okamoto Kanoko is a writer on the same level as Mori Ōgai and Natsume Sōseki. . . . All three manifest, as a seamless part of themselves, both the culture of the East and the civilization of the West. They have achieved the highest state, unable to be reached by other writers, combining the cultures of both East and West within that subtle point, Japan [*Nihon toiu bimyō na itten*].

Hayashi explains that Okamoto's appearance in the literary world is a "coincidence that can also be called a necessity," occurring simultaneously with the current drive to "return to Japan."[63] As an embodiment of transcendence, of both East and West, Okamoto is canonized by these men as a great Japanese writer.

Yet we can also see what these critics have overlooked in their interpretations. *Wheel of Life* is a reconsideration of the female quest for identity that is founded on modern love ideology; it is an attempt to redraw the relationship between woman and modernity, to refigure the meaning of female self-completion and progress. In grappling with the consequence of returning to the *Ur Mutter* and to eternal "monumental time" for modern female identity,[64] *Wheel of Life* illustrates the very dilemma of feminism during the 1930s: how to articulate a powerful maternal self separate from the demands of the nation-state, and whether this self can ever escape from erasure into collective myth.

Although the novel does not provide any easy answers, hope is expressed in Chōko's voice that continues to speak beyond the ending. Told in the first person by a narrator whose bodily presence keeps irrupting into the text despite her asexuality and mythic character, the narrative begins *in medias res* from a specific moment in Chōko's life, returns back to that departing point, and then continues on further. Although Chōko disappears into the sea at the end, her voice remains; in "real" terms, the novel concludes with the emergence of a female sailor who has told the entire story, an expansive monologue that gave voice to all of the numerous characters in the text. Although Ataka disappears into the fog forever as a mountain goddess, Chōko remains at large, continuing to speak from an undesignated space and time, harboring infinite possibilities for further transformations and identities.[65]

Just as Chōko continues to narrate her story, Okamoto's posthumously published text also continues to speak and wield influence since its author's death. By giving birth to a female narrator who freely navigates both the real and mythic worlds, the novel presents a unique perspective on the female search for true self. Despite Miyamoto's denunciation of Okamoto's works, many postwar female writers have found *Wheel of Life* an important source of inspiration. Ariyoshi Sawako (1931–1984), known for works such as *Ki no kawa* (*The River Ki*, 1959) and *Kōkotsu no hito* (*The Twilight Years*, 1972), claims that she would not have become a writer if she had not read Okamoto's works as a student; she remembers reading *Wheel of Life* and being profoundly moved by the "free writing style, the voluptuous images, and the passion that emanated from its pages."[66] Tsushima Yūko (1947–), whose works such as *Yama o hashiru onna* (*Woman Running in the Mountains*, 1980) challenge standard portrayals of motherhood and maternal love, explains that after discovering *Wheel of Life* in her youth she became possessed by "this monstrous novel" (*obake no shōsetsu*) and was overcome with the desire to become a writer.[67]

Wheel of Life is very much colored by the landscape of the 1930s, illustrated by the mythologization of maternal love and the articulation of the return to a transcendent female self. However, this novel is not simply a reflection of wartime nationalism and the rise of motherhood feminism. It is also a revisionary presentation of modern love ideology that affirms female identity and agency through maternal-self love. Although it is shaped by the discourses of its time, it also explores the possibilities for the discovery of an alternative originary mother—one who can escape the destiny of self-erasure and sacrifice for men and nation. Okamoto's novel looks back to the past and offers transcendence into myth, but it also projects ahead to the future through the haunting presence of Chōko's voice. After the war, the social, cultural, and legal landscape of Japan changed radically for women, allowing them to vote, own property, and gain, at least in the constitution, "equal rights." In the context of this social transformation, postwar women's literature would continue to grapple with the elusive meaning of maternal love. The mythic mother continues to be rediscovered and recreated in myriad ways, as we listen to the different voices that narrate the search for female identity.

Conclusion

In this book I have examined how discourses of love informed prewar concepts of female development and identity, and shaped the connection between gender and modernity. Using various ideas about same-sex love, love marriage, and maternal love, the women writers discussed here engaged profoundly with modern love ideology and the notion of love's progress. Beginning in the 1910s, Yoshiya Nobuko inserted same-sex love into the ideal course of female maturity, reworking sexological and early feminist notions about this love. While writing in different literary genres—girls' fiction, pure literature, and popular literature for women—she underscored same-sex love as an important part of modern female identity. Miyamoto Yuriko erased from the 1928 version of *Nobuko* as well as from its postwar interpretations the traces of love marriage ideology that had informed the 1924–1926 version. By analyzing Nobuko's story through its conversation with love marriage discourses; its ideas about reproduction, health, and divorce; and the emerging concern with class and sexual politics, we can retrieve the lost meaning of the Nobuko narratives. Okamoto Kanoko's late works portray maternal love as a powerful force that transcends the linear trajectory of betterment and completes the mythic female self. This rereading of the process of female development is part of the growing complicity of feminism with nationalism during the 1930s. By endorsing maternal love as the definitive aspect of female identity, however, her novels also illustrate the endpoint of modern love ideology. Okamoto's narratives must be read in tandem with feminist and nationalistic discourses about maternal love, with native ethnology's reclaiming of national identity, and with historical interest in matriarchy and matrilineality.

One of my goals in *Becoming Modern Women* has been to offer a new approach to these three prewar Japanese writers by reading their works not through the lenses of autobiography, literary traditions, or the unified notion of female authorship, but as texts produced within specific sociohistorical contexts, in dynamic conversation with a range of contemporary ideologies and issues. All the authors I examine were deeply influenced by prewar feminist discourse, and their works reveal unexpected meanings and complexities when read with ideas such as modern love ideology in mind. These writers also wrote intertextually, drawing on other prominent fields of knowledge, such as sexology, love tracts, and historiography, as well as other contemporary works of literature. Throughout my exploration I have endeavored to show the often overlooked connections between texts, ideologies, and debates, in ways that I hope help to illuminate both the literature and the history of the 1910s to 1930s.

My other goal has been to provide a new way of looking at love, an elusive notion recognized as an important factor in the development of modern Japanese literature. Discussions of love in the context of Japanese literary scholarship have focused on such issues as whether or not love is really a Western import from the Meiji period, how male and female characters experience love differently, or the relationship between love and sexuality. Love has always been a complex topic for analysis because it requires us to recognize that although human affection is a widely shared emotion and experience, its understanding and presentation change in different sociohistorical and literary/cultural settings. My approach is distinct from other investigations in that I focus on prewar modern love ideology and on specific forms of love that contributed to the creation of modern Japanese female identity.

It bears mentioning that some ideas rooted in modern love ideology are still valorized today and play a role in creating an often problematic view of the ideal Japanese woman. For example, the idea that self-completion through love is the desired process of female growth, the view that love marriage is superior to arranged marriage, and the concept that all women have an innate maternal feeling that is the highest form of love can be found in numerous postwar texts and discussions. My intent is not to make simplistic connections between the past and the present, but I do hope that my exploration of love and female identity in the early to mid-twentieth century offers some useful tools for thinking about the impact that love has had on female self-construction and representation in postwar Japan and beyond.

To be clear, love was not the only "technology of the self" available to prewar Japanese women in their pursuit of advancement. This book is by no means an exhaustive examination of all processes of becoming modern women, nor does it cover all women writers' narratives or experiences of progress; but by focusing on prewar concepts of love, *Becoming Modern Women* presents a fresh view of the symbiotic relationship between modernity and gender. As a figure embodying evolutionary process, the woman mirrors the broader issues of modernity. Her path of development through love resonates with Japan's own trajectory toward an imagined authenticity; she manifests both the progressive linearity of "becoming" and a problematic "overcoming" through the embracing of myth and the fetishization of a transcendent origin. Although it inspired women's sincere desires and hopes for modern transformation, the association of love's "evolution" with female progress was ultimately to facilitate a dangerous self-fashioning for both women and nation during the course of the 1930s and the Pacific War.

Like many of their counterparts around the world, early twentieth-century Japanese women who were concerned with women's advancement focused not "in *being*" where they were "massively misunderstood, but in *becoming*. . . . What might they become; what might they not become?"[1] This focus on "becoming" inevitably posed questions about the process itself. What did it actually mean for women to become modern and to express their true selves? What gauges determined success and where did such change lead? By highlighting these questions in the narratives and discourses explored here, we develop new critical perspectives for understanding modern Japanese women, their processes of self-construction, and the complex trajectories of modernity.

Reference Matter

Notes

Chapter One: Introduction

1. See Sidney L. Gulick, *The Evolution of the Japanese* (New York: Fleming H. Revell, 1903), 29–30, 54–55, 268. For more about Gulick, see Sandra C. Taylor, *Advocate of Understanding: Sidney Gulick and the Search for Peace with Japan* (Kent, OH: Kent State University Press, 1984).

2. See Indra Levy, *Sirens of the Western Shore: The Westernesque Femme Fatale, Translation, and Vernacular Style in Modern Japanese Literature* (New York: Columbia University Press, 2006), 51.

3. Franco Moretti, *The Way of the World: The* Bildungsroman *in European Culture* (London: Verso, 1987), 5. There are many ways to characterize the *bildungsroman* as a genre, and various interpretations of what a *bildungsroman* plot structure entails.

4. Technically, Japan was already engaged in war from the 1930s on: the so-called Fifteen-Year War (1931–1945) started with Japan's aggressive incursions into China and includes the China War (1937–1945). For the sake of simplicity and consistency, however, throughout this book I use the term *prewar period* to refer to the 1910s through 1930s.

5. See, for example, Rita Felski, *The Gender of Modernity* (Cambridge, MA: Harvard University Press, 1995); Rey Chow, *Woman and Chinese Modernity: The Politics of Reading Between West and East* (Minneapolis: University of Minnesota Press, 1991); Miriam Silverberg, "The Modern Girl as Militant," in *Recreating Japanese Women, 1600–1945,* ed. Gail Lee Bernstein (Berkeley: University of California Press, 1991), 239–266; *Erotic Grotesque Nonsense: The Mass Culture of Japanese Modern Times* (Berkeley: University of California Press, 2006), 51–107, 143–174; Barbara Sato, *The New Japanese Woman: Modernity, Media, and Women in Interwar Japan* (Durham, NC: Duke University Press, 2003); Barbara Hamill Sato, "Japanese Women and Modanizumu: The Emergence of a New Women's Culture in the 1920s" (Ph.D. diss., Columbia University, 1994); Jennifer Robertson, *Takarazuka: Sexual Politics and Popular Culture in Modern Japan* (Berkeley: University of California Press, 1998); Harry Harootunian, *Overcome by Modernity: History, Culture, and Community in Interwar Japan* (Princeton, NJ: Princeton University Press, 2000); Miyako Inoue, *Vicarious Language: Gender and Linguistic Modernity in Japan* (Berkeley: University of California Press, 2006).

6. For Hirabayashi Hatsunosuke's (1892–1931) notion of "feminization of culture," see Sato, *New Japanese Woman*, 39; Harootunian, 11. For examples of works that discuss connections between *modanizumu*, *modan*, and gender, see the works by Sato and Silverberg cited in notes 5 and 12.

7. Miriam Silverberg, "Constructing a New Cultural History of Prewar Japan," in *Japan in the World*, ed. Masao Miyoshi and H. D. Harootunian (Durham, NC: Duke University Press, 1993), 141.

8. Hiratsuka Raichō, "Henshūgo no zakkansō (*Seitō* daisangō no henshūkōki)," in *Hiratsuka Raichō chosakushū*, vol. 1, ed. Hiratsuka Raichō chosakushū henshū iinkai (Ōtsuki shoten, 1983), 50–51; originally published in *Seitō* 1, no. 3 (1911).

9. Ibid., 51.

10. See "Shomeishi no iwayuru 'fujin mondai' ni tsuite," in *Hiratsuka Raichō chosakushū*, vol. 1, 262.

11. Inoue, *Vicarious Language*, 67. Harootunian's notion of "co-eval modernity," as opposed to "alternative" modernity, has been important in establishing the view that Japanese modernity is not a delayed or lesser phenomenon but one that shares "the same temporality" as "other modernities" (xvi). See also Marilyn Ivy, *Discourses of the Vanishing: Modernity, Phantasm, Japan* (Chicago: University of Chicago Press, 1995), 4–8.

12. Many scholars have written on these identities. For some examples, see Jan Bardsley, *The Bluestockings of Japan: New Woman Essays and Fiction from* Seitō, *1911–16* (Ann Arbor: Center for Japanese Studies, University of Michigan, 2007); Dina Lowy, *The Japanese "New Woman": Images of Gender and Modernity* (New Brunswick: Rutgers University Press, 2007); Sharon L. Sievers, *Flowers in Salt: The Beginnings of Feminist Consciousness in Modern Japan* (Stanford, CA: Stanford University Press, 1983); Laurel Rasplica Rodd, "Yosano Akiko and the Taishō Debate Over the 'New Woman,'" in *Recreating Japanese Women*, 175–198; Hasegawa Kei, "Atarashii onna no tankyū: Furoku 'Nora,' 'Magda,' 'Atarashii onna, sonota fujin mondai ni tsuite,'" in Seitō *o yomu*, ed. Shin feminizumu hihyō no kai (Gakugei shorin, 1998), 285–304; Silverberg, "The Modern Girl as Militant"; *Erotic Grotesque Nonsense*, 51–107, 143–174; "The Café Waitress Serving Modern Japan," in *Mirror of Modernity: Invented Traditions of Modern Japan*, ed. Stephen Vlastos (Berkeley: University of California Press, 1998), 208–225; "After the Grand Tour: The Modern Girl, the New Woman, and the Colonial Maiden," in *The Modern Girl Around the World: Consumption, Modernity, and Globalization*, ed. The Modern Girl Around the World Research Group (Durham, NC: Duke University Press, 2008), 354–361; Sato, *New Japanese Woman*; "Japanese Women and Modanizumu"; "Josei: Modanizumu to kenri ishiki," in *Shōwa bunka 1925–1945*, ed. Minami Hiroshi and Shakai shinri kenkyūjo (Keisō shobō, 1992), 198–231; "Contesting Consumerisms in Mass Women's Magazines," in *Modern Girl Around the World*, 263–287; Hiratsuka Raichō, "Kaku arubeki modan gaaru," in *Hiratsuka Raichō chosakushū*, vol. 4 (1983), 290–297; Ōya Sōichi, "Hyaku paasento moga," in *Ōya Sōichi senshū*, vol. 2 (Chikuma shobō, 1959), 222–226; Sarah Frederick, *Turning Pages: Reading and Writing Women's Magazines in Interwar Japan* (Honolulu: University of Hawai'i Press, 2006); Ruri

Ito, "The 'Modern Girl' Question in the Periphery of Empire: Colonial Modernity and Mobility Among Okinawan Women in the 1920s and 1930s," in *Modern Girl Around the World*, 240–262; Margit Nagy, "Middle-Class Working Women During the Interwar Years," in *Recreating Japanese Women*, 199–216; Barbara Molony, "Activism Among Women in the Taishō Cotton Textile Industry," in *Recreating Japanese Women*, 217–238; Yoshiko Miyake, "Doubling Expectations: Motherhood and Women's Factory Work Under State Management in Japan in the 1930s and 1940s," in *Recreating Japanese Women*, 267–295; Janet Hunter, "Gendering the Labor Market: Evidence from the Interwar Textile Industry," in *Gendering Modern Japanese History*, ed. Barbara Molony and Kathleen Uno (Cambridge, MA: Harvard University Asia Center, 2005), 359–383; Elyssa Faison, *Managing Women: Disciplining Labor in Modern Japan* (Berkeley: University of California Press, 2007); Mikiso Hane, trans. and ed., *Reflections on the Way to the Gallows: Rebel Women in Prewar Japan* (Berkeley: University of California Press, 1988); Kimura Ryōko, "Jogakusei to jokō: 'Shisō' to no deai," in *Onna no bunka*, vol. 8 of Kindai Nihon bunkaron, ed. Aoki Tamotsu and others (Iwanami shoten, 2000), 73–95; Vera Mackie, *Creating Socialist Women in Japan: Gender, Labour and Activism, 1900–1937* (Cambridge, UK: Cambridge University Press, 1997); Ronald P. Loftus, *Telling Lives: Women's Self-Writing in Modern Japan* (Honolulu: University of Hawai'i Press, 2004); Jordan Sand, *House and Home in Modern Japan: Architecture, Domestic Space, and Bourgeois Culture, 1880–1930* (Cambridge: Harvard University Asia Center, 2003), 55–94; Elise K. Tipton, "The Café: Contested Space of Modernity in Interwar Japan," in *Being Modern in Japan: Culture and Society from the 1910s to the 1930s*, ed. Elise K. Tipton and John Clark (Honolulu: University of Hawai'i Press, 2000), 119–136.

Other important female figures of the time include the schoolgirl (*jogakusei*) and Good Wife, Wise Mother. For more on the schoolgirl, see, for example, Inoue, *Vicarious Language*; Levy; Honda Masuko, *Jogakusei no keifu: Saishoku sareru Meiji* (Seidosha, 1990). Girls (*shōjo*) and other related figures of youth are discussed in depth in the following two chapters. For examples of work on Good Wife, Wise Mother, see Koyama Shizuko, *Ryōsai kenbo to iu kihan* (Keisō shobō, 1992); Kathleen S. Uno, "The Death of 'Good Wife, Wise Mother'?" in *Postwar Japan as History*, ed. Andrew Gordon (Berkeley: University of California Press, 1993), 293–322; "Womanhood, War and Empire: Transmutations of 'Good Wife, Wise Mother' Before 1931," in *Gendering Modern Japanese History*, 493–519; Muta Kazue, "'Ryōsai kenbo' shisō no omoteura: Kindai Nihon no katei bunka to feminizumu," in *Onna no bunka*, 23–46.

13. Felski, 21.

14. Ōtsuka Eiji suggests that in premodern society, entry into female maturity was clearly delineated by menarche. *Shōjo minzokugaku: Seikimatsu no shinwa o tsumugu "iko no matsuei"* (Kōbunsha, 1997), 18.

15. In discussing notions of *self*, *selfhood*, and *individual*, I specifically avoid using the terms *subject* and *subjectivity*. The former terms better reflect the notion of what Tomi Suzuki calls "an independent social and moral entity" conceptualized within the discourse of prewar liberal humanism; see *Narrating the Self: Fictions of*

Japanese Modernity (Stanford, CA: Stanford University Press, 1996), 8. This is not to say, however, that the writers I discuss are oblivious to the notion of subjectivity. Their writings reveal an understanding of the complex relationships between ideology, self, agency, and discourse; although they present the completion of the self as a crucial goal for women, these novels also show that the individual is constructed through interpellation and is in effect a series of different "subject-positions" created through "discourses and the world that he / she inhabits." See Paul Smith, *Discerning the Subject* (Minneapolis: University of Minnesota Press, 1988), xxxv.

16. Karatani Kōjin, *Origins of Modern Japanese Literature*, trans. and ed. Brett de Bary (Durham, NC: Duke University Press, 1993), 61.

17. For more on discourses about *kyōyō*, *jinkaku*, and *shūyō*, see Kyoko Inoue, *Individual Dignity in Modern Japanese Thought: The Evolution of the Concept of Jinkaku in Moral and Educational Discourse* (Ann Arbor: Center for Japanese Studies, University of Michigan, 2001); Kano Masanao, *Kindai Nihon shisō annai* (Iwanami shoten, 2000), 176–191; Minami Hiroshi and Shakai shinri kenkyūjo, eds., *Taishō bunka* (Keisō shobō, 1977), 316–333; Sato, *New Japanese Woman*; "Japanese Women and Modanizumu"; "Commodifying and Engendering Morality: Self-Cultivation and the Construction of the 'Ideal Woman' in 1920s Mass Women's Magazines," in *Gendering Modern Japanese History*, 99–130; Michiko Suzuki, "Progress and Love Marriage: Rereading Tanizaki Jun'ichirō's *Chijin no ai*," *Journal of Japanese Studies* 31, no. 2 (2005): 357–384; Tsutsui Kiyotada, "Kindai Nihon no kyōyō shugi to shūyō shugi," *Shisō* 812 (February, 1992): 151–174. According to Tsutsui (165–166), *shūyō* was understood as a Japanese translation of the German word *bildung*, a concept intrinsically associated with the development of the individual.

18. Suzuki, *Narrating the Self*, 52.

19. Kobayashi Tomie notes that Hiratsuka liked the visual appearance of *White Birch* and used it as a model in producing *Bluestocking*, even hiring the same printing firm; *Hiratsuka Raichō*, vol. 71 of Hito to shisō (Shimizu shoin, 2001), 93. Both journals also focus on the publication of fiction. Hiroko Tomida suggests that the *Bluestocking* women were inspired by the humanitarian stance of *White Birch*; see *Hiratsuka Raichō and Early Japanese Feminism* (Leiden: Brill, 2004), 143.

20. Michel Foucault, *Technologies of the Self: A Seminar with Michel Foucault*, ed. Luther H. Martin, Huck Gutman, and Patrick H. Hutton (Amherst: University of Massachusetts Press, 1988), 18.

21. Tomi Suzuki sees the popularity of Marxism as a result of the intellectuals' "larger concern for the 'true' and 'genuine' self." *Narrating the Self*, 8.

22. Fredric Jameson, *The Political Unconscious: Narrative as a Socially Symbolic Act* (Ithaca, NY: Cornell University Press, 1981), 87.

23. Hiratsuka Raichō, *Hiratsuka Raichō chosakushū*, vol. 1, 290; originally published in *Seitō* 4, no. 2 (1914). For commentary and a full translation of the letter, see Bardsley, *Bluestockings of Japan*, 92–94, 107–115.

24. "Fujin no chii," *Jogaku zasshi* 2 (August 1885), 22–23. Quoted in Saeki Junko, *"Iro" to "ai" no hikaku bunkashi* (Iwanami shoten, 1999), 10. Karatani's statement that "there was *koi* in premodern Japan, but not romantic love (*ren'ai*)"

(82) and Saeki's schema of *ai* as superceding *iro* and *koi* are currently considered basic frameworks for understanding ideas about love since the Meiji period. Instead of exploring such distinctions between *ai* or *ren'ai* and *iro* or *koi*, my project looks at how different notions of love are used by Japanese writers, not as "superior" Western values but as definitive modern experiences or concepts perceived to have the power to dramatically create and transfigure selves. Additionally, by focusing on specific forms, discourses, and ideologies of love, I avoid retracing areas of discussion that have been central to studies of love and modern Japanese literature for scholars in Japan: sex / gender differences in experiences, narratives, and discourses of love; and the relationship between love and sexuality. Because these issues were important concerns for prewar women writers depicting love, I touch on them where relevant but do not explore them in depth. For studies that emphasize such sex / gender differences, that explore love in relation to sexuality, or both, see, for example, Saeki; Koyano Atsushi, *"Otoko no koi" no bungakushi* (Asahi shinbunsha, 1997); Kanno Satomi, *Shōhisareru ren'ai ron: Taishō chishikijin to sei* (Seikyūsha, 2001). For a broad conceptualization of love and its place in the history of modern Japanese popular literature and culture, see Koyano Atsushi, *Ren'ai no Shōwashi* (Bungei shunjū, 2005). For a history of the vocabulary associated with love and sexuality, see Koyano Atsushi, *Sei to ai no Nihongo kōza* (Chikuma shobō, 2003). For an anthropological work in English, see Sonia Ryang, *Love in Modern Japan: Its Estrangement from Self, Sex, and Society* (London: Routledge, 2006).

25. Gulick, 56.

26. For a study of *Jogaku zasshi* and Meiji women's literature, see Rebecca L. Copeland, *Lost Leaves: Women Writers of Meiji Japan* (Honolulu: University of Hawai'i Press, 2000).

27. From the 1890s on, *ai* was also used to denote male-female love and not necessarily to indicate Christian love, or parental or fraternal love. For example, Mori Ōgai (1862–1922) uses *"ai"* to refer to heterosexual love in *Maihime* (The dancer, 1890); see Sōgō Masaaki and Hida Yoshifumi, eds., *Meiji no kotoba jiten* (Tokyodō shuppan, 1998), 3.

28. For a discussion of the term *ren'ai*, see Saeki, 16; Sōgō and Hida, 602; Yanabu Akira, *Honyakugo seiritsu jijō* (Iwanami shoten, 1982), 87–105; Karatani, 82.

29. According to Furukawa Makoto, the earliest usage of *"dōseiai"* (as male-male sexuality) is found in a 1922 work of sexology. He also notes that even as this new word was replacing the traditional term used to refer to male-male love and / or sexuality (*"nanshoku"*), *"dōseiai"* came to be associated strongly with female-female love and / or sexuality during the 1910s to 1930s; see "Dōsei 'ai' kō," *Imago* 6, no. 12 (1995): 205–207. Although the term *dōseiai* is used to connote both male and female same-sex love, I focus only on the latter in this book, using the term to mean "female same-sex love." For more on the history of male-male love and sexuality in Japan, see Gregory M. Pflugfelder, *Cartographies of Desire: Male-Male Sexuality in Japanese Discourse, 1600–1950* (Berkeley: University of California Press, 1999).

The compound *"boseiai"* (maternal love) came into common usage sometime during the late 1920s. See Kanō Mikiyo, "Bosei fashizumu no fūkei," in *Bosei fashizumu,* ed. Kanō Mikiyo, vol. 6 of Nyū feminizumu rebyū [New Feminism Review] (Gakuyō shobō, 1995), 41.

30. Kitamura Tōkoku, "Ensei shika to josei," in *Kitamura Tōkoku shū,* ed. Odagiri Hideo, vol. 29 of Meiji bungaku zenshū (Chikuma shobō, 1976), 64, 66–67. Emphasis in original. For further discussion of this essay, see Copeland, *Lost Leaves,* 187; Suzuki, *Narrating the Self,* 75; Takahashi Yōji, ed., *Kindai ren'ai monogatari 50,* vol. 26 of Bessatsu Taiyō (Heibonsha, 1997), 20; Nishimura Hiroko, Sekiguchi Hiroko, Sugano Noriko, and Esashi Akiko, eds., *Bungaku ni miru Nihon josei no rekishi* (Yoshikawa kōbunkan, 2000), 192–195.

31. Shimizu Shikin, "Koware yubiwa," in *Ai to sei no jiyū: "Ie" kara no kaihō,* ed. Esashi Akiko (Shakai hyōronsha, 1989), 22–33; originally published in *Jogaku zasshi* 246 (January 1891) under the penname Tsuyuko. For the English translation, see "The Broken Ring," trans. Rebecca Jennison, in *The Modern Murasaki: Writing by Women of Meiji Japan,* ed. Rebecca L. Copeland and Melek Ortabasi (New York: Columbia University Press, 2006), 232–239. On Shimizu and her works, see Copeland, *Lost Leaves,* 159–214; Rebecca Jennison, "Shimizu Shikin (1868–1933)," in *Modern Murasaki,* 222–227.

32. Yosano Akiko, "Midaregami," in *Ai to sei no jiyū,* 52–72. For more on Yosano and her poetry, see Janine Beichman, *Embracing the Firebird: Yosano Akiko and the Birth of the Female Voice in Modern Japanese Poetry* (Honolulu: University of Hawai'i Press, 2002); Rodd, "Yosano Akiko and the Taishō Debate"; Sarah M. Strong, "Passion and Patience: Aspects of Feminine Poetic Heritage in Yosano Akiko's *Midaregami* and Tawara Machi's *Salad kinenbi,*" *Journal of the Association of Teachers of Japanese* 25, no. 2 (1991): 177–194; Laurel Rasplica Rodd, ed., "Yosano Akiko (1878–1942)," Special Issue, *Journal of the Association of Teachers of Japanese* 25, no. 1 (1991). Yosano published many poems in *Bluestocking* and was an official supporter. For more on her involvement with the journal, see Raichō kenkyūkai, ed., *Seitō jinbutsu jiten: 110 nin no gunzō* (Taishūkan shoten, 2001), 188–189; Bardsley, *Bluestockings of Japan,* 246–258.

33. "Genshi josei wa taiyō de atta: *Seitō* hakkan ni saishite," in *Hiratsuka Raichō chosakushū,* vol. 1, 18; originally published in *Seitō* 1, no. 1 (1911). This quote is not the opening paragraph of the essay but is from the middle of the text. In translating this excerpt I have consulted Copeland's translation of the opening paragraph and her discussion of the essay; see Rebecca L. Copeland, "Hiratsuka Raichō," in *Japanese Women Writers: A Bio-Critical Sourcebook,* ed. Chieko I. Mulhern (Westport, CT: Greenwood Press, 1994), 140–141; "Introduction: Meiji Women Writers," in *Modern Murasaki,* 1–2. For an introduction and full translation of the essay, see Bardsley, *Bluestockings of Japan,* 88–91, 94–103.

34. See Hiratsuka Raichō, *Hiratsuka Raichō jiden: Genshi josei wa taiyō de atta,* vol. 2 (Ōtsuki shoten, 1971), 505; *In the Beginning, Woman Was the Sun: The Autobiography of a Japanese Feminist,* trans. Teruko Craig (New York: Columbia University Press, 2006), 239. *In the Beginning, Woman Was the Sun* is the English translation

of *Hiratsuka Raichō jiden*, the two-volume autobiography of Hiratsuka Raichō. Although I do not use this translation in quoting from *Hiratsuka Raichō jiden*, I note corresponding pages from it when appropriate. When the corresponding pages are not noted, it means the translation does not include parts of the original text that are relevant to my argument.

35. The term *atarashii onna* was first used in 1910 by Tsubouchi Shōyō (1859–1935) and later popularized. It was used to refer to women who went against tradition and was often associated with members of the Bluestocking Society. See Muta Kazue and Shin Chi Won, "Kindai no sexuaritii no sōzō to 'atarashii onna': Hikaku bunseki no kokoromi," *Shisō* 886 (April 1998): 91.

36. See, for example, Shin feminizumu hihyō no kai, ed., *Seitō o yomu* (Gakugei shorin, 1998); Yoneda Sayoko and Ikeda Emiko, eds., *Seitō o manabu hito no tame ni* (Kyoto: Sekai shisōsha, 1999); Raichō kenkyūkai; Iwata Nanatsu, *Bungaku to shite no Seitō* (Fuji shuppan, 2003); Setouchi Harumi, *Seitō* (Chūō kōronsha, 1987); Horiba Kiyoko, ed., *Seitō josei kaihō ronshū* (Iwanami shoten, 1999); Iida Yūko, ed., *Seitō to iu ba: Bungaku, jendaa, "atarashii onna"* (Shinwasha, 2002); Kōuchi Nobuko, ed., *Shiryō bosei hogo ronsō*, vol. 1 of Ronsō shiriizu (Domesu shuppan, 1988); Orii Miyako, ed., *Shiryō sei to ai o meguru ronsō*, vol. 5 of Ronsō shiriizu (Domesu shuppan, 1991); Jan Bardsley, "*Seitō* and the Resurgence of Writing by Women," in *The Columbia Companion to Modern East Asian Literature*, ed. Joshua S. Mostow, Kirk A. Denton, Bruce Fulton, and Sharalyn Orbaugh (New York: Columbia University Press, 2003), 93–98; Lowy, *Japanese "New Woman,"* 1–99; Sievers, 163–188; Tomida, 139–261. For analyses and translations of selected writing from *Bluestocking*, see Bardsley, *Bluestockings of Japan*.

37. Itō Noe (1895–1923) was publisher and editor beginning with *Seitō* 5, no. 1 (1915); see Raichō kenkyūkai, 41. For more on Hiratsuka, see Raichō kenkyūkai, 142–143; Setouchi, *Seitō*; Kobayashi; Yoneda Sayoko, *Hiratsuka Raichō: Kindai Nihon no demokurashii to jendaa* (Yoshikawa kōbunkan, 2002); Ōmori Kaoru, *Hiratsuka Raichō no hikari to kage* (Daiichi shorin, 1997); *Hiratsuka Raichō jiden*, vols. 1 and 2; Hiratsuka, *In the Beginning*; Bardsley, *Bluestockings of Japan*, 80–118; Copeland, "Hiratsuka Raichō," 132–143; Lowy, *Japanese "New Woman,"* 1–99; Tomida. The official chronology is "Hiratsuka Raichō nenpu," in *Hiratsuka Raichō chosakushū ho: Shashin, shokan, nenpu, chosaku mokuroku*, ed. Hiratsuka Raichō chosakushū henshū iinkai (Ōtsuki shoten, 1984), 159–192.

38. For more on this scandal known as the Shiobara (Baien) incident, see Sasaki Hideaki, *"Atarashii onna" no tōrai: Hiratsuka Raichō to Sōseki* (Nagoya: Nagoya daigaku shuppankai, 1994); Bardsley, *Bluestockings of Japan*, 82; Copeland, "Hiratsuka Raichō," 133–134; Lowy, *Japanese "New Woman,"* 66–68; Tomida, 107–137; Hiratsuka, *Hiratsuka Raichō jiden*, vol. 1, 211–252; *In the Beginning*, 104–123; Morita Sōhei, *Baien* (Iwanami shoten, 1940). Hiratsuka wrote her own version of this incident in a newspaper serial entitled "Tōge" (The hill) published in *Jiji shinpō* (April 1–21, 1915). Due to her poor health at the time, this work was never completed. See *Hiratsuka Raichō chosakushū*, vol. 2 (1983), 61–105.

39. Felski, 1.

40. Narita Ryūichi suggests that Bluestocking Society writers used the idea of love to find a woman's "personal dignity" and "individuality." See *Taishō demokurashii*, vol. 4 of Shiriizu Nihon kingendaishi (Iwanami shoten, 2007), 40.

41. Many Japanese critics conflate *kindai ren'ai ideorogii* with a similar term, (*kindai*) *ren'ai kekkon ideorogii* ([modern] love marriage ideology), which connotes the new ideal of marrying for love. As I discuss fully in Chapter Four, love marriage ideology comes out of the new ideal of love expressed by Hiratsuka's writings but should be kept separate from what I call *modern love ideology*.

42. See Raichō kenkyūkai, 209; Dina Lowy, "Love and Marriage: Ellen Key and Hiratsuka Raichō Explore Alternatives," *Women's Studies* 33 (2004): 361–380. For more on Ellen Key, see Ronald William De Angelis, "Ellen Key: A Biography of the Swedish Reformer" (Ph.D. diss., University of Connecticut, 1978).

43. For Hiratsuka's comments on *Love and Marriage*, see "*Ren'ai to kekkon* (Ellen Key cho) rensai ni attate," in *Hiratsuka Raichō chosakushū*, vol. 1, 177–181; originally published in *Seitō* 3, no. 1 (1913). See also *Hiratsuka Raichō jiden*, vol. 2, 424–426; *In the Beginning*, 202–203. In addition to selections from *Love and Marriage*, other writings by Key were also translated and published in *Bluestocking*. A complete Japanese translation of *Love and Marriage* (from the English edition) was published by educator Harada Minoru in 1920. For a history of the introduction of this text in Japan, see Kaneko Sachiko, *Kindai Nihon joseiron no keifu* (Fuji shuppan, 1999), 132–133. The original Swedish work was published in 1903 as *Lifslinjer* (Life's lines), vol. 1. The English *Love and Marriage* is different from the original Swedish in that it abridges some parts of the text. My quotations from *Love and Marriage* are either translations of the Japanese text published in *Bluestocking* or from the English version: *Love and Marriage*, trans. Arthur G. Chater (New York: G. P. Putnam's Sons, 1911). I have also consulted the most recent Japanese translation: *Ren'ai to kekkon*, 2 vols., trans. Onodera Makoto and Onodera Yuriko (Iwanami shoten, 1975–1976).

44. *Hiratsuka Raichō jiden*, vol. 2, 490–491; see also *In the Beginning*, 232–233. In terms of sexual experience, Hiratsuka was not a virgin when she met Okumura. See *Hiratsuka Raichō jiden*, vol. 1, 283–287; *In the Beginning*, 138–139.

45. *Love and Marriage*, 182; "Boken," trans. Hiratsuka Raichō, *Seitō* 4, no. 9 (1914): 20.

46. Key, "Ren'ai to dōtoku," trans. Itō Noe, *Seitō* 3, no. 5 (1913): furoku 19–20.

47. Kaneko, 130; see also De Angelis.

48. "Ellen Key joshi," in *Hiratsuka Raichō chosakushū*, vol. 1, 405; originally published in *Shin Nihon* (September 1914).

49. Key describes the distinction between male and female experiences of love: "That with women love usually proceeds from the soul to the senses and sometimes does not reach that far; that with man it usually proceeds from the senses to the soul and sometimes never completes the journey—this is for both the most painful of the existing distinctions between man and woman." *Love and Marriage*, 98–99. The Japanese translation of this section is presented under the title: "Danjo ren'ai no sabetsu" (The difference between male and female love) in *Seitō* 4, no. 5 (1914): 1. See also Hiratsuka's comment on this quote in "Shōkan ni, san," in *Hiratsuka*

Raichō chosakushū, vol. 1, 316–317; original essay published as "Yonda mono no hyō to saikin zakkan," *Seitō* 4, no. 5 (1914).

50. See Kawamura Kunimitsu, *Sexuariti no kindai* (Kōdansha, 1996), 119–120.

51. Joan E. Ericson discusses the issues surrounding the problematic view that women's literature has only one unified style and is less important than writings by men; see *Be a Woman: Hayashi Fumiko and Modern Japanese Women's Literature* (Honolulu: University of Hawai'i Press, 1997), 3–38. Some examples of essays that reflect such views are collected in Rebecca L. Copeland, ed., *Woman Critiqued: Translated Essays on Japanese Women's Writing* (Honolulu: University of Hawai'i Press, 2006).

52. See Suzuki, *Narrating the Self*, 6–7.

53. For an exploration of this issue as reflected in critical writings about women writers, see Copeland, *Woman Critiqued*.

54. Meiji humanists such as Iwamoto Yoshiharu promoted the idea of love in the home and the importance of love for husband-wife relationships. Such notions lay the groundwork for love marriage ideology by promoting the desirability of marital love. The difference between these Meiji period concepts and love marriage ideology is discussed in detail in Chapter Four.

55. Kubokawa Ineko, "Haha no jikaku to konran," in *Jiga no kanata e: Kindai o koeru feminizumu*, ed. Kanō Mikiyo (Shakai hyōronsha, 1990), 216–218. From the late 1920s to 1945, Sata used her married name, Kubokawa Ineko. A year after her divorce in 1946 she began using the name Sata, by which she is better known. See "Nenpu," in *Sata Ineko shū*, ed. Sasaki Kiichi, vol. 39 of Nihon bungaku zenshū (Shinchōsha, 1965), 425.

56. "Okamoto Kanoko nenpu," in *Okamoto Kanoko zenshū*, vol. 12 (Chikuma shobō, 1994), 454; "Hiratsuka Raichō nenpu," in *Hiratsuka Raichō chosakushū ho*, 164.

Part One: Girls and Virgins

Several sections in Chapters Two and Three were published in an earlier form in "Writing Same-Sex Love: Sexology and Literary Representation in Yoshiya Nobuko's Early Fiction," *Journal of Asian Studies* 65, no. 3 (2006). Reprinted with permission of the Association for Asian Studies. Several paragraphs about virginity in Chapter Three appeared in an earlier form in "Becoming a Virgin: Female Growth and Sexuality in *Yaneura no nishojo*," in *Across Time and Genre: Reading and Writing Japanese Women's Texts*, ed. Janice Brown and Sonja Arntzen (Edmonton: Department of East Asian Studies, University of Alberta, 2002).

Chapter Two: Same-Sex Love

1. Kōtō jogakkō kenkyūkai, ed., *Kōtō jogakkō kenkyū: Seidoteki enkaku to setsuritsu katei* (Ōzorasha, 1994), shiryōhen 25–32. According to Maeda Ai, from 1918 to 1926 the number of such schools more than doubled and student numbers tripled; see *Kindai dokusha no seiritsu* (Iwanami shoten, 1993), 220. There were both public and private higher girls' schools, and from 1911 there was also the practical higher

girls' school (*jikka kōtō jogakkō*), which focused on domestic subjects. For a general introduction to higher girls' schools and student culture, see Inagaki Kyōko, *Jogakkō to jogakusei: Kyōyō, tashinami, modan bunka* (Chūōkōron shinsha, 2007). For more on the statistics, laws, and history of these schools, see Kōtō jogakkō kenkyūkai; Sakurai Mamoru, *Joshi kyōikushi* (Osaka: Zōshindō, 1943).

2. See Saeki; Levy; Honda, *Jogakusei no keifu.*

3. Ubukata Toshirō, *Meiji Taishō kenbunshi* (Chūō kōronsha, 1995), 101.

4. See Furukawa, "Dōsei 'ai' kō," 205–207. He notes that it is unclear when "*dōseiai*" was used as a compound for the first time. He also documents the use of terms such as "*dōsei no ai,*" "*dōsei no koi,*" and "*dōsei ren'ai*" during the 1910s.

5. The use of *ome* has a complicated history. In 1910, a commentator writing under the name Tatsuko explained the term as a romantic friendship between an older student and a younger student in higher girls' schools. The practice entailed looking into each other's eyes and shaking hands during recess. The younger girl publicly displayed the relationship by wearing a hair ribbon given to her by "her lover." Tatsuko notes that it is difficult to determine the origins of the term but explains that some believe it comes from "*Futari no ai natte omedetai*" (It is *auspicious* that the two girls' love has been fulfilled) or "*Ome ni kakkata ga ai no itoguchi*" (Love started once they *saw/met* each other). See "Jogakusei dōshi no aijin: 'Omesan' no ryūkō," reprinted in Okano Yukie, ed., *Ansorojii onna to seikatsu,* vol. 22 of Josei no mita kindai (Yumani shobō, 2001), 69–71; originally published in *Murasaki* 6, no. 10 (1910).

The meaning of *ome*, however, seems to have changed quickly. Poet Yosano Akiko noted in 1917 that she was told "seven or eight years ago" that "*ome*" means "*Ano kata to ano kata wa omedetai*" (That person and that person are *happily friendly with each other*), signifying a purely innocent friendship, but now it has come to be seen as a word with a meaning that is "disgusting even to think about." This explanation seems to refer to the understanding of *ome* as a sexual relationship between a masculine female and a feminine female, what is now termed *butch-femme.* "*Ome*" in this case, Yosano notes, comes from a reading of 男女, that is, "male-female" or "man-woman." See "Dōsei no ai: Jiden no issetsu," in *Yosano Akiko hyōron chosakushū,* vol. 18 (Ryūkei shosha, 2002), 53–55. Jennifer Robertson interprets "*ome*" as butch-femme couples; see *Takarazuka,* 68–70; "Dying to Tell: Sexuality and Suicide in Imperial Japan," *Signs: Journal of Women in Culture and Society* 25, no. 1 (1999): 8. She explains that it derives from a combination of "*osu*" (male) and "*mesu*" (female), terms usually used for animals; see "Dying to Tell," 8. There seems to have been some overlap, depending on the context and time, in the use of *ome* as both romantic friendship and butch-femme sexuality. Furukawa, for example, quotes a 1910 magazine article that describes "*ome*" as "an aberrant love . . . the female equivalent of *nanshoku* [male-male love]." Furukawa Makoto, "Sexuaritii no henyō: Kindai Nihon no dōseiai o meguru mittsu no kōdo," *Nichibei josei jaanaru* 17 (1994): 43. In the 1926 "Jogakusei kakushi kotoba jiten" (School-girls' secret language dictionary) published in the girls' magazine, *Shōjo gahō* (Girls' graphic), however, "*ome*" is defined as a specific kind of romantic friendship, the love that a student has for a younger, beautiful student; see Imada Erika, *"Shōjo" no shakaishi* (Keisō shobō, 2007), 190–191. Gregory M. Pflugfelder's interviews suggest that there may have been a sense among schoolgirls that *"ome"* was simply an earlier term superceded by *"S"* (or that these terms were used more or less interchangeably) and thus *"ome"* did not always necessarily convey the sense of sexual and / or clearly gendered butch-femme relations; see "'S' Is for Sister: Schoolgirl Intimacy and 'Same-Sex Love' in Early Twentieth-Century Japan," in *Gendering Modern Japanese History*, 137–138.

"S" (or *"esu"*), as Pflugfelder points out, was a "generic signifier for schoolgirl intimacy" during the "early twentieth century." It was commonly seen as a shortened term for the English word *"sister,"* signifying the lover or the relationship; see Pflugfelder, "'S' Is for Sister," 136–137; Imada, 190–191. Robertson notes that it can also mean *"shōjo,"* "sex," or a combination of all three meanings; see *Takarazuka*, 68. For more on these and other terms, see Furukawa, "Sexuaritii no henyō," 43–44; Robertson, *Takarazuka*, 67–70; "Dying to Tell," 8–10; Pflugfelder, "'S' Is for Sister," 134–140; Imada, 190–191.

6. Furukawa, "Sexuaritii no henyō," 43; "Dōsei 'ai' kō," 205; Yoshikawa Toyoko, "'Josei dōseiai' toiu 'yamai' to jendaa," in *Jendaa no Nihon kindai bungaku*, ed. Nakayama Kazuko, Egusa Mitsuko, and Fujimori Kiyoshi (Kanrin shobō, 1998), 114; "Kindai Nihon no 'lezubianizumu': 1910 nendai no shōsetsu ni egakareta lezubiantachi," in *Sei gensō o kataru*, ed. Kondō Kazuko, vol. 2 of Kindai o yomikaeru (San'ichi shobō, 1998), 84; Peichen Wu, "Performing Gender Along the Lesbian Continuum: The Politics of Sexual Identity in the Seitō Society," *U.S.-Japan Women's Journal English Supplement* 22 (2002): 67; Pflugfelder, "'S' Is for Sister," 153–158.

7. "Extremely close friendship" is emphasized in the original. "Dōsei no ai: Shasetsu," *Fujo shinbun*, August 11, 1911. Reprinted in facsimile form in Furukawa Makoto and Akaeda Kanako, eds., *Senzenki Dōseiai kanren bunken shūsei*, vol. 3 (Fuji shuppan, 2006), 36. Also quoted in Yoshikawa, "Kindai Nihon no 'lezubianizumu,'" 103–104. Articles about the 1911 love suicide as well as other prewar texts on female same-sex love have been recently collected in Furukawa and Akaeda, 21–366.

8. Wu, 70; Pflugfelder, "'S' Is for Sister," 157–158. See also the warning to female educators about dangerous passionate friendships presented in "Dōsei no ai: Shasetsu."

9. "Dōsei no ai: Shasetsu." Also quoted in Yoshikawa, "Kindai Nihon no 'lezubianizumu,'" 104.

10. Sabine Frühstück, *Colonizing Sex: Sexology and Social Control in Modern Japan* (Berkeley: University of California Press, 2003), 5.

11. Erwin J. Haeberle, *The Birth of Sexology: A Brief History in Documents*, pamphlet published for the Sixth World Congress of Sexology, Washington, DC (1983).

12. See Furukawa, "Dōsei 'ai' kō"; "Sexuaritii no henyō"; Yoshikawa, "Kindai Nihon no 'lezubianizumu'"; Robertson, "Dying to Tell"; Donald Roden, "Taishō Culture and the Problem of Gender Ambivalence," in *Culture and Identity: Japanese*

Intellectuals During the Interwar Years, ed. J. Thomas Rimer (Princeton, NJ: Princeton University Press, 1990), 45–46; Frühstück; Pflugfelder, "'S' Is for Sister."

13. *Psychopathia Sexualis* was translated as *Hentai seiyoku shinri* (Psychology of abnormal sexual desires, 1913); see Furukawa, "Dōsei 'ai' kō," 203. Another work heavily based on *Psychopathia Sexualis* was *Hentai seiyoku ron* (Theories of abnormal sexual desires, 1915), authored by sexologists Habuto Eiji and Sawada Junjirō; this work was "reprinted eighteen times over the next decade"; see Roden, 45. See also Frühstück, 106. Excerpts from *Studies in the Psychology of Sex* were translated and published in Japan from the 1910s to the 1930s. The complete work by Ellis is a seven-volume set published from 1899 to 1928; the initial version was published under the title *Sexual Inversion* in 1897. See Ruth M. Pettis, "Ellis, Havelock," in *glbtq: An Encyclopedia of Gay, Lesbian, Bisexual, Transgender, and Queer Culture*, http:// www .glbtq.com/social-sciences/ellis_h.html (accessed January 13, 2005).

14. See Habuto Eiji, *Kyōiku shiryō: Ippan seiyokugaku* (Jitsugyō no Nippon sha, 1921), 240–241; Frühstück, 70; Yasuda Tokutarō, "Dōseiai no rekishikan," *Chūō kōron* 50, no. 3 (1935): 146–152; Pflugfelder, "'S' Is for Sister," 140–150.

15. Erisu [Havelock Ellis], "Joseikan no dōsei ren'ai," trans. Nomo, foreword by Hiratsuka Raichō, *Seitō* 4, no. 4 (1914): furoku 1–24. The foreword is reprinted as "*Joseikan no dōsei ren'ai* (Ellis cho, Nomo yaku) no jogen," in *Hiratsuka Raichō chosakushū*, vol. 1, 305–306. Nomo is the pseudonym for Bluestocking Society member Takada (Sakamoto) Makoto (1889–1954). See Hiratsuka, *Hiratsuka Raichō jiden*, vol. 2, 543; *In the Beginning*, 257–258; Raichō kenkyūkai, 112–113. For the original text, see Havelock Ellis, *Studies in the Psychology of Sex*, vol. 1 (New York: Random House, 1942), 195–263. Hiratsuka explains that she learned of this work from sexologist Ogura Seizaburō (1882–1941), who published essays on sexology in *Bluestocking*; see *Hiratsuka Raichō jiden*, vol. 2, 543; *In the Beginning*, 257.

16. Edward Carpenter, *The Intermediate Sex: A Study of Some Transitional Types of Men and Women* (London: George Allen and Unwin, 1930). Yamakawa's abridged translation was published in *Safuran* (Saffron), a magazine published by Otake Kōkichi in 1914 after she left the Bluestocking Society in 1912. The translation in book form was published as a combined volume with Sakai Toshihiko's translation of a section from Lester Ward's *Pure Sociology: Resutaa Wōdo* [Lester Ward] and Edowaado Kaapentaa [Edward Carpenter], *Josei chūshinsetsu to Dōseiai*, trans. Sakai Toshihiko and Yamakawa Kikue (Arususha, 1919).

17. Ellis, *Studies*, vol. 1, 218, 368, 374; "Joseikan," 12.

18. Yosano Akiko, "Fujin to seiyoku," in *Yosano Akiko hyōron chosakushū*, vol. 4 (2001), 292; facsimile edition of *Warera nani o motomuru ka* (Tengendō, 1917). Quotation also in Yoshikawa, "Kindai Nihon no 'lezubianizumu,'" 103.

19. Numata Rippō, *Gendai shōjo to sono kyōiku*, vol. 15 of Kindai Nihon joshi kyōiku bunkenshū, ed. Nakajima Kuni (Nihon tosho sentaa, 1984), 47–50; facsimile edition of the 1916 book published by Dōbunkan. Numata was editor of *Shōjo sekai* (Girls' world) when the fourteen-year-old Yoshiya Nobuko won a special prize from the magazine for her contributions in 1910. See "Nenpu" and "Tōsho jidai," in

Yoshiya Nobuko zenshū, vol. 12 (Asahi shinbunsha, 1976), 408–410, 549, 555. Yoshiya reads Numata's name as Ryūhō, but scholars currently refer to him as Rippō.

20. Frühstück, 70. Pflugfelder notes that almost all sexologists saw same-sex relationships between schoolboys as "more likely to involve a physical dimension than those of their schoolgirl contemporaries"; see "'S' Is for Sister," 148.

21. Habuto, 354. Frühstück (113–114) notes that a number of works by Habuto, including *General Sexology*, "were advertised constantly in women's magazines, and some had appeared in their fifteenth edition by as early as 1921."

22. Yasuda Tokutarō, 150–151. Pflugfelder suggests that such "constructions of 'same-sex love' as a necessary and even beneficial stage in psychological development became increasingly common during the 1930s and 1940s, reflecting the growing influence of Sigmund Freud"; see "'S' Is for Sister," 147.

23. See Robertson, "Dying to Tell," 21. She translates this term as "deviant homosexual love." I use the word *abnormal* for "*hentai*" here because it underscores that it is the opposite of *normal (jōtai)*.

24. See Roden; Robertson, "Dying to Tell"; Ellis, *Studies*, vol. 1, 222; "Joseikan," 15; Yasuda Tokutarō, 151.

25. Robertson, "Dying to Tell," 11–12, 21.

26. Yasuda Tokutarō, 150–151.

27. See Carroll Smith-Rosenberg, *Disorderly Conduct: Visions of Gender in Victorian America* (Oxford, UK: Oxford University Press, 1985), 276–277; Martha Vicinus, "'They Wonder to Which Sex I Belong': The Historical Roots of the Modern Lesbian Identity," in *Lesbian and Gay Studies Reader*, ed. Henry Abelove, Michèle Aina Barale, and David M. Halperin (New York: Routledge, 1993), 441; Ellis, *Studies*, vol. 1, 217–218; "Joseikan," 11–12; Yasuda Tokutarō, 151.

28. Tamura Toshiko, "Akirame," in *Tamura Toshiko sakuhinshū*, vol. 1 (Orijin shuppan sentaa, 1987), 53; first serialized in *Osaka Asahi shinbun*, Jan. 1–March 21, 1911. For an analysis of Tamura's same-sex love writing, see Yoshikawa, "Kindai Nihon no 'lezubianizumu,'" 88–110. Tamura is said to have had same-sex love relationships with *Bluestocking* contributor Naganuma Chieko (1886–1938) and Yuasa Yoshiko (1896–1990), who later lived with Miyamoto Yuriko. For more on Tamura's life and publications, see "Nenpu," in *Tamura Toshiko sakuhinshū*, vol. 3 (1988), 445–465; Raichō kenkyūkai, 122–123; Kyoko Nagamatsu, "Tamura Toshiko," in *Japanese Women Writers*, 389–397; Edward Fowler, "Tamura Toshiko (1884–1945)," in *Modern Murasaki*, 339–347. For the translation of "Ikichi," Tamura's 1911 story published in the inaugural issue of *Bluestocking*, see "Lifeblood," trans. Edward Fowler, *Modern Murasaki*, 348–357.

29. Kawada Yoshi, "Onna tomodachi," *Seitō* 5, no. 3 (1915): 73–88. See Watanabe Mieko, "*Seitō* ni okeru lezubianizumu," in *Seitō o yomu*, 272–273.

30. Sugawara Hatsu, "Junjitsu no tomo," *Seitō* 5, no. 3 (1915): 42–66. Another same-sex love story is Kanzaki Tsune's (1890–1975) "Zōkibayashi" (The woods), *Seitō* 3, no. 1 (1913): 129–135. For a different reading, see Watanabe, "*Seitō* ni okeru lezubianizumu," 276–284.

31. Lillian Faderman, *Odd Girls and Twilight Lovers: A History of Lesbian Life in Twentieth-Century America* (New York: Penguin Books, 1992), 12.

32. See Muta and Shin, 108.

33. For more on their relationship, see Kurosawa Ariko, "1912 nen no Raichō to Kōkichi: 'Josei kaihō' to lezubianizumu o megutte," in *Bungaku shakai e chikyū e*, ed. Nishida Masaru tainin taishoku kinen bunshū henshū iinkai (San'ichi shobō, 1996), 309–327; Yoshikawa, "Kindai Nihon no 'lezubianizumu,'" 77–82; Wu, 64–86; Pflugfelder, "'S' Is for Sister," 166–168; Bardsley, *Bluestockings of Japan*, 85–87; Lowy, *Japanese "New Woman,"* 68–72.

34. Hiratsuka Raichō, "Marumado yori," in *Hiratsuka Raichō chosakushū*, vol. 1, 127, 129. Originally published as "Marumado yori: Chigasaki e Chigasaki e (Zatsuroku)," *Seitō* 2, no. 8 (1912). Otake married artist Tomimoto Kenkichi (1886–1963). See Kurosawa, "1912 nen," 324; Raichō kenkyūkai, 68–69, 201.

35. Hiratsuka Raichō, "Ichinenkan," *Seitō* 3, no. 2 (1913): 87–100; "Ichinenkan (Tsuzuki)," *Seitō* 3, no. 3 (1913): 78–85; "Ichinenkan (Tsuzuki)," *Seitō* 3, no. 12 (1913): 2–21. All of these articles are reprinted as "Ichinenkan," in *Hiratsuka Raichō chosakushū*, vol. 1, 182–215. The serialization was never completed.

36. "*Joseikan no dōsei ren'ai* (Ellis cho, Nomo yaku) no jogen," in *Hiratsuka Raichō chosakushū*, vol. 1, 305.

37. Kurosawa, "1912 nen," 319.

38. *Hiratsuka Raichō jiden*, vol. 2, 388; see also *In the Beginning*, 186.

39. Pflugfelder, "'S' Is for Sister," 167.

40. "Danshō" (Literary fragment), *Seitō* 6, no. 1 (1916): 105–106; "Chiisaki mono" (The little one), *Seitō* 6, no. 2 (1916): 28–38.

41. There are many conflicting reports about the dates and details of the Yamadas' reading group. Yoshiya's official chronology, "Nenpu," notes that Yoshiya studied *Love and Marriage* with the Yamadas in 1917; see *Yoshiya Nobuko zenshū*, vol. 12, 551. In her autobiography Hiratsuka says she studied in the same group as Yoshiya but does not mention dates; see *Hiratsuka Raichō jiden*, vol. 2, 572. In a 1937 essay Hiratsuka comments that Yoshiya was a member of the reading group, but she incorrectly says she was never a part of their "movement," despite the fact that Yoshiya published in *Bluestocking*; see "Seitō jidai," in *Hiratsuka Raichō chosakushū*, vol. 6 (1984), 186. Yoshikawa Toyoko suggests that Yoshiya studied with the Yamadas from 1915 to 1917; see "*Seitō* kara 'taishū shōsetsu' sakka e no michi: Yoshiya Nobuko *Yaneura no nishojo*," in *Feminizumu hihyō e no shōtai: Kindai josei bungaku o yomu*, ed. Iwabuchi Hiroko, Kitada Sachie, and Kōra Rumiko (Gakugei shorin, 1995), 124–126. For more on Yamada Waka, see Raichō kenkyūkai, 184–185; Bardsley, *Bluestockings of Japan*, 232–245.

42. Kume Yoriko, "Shōjo shōsetsu: Sai to kihan no gensetsu sōchi," in *Media, hyōshō, ideorogii: Meiji 30 nendai no bunka kenkyū*, ed. Komori Yōichi, Kōno Kensuke, and Takahashi Osamu (Ozawa shoten, 1997), 212–213.

43. Matsuzaki Tenmin, "Shakai kansatsu mannenhitsu," in *Ningen seken*, ed. Minami Hiroshi, Namase Katsumi, and Sakata Minoru, vol. 1 of Kindai shomin seikatsushi, ed. Minami Hiroshi (San'ichi shobō, 1991), 28.

44. See Honda, *Jogakusei no keifu*, 186–191; Kawamura Kunimitsu, *Otome no inori: Kindai josei imeeji no tanjō* (Kinokuniya shoten, 1993); Nagai Kiyoko, "Tanjō shōjotachi no kaihōku: *Shōjo sekai* to 'shōjo dokushakai,'" in *Semegiau onna to okoto: Kindai*, ed. Okuda Akiko, vol. 5 of *Onna to otoko no jikū: Nihon joseishi saikō*, ed. Tsurumi Kazuko, Kōno Nobuko, and others (Fujiwara shoten, 1995), 278–311; Inoue, *Vicarious Language*, 125–130.

45. Yoshiya published in girls' magazines beginning in 1908 (when she was twelve) and won a number of prestigious prizes. In 1911 she started submitting works to general literary magazines, and by 1914 she had stopped writing as an amateur who sent in contributions without compensation. See "Nenpu," in *Yoshiya Nobuko zenshū*, vol. 12, 548–550.

Chapter Three: Yoshiya Nobuko and the Romance of Sisterhood

1. Tanabe Seiko, *Yume haruka Yoshiya Nobuko: Aki tomoshi tsukue no ue no ikusanga*, vol. 2 (Asahi shinbunsha, 1999), 111.

2. See "Nenpu," in *Yoshiya Nobuko zenshū*, vol. 12, 545–577; Tanabe, *Yume haruka Yoshiya Nobuko*, vols. 1 and 2. For a biographical introduction in English, see Jennifer Robertson, "Yoshiya Nobuko: Out and Outspoken in Practice and Prose," in *The Human Tradition in Modern Japan*, ed. Anne Walthall (Wilmington, DE: Scholarly Resources, 2002), 155–174.

3. "Dōsei no ai," in *Yosano Akiko hyōron chosakushū*, vol. 18, 53.

4. The official chronology and most scholars count fifty-two stories in *Flower Tales*, which was first serialized in *Girls' Graphic* from 1916 to 1924. Komatsu Satoko adds two more stories, serialized in *Shōjo kurabu* (Girls' club) from 1925 to 1926. Fifty are included in the collected works edition; see "Hanamonogatari," in *Yoshiya Nobuko zenshū*, vol. 1 (1975), 3–356. For publication details and different viewpoints about the total number of stories, see "Nenpu," in *Yoshiya Nobuko zenshū*, vol. 12, 551, 554; Komatsu Satoko, "Yoshiya Nobuko *Hanamonogatari* no buntai," *Ochanomizu joshi daigaku ningen bunka kenkyū nenpō* 18 (1994): 2-48, 2-54; Kanai Harumi, "Yoshiya Nobuko no shōjo shōsetsu ni okeru shōjozō: *Hanamonogatari* no shōjozō," *Yamaguchi kokugo kyōiku kenkyū* 5 (1995): 12; Tanabe, *Yume haruka*, vol. 1, 266.

5. Kume, "Shōjo shōsetsu," 196–201, 220; "Kōseisareru 'shōjo': Meijiki 'shōjo shōsetsu' no janru keisei," *Nihon kindai bungaku* 68 (2003): 2.

6. Kume points out that the theme of close girlhood friendships was not invented by Yoshiya but derives from earlier girls' fiction; see "Kōseisareru 'shōjo,'" 9–10. Although such earlier influence is important in understanding *Flower Tales*, I suggest that this work by Yoshiya is a departure; it is a unique and complex work that strategically utilizes accepted ideas about pure love and girlhood while simultaneously subverting them. For more on Kume's view of romantic friendships in girls' fiction, see "Kōseisareru 'shōjo,'" 10–13.

7. "Hanamonogatari," 83. Subsequent quotes from the work are noted directly in the text in parentheses. For more about the white lily and its use as a symbol of purity and girls in the context of Meiji girls' schools and girls' magazines, see

Watanabe Shūko, *"Shōjo" zō no tanjō: Kindai Nihon ni okeru "shōjo" kihan no keisei* (Shinsensha, 2007), 269–303.

8. Martha Vicinus, "Distance and Desire: English Boarding-School Friendships," *Signs: Journal of Women in Culture and Society* 9, no. 4 (1984): 604–605.

9. "Dōsei o aisuru saiwai," in *Akogare shiru koro* (Kōransha, 1923), 16, 18–21. This book is a collection of Yoshiya's juvenilia.

10. See "Dōsei o aisuru saiwai," 19; "Aishiau kotodomo," in *Shojo dokuhon*, vol. 35 of Sōsho Joseiron, ed. Yamazaki Tomoko (Ōzorasha, 1997), 103–104; Carpenter, *Intermediate Sex*, 83–106; Wōdo [Ward] and Kaapentaa [Carpenter], 227–241. "Aishiau kotodomo" is an extremely abbreviated version of "Dōsei o aisuru saiwai." I use the version of "Aishiau kotodomo" from *Shojo dokuhon*, a facsimile edition of the 1936 Kenbunsha publication. For Pflugfelder's discussion of this essay, see "'S' Is for Sister," 164, 171, 186–187, 189. As he notes, "Aishiau kotodomo" was published earlier in *Shin shōsetsu* (January 1921). The facsimile of this article is also collected in Furukawa and Akaeda, 151.

11. For more on this bifurcated association of the male with sexual desire and the female with love, particularly in relation to same-sex sexuality, see Furukawa, "Dōsei 'ai' kō," 207; Pflugfelder, "'S' Is for Sister," 148.

12. Perhaps Yoshiya is also tapping into the Meiji educational discourse that promoted *aijō* as an innate female virtue. In this discourse, *aijō* is discussed as a selfless, pure love, associated with being a Good Wife, Wise Mother. By using such terms as *aijō* to make her point about the value of youthful, pure love, Yoshiya strategically aligns her stories with the moral teachings promoted in school. For *aijō* and purity in Meiji educational discourse, see Watanabe Shūko, 31–86.

13. Honda Masuko, *Ibunka to shite no kodomo* (Chikuma shobō, 1992), 187.

14. The six-dot ellipses (……) in quotes from Yoshiya's works are typographic marks in the actual text and should not be confused with the three spaced periods (. . .) commonly used in citations to signify the omission of a word or words. I discuss this textual symbol in detail later in the chapter.

15. Terry Castle, *The Apparitional Lesbian: Female Homosexuality and Modern Culture* (New York: Columbia University Press, 1993), 85.

16. Numata, 67–68, 221; Smith-Rosenberg, 186.

17. Various critics have read *Flower Tales* as expressing some form of female resistance, agency, or liberation. See Honda, *Ibunka*, 202–219; Kurosawa Ariko, "Shōjotachi no chikadōmei: Yoshiya Nobuko no *Onna no yūjō* o megutte," in *Onna to hyōgen: Feminizumu hihyō no genzai*, ed. Mizuta Noriko, vol. 2 of Nyū feminizumu rebyū [New Feminism Review] (Gakuyō shobō, 1991), 87–88; Kami Shōichirō, *Nihon jidō bungaku no shisō* (Kokudosha, 1976), 235; Kano Masanao, *Taishō demokurashii*, vol. 27 of Nihon no rekishi, ed. Kodama Kōta, Inoue Mitsusada, and Nagahara Keiji (Shōgakkan, 1976), 235–236; Yoshitake Teruko, *Nyonin Yoshiya Nobuko* (Bungei shunjū, 1982), 12; Komashaku Kimi, *Yoshiya Nobuko kakure feminisuto* (Libroporto, 1994), 24–30; Hitomi Tsuchiya Dollase, "Early Twentieth Century Japanese Girls' Magazine Stories: Examining Shōjo Voice in *Hanamonogatari* (Flower Tales)," *Journal of Popular Culture* 36, no. 4 (2003): 736–740; Kanai, 13.

18. Homi K. Bhabha, "Postcolonial Authority and Postmodern Guilt," in *Cultural Studies*, ed. Lawrence Grossberg, Cary Nelson, and Paula A. Treichler (New York: Routledge, 1992), 65–66. See also Judith Butler's reading in *The Psychic Life of Power: Theories in Subjection* (Stanford, CA: Stanford University Press, 1997), 190.

19. For discussion of the emergence of the *Flower Tales* narrative style, see Honda, *Ibunka*, 188–201; Nagai, 286–288, 306–308.

20. Dollase, "Early Twentieth Century," 731–732, 748.

21. Honda, *Ibunka*, 190–192.

22. Komori Yōichi, *Buntai to shite no monogatari* (Chikuma shobō, 1994), 234–235; Suga Hidemi, *Nihon kindai bungaku no "tanjō": Genbun-itchi undō to nashonarizumu* (Ōta shuppan, 1995), 144–145.

23. Suga, 143. Iwaya Daishi claims that Yamada was the first writer to use such textual symbols in Japan; see *Bundan monoshiri chō* (Kawade shobō, 1981), 181. Whether or not this is accurate, Yamada is considered an innovator in regard to such punctuation. See Maeda Ai and Hasegawa Izumi, eds., *Nihon bungaku shinshi: Kindai* (Shibundō, 1990), 100–101; Suzuki, *Narrating the Self*, 44.

24. Suga, 144–145. Here Suga discusses the illogic suggested by these symbols as the representation of femininity in a work by Hirotsu Ryūrō. I would underscore, however, that because these symbols were used for both male and female speech in *genbun-itchi* writing, they cannot be considered *a priori* to be linked to femininity or female identity.

25. Gilles Deleuze, "He Stuttered," in *Essays Critical and Clinical*, trans. Daniel W. Smith and Michael A. Greco (Minneapolis: University of Minnesota Press, 1997), 111–113.

26. Yoshiya Nobuko, "Wakaki tamashii no sudachi," *Kuroshōbi* 3 (1925): 16–17, 23–25. For quotes from *Kuroshōbi* I use the reissued facsimile collected edition, *Fukkokuban Kuroshōbi* (Fuji shuppan, 2001).

27. Yoshikawa calls *Two Virgins in the Attic* "lesbian-feminist"; see "*Seitō*," 136. Komashaku (57–71) points out the importance of same-sex love and feminism in the novel. Komashaku, Yoshitake, and the official chronology all describe the work as being "close to an I-novel"; see Komashaku, 59; Yoshitake, 21; "Nenpu," in *Yoshiya Nobuko zenshū*, vol. 12, 552. Yoshiya studied at Gyokusei hobo yōseijo (Gyokusei school for kindergarden teachers) in Tokyo. "Nenpu" notes that she entered the school in 1917 (551), but according to Yoshikawa, she studied there from 1918 to 1919; see "*Seitō*," 127. In 1918, Yoshiya moved into a dormitory run by the YWCA (Nihon kirisutokyō joshi seinenkai; Young Women's Christian Association of Japan), where she met Kikuchi Yukie, the supposed model for Miss Akitsu. For details of their relationship, see Yoshitake (83–127), who refers to Kikuchi by the pseudonym Hanawa Toshiko. Tanabe discusses the Yoshiya-Kikuchi relationship at length; she reads *Two Virgins in the Attic* as a work of nonfiction that depicts the actual relationship between the two women; see *Yume haruka*, vol. 1, 282–371.

28. Yoshiya Nobuko, "Shosai yori (Sono 7)," in *Yoshiya Nobuko zenshū geppō* 7 (Shinchōsha, 1935), 4; "Atogaki," in *Yoshiya Nobuko zenshū*, vol. 1, 551.

29. See "Nenpu," in *Yoshiya Nobuko zenshū*, vol. 12, 552.

30. Hiromi Tsuchiya Dollase interprets *Two Virgins in the Attic* as a "girls' narrative"; see "Yoshiya Nobuko's 'Yaneura no nishojo': In Search of Literary Possibilities in *Shōjo* Narratives," *U.S.-Japan Women's Journal English Supplement* 20 (2001): 151–178. Sarah Frederick also views this novel as girls' fiction; see "Not That Innocent: Yoshiya Nobuko's Good Girls," in *Bad Girls of Japan*, ed. Laura Miller and Jan Bardsley (New York: Palgrave MacMillan, 2005), 70.

31. In 1920, 125,588 women were enrolled in higher girls' schools while only 2,795 were enrolled in post higher girls' school institutions. See Watanabe Yōko, *Kindai Nihon joshi shakai kyōiku seiritsu shi: Shojokai no zenkoku soshikika to shidō shisō* (Akashi shoten, 1997), 45.

32. "Yaneura no nishojo," in *Yoshiya Nobuko zenshū*, vol. 1, 439. Subsequent quotes are noted parenthetically in the text.

33. The dormitory is referred to as "YWA," not YWCA. Yoshikawa suggests that the main reason the name of the dormitory has been altered is to promote strategically the idea of a "young women's association," that is, an "alliance" among women; see "*Seitō*," 137, 146. As I suggest later in the chapter, however, this removal of the *C* strongly symbolizes the critique of Christianity in the text. "ATTIC" is in English, in upper case. The attic is also referred to in Japanese, as "*yaneura*."

34. Frances Hodgson Burnett, *A Little Princess* (New York: Bantam Books, 1987). The online catalog of Kokuritsu kokkai toshokan (National Diet Library) lists a 1910 translation of *A Little Princess* by Fujii Shigeichi (Haku'unshi) published by Shūseidō. A number of other translations were published throughout the 1920s and later, including some by writers who had personal ties with Yoshiya, such as Sasaki Mosaku (1924, published by Tōkōkaku) and Kikuchi Kan (1927, published by Kōbunsha); see http://opac.ndl.go.jp. Kawasaki Kenko mentions a 1931 translation titled *Yaneura no ōjo* (The princess of the attic), published in a girls' magazine alongside a serialization of Yoshiya's girls' fiction; see *Shōjo biyori* (Seikyūsha, 1990), 16. In one of the *Flower Tales* stories, "Ukonzakura" (Saffron cherry), Sara Crewe is mentioned by name; see "Hanamonogatari," 31.

35. Yoshiya Nobuko, *Mittsu no hana* (Kateisha, 1947), 3. First serialized in *Girls' Club* (April 1926–June 1927).

36. Kume notes that in early girls' fiction, an important lesson for girls was to remain obediently inside the house. This was in sharp contrast to boys' fiction, which depicted adventure, encouraging bravery and vigorous activity; see "Shōjo shōsetsu," 195–205; "Kōseisareru 'shōjo,'" 2. It should be noted that such gendered aspects of ideal childhood behavior also reflect specific class-based values and expectations. On the dangers of imagination in girlhood, see Numata, 67–72, 226–232. For more on Akiko's imagination and language, see Suzuki Michiko, "Kindaiteki shutai tankyū: Female Bildungsroman to shite no *Yaneura no nishojo* ni okeru sōzō to kotoba," in *Kotoba to sōzōryoku*, ed. Kaneko Yūji and Ōnishi Naoki (Kaibunsha, 2001), 198–214.

37. Sarah Frederick interprets the typographical ellipses in this novel as a way for readers themselves to fill in and complete the meanings of statements; see "Aposiopesis and Completion: Yoshiya Nobuko's Typographic Melodrama," *Proceedings of*

the Association for Japanese Literary Studies 7 (2006): 74–77. I agree with Frederick that there is such a reader-response aspect to this typography, but additional interpretations are also possible, as I suggest in this section and in my analyses of *Flower Tales* in the previous section. Also see my discussion of these textual symbols as addressing the issue of girls' imagination in Suzuki, "Kindaiteki shutai."

38. Honda, *Ibunka*, 207–212.

39. For more on these ideas about same-sex environments, see Kawamura Kunimitsu, *Otome no shintai: Onna no kindai to sexuariti* (Kinokuniya shoten, 1994), 120–121; Takahashi Jukei, *Joji no seikyōiku*, vol. 21 of Kindai Nihon joshi kyōiku bunkenshū, ed. Nakajima Kuni (Nihon tosho sentaa, 1984), 163–164; facsimile of the 1925 book published by Meiji tosho. Havelock Ellis had similar ideas about such "unwholesome" environments; see Smith-Rosenberg, 276–277.

40. The parentheses in this quotation are in the original.

41. Yoshikawa, "*Seitō*," 135–136. She also suggests that the Hatanakas, the censorious couple in the story, are modeled on Yamada Kakichi and Waka, who helped Yoshiya and Hiratsuka read Ellen Key in English (126–130).
"Black Hand" refers to the matching black gloves the members wear. The Black Hand society may also be a reference to *Kaizoku gumi* (Band of Pirates), a group that Hiratsuka created with her schoolmates in 1900. Hiratsuka explains that this group was created with the idea of rebelling against the stifling atmosphere of the school. See *Hiratsuka Raichō jiden*, vol. 1, 94–95; *In the Beginning*, 46. In 1964, Yoshiya wrote a short biographical sketch of Hiratsuka titled "Hiratsuka Raichō shōden," in which she discusses Hiratsuka's "Band of Pirates"; see *Yoshiya Nobuko zenshū*, vol. 12, 374–375.

42. *Hiratsuka Raichō jiden*, vol. 1, 190–191. Noted in Yoshikawa, "*Seitō*," 132. In "Nikki" (Diary), a 1913 short story by Tamura Toshiko, a character named "H" (considered to be Hiratsuka) is described as usually wearing a *hakama* and clogs with "supports that make sounds" and as spreading her legs wide and crossing her arms over her chest in a masculine manner; see "Nikki," in *Tamura Toshiko sakuhinshū*, vol. 3 (1988), 341, 347. Noted in Wu, 76.

43. Although *otome* and *musume* have their own nuances, here I focus on *shojo* as the central concept in this work. See Kawamura, *Otome no shintai* for a discussion of such terminology.

44. Muta Kazue, *Senryaku to shite no kazoku: Kindai Nihon no kokumin kokka keisei to josei* (Shinyōsha, 1998), 138.

45. The concept of the existence of the hymen (*shojomaku*) was first introduced in Japan through James Ashton's *The Book of Nature* (1865), translated into Japanese as *Zōkakiron* in 1875. See Kawamura Kunimitsu, "'Shojo' no kindai: Fūin sareta nikutai," in *Sexuariti no shakaigaku*, vol. 10 of Iwanami kōza gendai shakaigaku, ed. Inoue Shun, Ueno Chizuko, and others (Iwanami shoten, 1999), 133–134.

46. This sense is suggested in Yoshiya's novel *Sora no kanata e* (Beyond the sky), serialized in 1927 and 1928, in which a character is given new clothes to celebrate "her growth from a 'girl' [*shōjo*] to a 'virgin' [*shojo*] that happened this summer"; *Yoshiya Nobuko zenshū*, vol. 2 (1975), 303. For a discussion of this story in relation

to the original venue of serialization, *Shufu no tomo* (Friend of the housewife), see Frederick, *Turning Pages*, 126–136. In 1935, educator Ichikawa Genzō specifically located eight- to fifteen-year-old girls in *"shōjoki"* (girlhood) and sixteen- to twenty-five-year-olds in *"seinenki"* (youth). *Seinen* is often used to mean "young men," but in scientific or formal discourse it is used as a gender neutral term. Alternative female-specific terms during the prewar period were *shojo* and *seinen joshi* (female youth). Ichikawa notes that girls enter the "youth" phase with menarche and that the average age of menarche is fourteen years and ten months old; see *Josei bunka kōwa*, vol. 27 of Kindai Nihon joshi kyōiku bunkenshū, ed. Nakajima Kuni (Nihon tosho sentaa, 1984), 116–117; facsimile of the 1935 book published by Meiji tosho.

47. The central headquarters for virgin groups was established in 1917. For the history and analyses of *shojokai*, see Watanabe, *Kindai Nihon*; Hirakawa Keiko, "Kokumin kokka keiseiki ni okeru shojokai: Joshi seinendan no soshikika," in *Sei gensō o kataru*, 111–145.

48. Ikuta Hanayo, "Taberu koto to teisō to," *Hankyō* (September 1914); reprinted in Orii, 13–18. Yasuda Satsuki, "Ikiru koto to teisō to: *Hankyō* 9 gatsu gō 'Taberu koto to teisō to' o yonde," *Seitō* 4, no. 11 (1914); reprinted in Orii, 18–24. For an introduction to Ikuta and Yasuda, see Raichō kenkyūkai, 36–37, 176–177. For more on Yasuda and for a translation of a story she published in *Bluestocking*, see Bardsley, *Bluestockings of Japan*, 48–79. For more on the Virginity or Chastity Debates, see Orii, 11–130, 274–284; Iwabuchi Hiroko, "Sexuaritii no seijigaku e no chōsen: Teisō, datai, haishō ronsō," in Seitō o yomu, 305–314; Bardsley, *Bluestockings of Japan*, 51–59.

49. Muta, *Senryaku*, 138–141. Muta believes that the physical aspect of the notion of virginity also became central as a result of the literary works of Yosano Akiko, who romanticized and praised the purity of the virgin's body that is given to her lover. As Muta herself notes, however, Yosano did not use the term *virgin*.

50. Ibid., 142.

51. Kawamura, *Otome no shintai*, 189–191, 197; "'Shojo' no kindai," 137.

52. See Muta, *Senryaku*, 142–143; Kawamura, *Otome no shintai*, 239–248; "'Shojo' no kindai," 140–145. Some scientists at the time believed that when a woman lost her virginity, her blood was permanently altered by her partner. Thus, if she went on to have a child with another man, the child would not be completely his. This idea is discussed by Itō Noe in "Teisō ni tsuite no zakkan," *Seitō* 5, no. 2 (1915), reprinted in Orii, 58–65. Kawamura discusses this belief at length, viewing it as one of the reasons for the heightened promotion of virginity and increased control over female sexuality that developed during the early twentieth century in Japan.

53. "Shojo no shinka," in *Hiratsuka Raichō chosakushū*, vol. 2, 58. First published as "Shojo no shinkachi" in *Shin kōron* (March 1915).

54. See Yoshikawa, "Seitō," 138.

55. From *Musume to tsuma to haha no eisei dokuhon*, a supplement to the August 1937 issue of *Shufu no tomo*. Quoted in Kawamura, *Sexuariti no kindai*, 182. *Rōjo* is usually a generic term for "old woman." Here I have translated it as "old maid" to best reflect the conveyed meaning. Although this work was published much later

than *Two Virgins in the Attic*, I believe the sentiment would have been perceived as a common view even during the late 1910s and early 1920s.

56. Yoshiya Nobuko, "Sanruishō," in *Safuran* (Hōbunkan, 1928), 256.

57. In Kume Yoriko's reading, the ending avoids actual confrontation with mainstream social values; the heroines disappear in a beautiful way, just like the girls in *Flower Tales*; see "Esu: Yoshiya Nobuko *Hana monogatari, Yaneura no nishojo*," *Kokubungaku kaishaku to kyōzai no kenkyū* 46, no. 3 (2001): 154.

58. *Yoshiya Nobuko zenshū geppō* 6 (Shinchōsha, 1935), 3. The phrase I translate here as "youthful days" is "*wakaki shojo no hi*," which literally means "youthful virgin days," suggesting the state of being young virgins, that is, girls.

59. Kami Shōichirō, "Kaisetsu *Kuroshōbi* to Yoshiya Nobuko," in *Fukkokuban Kuroshōbi*, 4–5. Some critical texts refer to the title as *Kurosōbi*, but Yoshiya personally requested her readers to read it as "*Kuroshōbi*"; see *Kuroshōbi* 1: 67. Quotes from the magazine are noted parenthetically in the text. Yoshiya explains that she considered formally calling this a "*kojin zasshi*" (private magazine) but decided to call it a "*panfuretto*" (pamphlet), implying that this would allow it to more easily avoid government oversight; see *Kuroshōbi* 1: 67; Yoshitake, 24. The cover reads "Yoshiya Nobuko *panfuretto Kuroshōbi*." *Black Rose* was published by Kōransha and, according to Yoshitake (37), had a circulation of about fifteen thousand copies. For more on *Black Rose* and the exchange of letters about the venture between Yoshiya and her partner Monma, see Yoshitake, 24–38; Tanabe, *Yume haruka*, vol. 1, 502–511. For a discussion of *Black Rose* as a private magazine, see Kami, "Kaisetsu *Kuroshōbi*," 3–14.

60. One example of this stance can be seen in the frontispiece to the first issue, a depiction of "Sappho under the sea."

61. Kami, "Kaisetsu *Kuroshōbi*," 10–11.

62. In the last issue, Yoshiya requests "a little rest" from publishing this magazine and announces the cancellation; see *Kuroshōbi* 8: 78.

63. Emphasis in original.

64. Ellis, *Studies*, vol. 1, 216, 219, 222; "Joseikan," 7, 12–13, 15, 16. In the abridged 1914 Japanese translation of "Sexual Inversion in Women," "Joseikan no dōsei ren'ai," published in *Bluestocking*, *normal* and *abnormal* are frequently written in the phonetic *katakana* syllabary as "*nōmaru*" and "*abunōmaru*." The first time the word "*hentai*" is used, the provided phonetic guide (*furigana*) is "*abunōmaritii*"; see "Joseikan," 2. In the original English, "*hontō ni sei no tentō shita onna*" is "actively inverted woman" and "*seiteki hentai*" is "sexual perversion."

65. Radclyffe Hall, *The Well of Loneliness* (New York: Anchor Books, 1990). For a discussion of the "invert" as an important choice for Hall's depiction of lesbianism, see Vicinus, "They Wonder," 445–446; Judith Halberstam, *Female Masculinity* (Durham, NC: Duke University Press, 1998), 75–110.

66. Faderman, 57–61.

67. *Intermediate Sex*, 54, 55, 57, 61; Wōdo [Ward] and Kaapentaa [Carpenter], 206, 207, 209, 211.

68. "Sexual connection" is in English.

69. Ellis, *Studies*, vol. 1, 222; "Joseikan," 15.

70. Smith-Rosenberg, 272.

71. Miyako Inoue notes that this new form of speech, also known as "*teyo-dawa* speech" (*teyo dawa kotoba*), ultimately became a "pure *gender marker*"—a "women's language" that signified "the ideal modern Japanese woman"; see *Vicarious Language*, 37, 114. For Akiko, it also functions as a marker of "standard" (Tokyo-centered), educated speech. For a full study of *teyo-dawa* speech, its historical and cultural shifts and its significance within modernity, see *Vicarious Language*, 37–159; Honda, *Jogakusei no keifu*, 107–134.

72. In *Two Virgins in the Attic*, Kudō is the only one who consistently speaks in male speech.

73. Judith Butler, *Gender Trouble: Feminism and the Subversion of Identity* (New York: Routledge, 1990), 25.

74. For further discussion of gendered speech and specific narration style in this story, see Michiko Suzuki, "Writing Same-Sex Love: Sexology and Literary Representation in Yoshiya Nobuko's Early Fiction," *Journal of Asian Studies* 65, no. 3 (2006): 590–592.

75. The rape can be inferred from the (presumably) self-censored text that explains through dialogue: "*keisatsu dewa······sareteirutte iundesutte*" (the police says she had been······ed.) (8:64)

76. Suzuki, *Narrating the Self*, 1.

77. See "Nenpu," in *Yoshiya Nobuko zenshū*, vol. 12, 555.

78. See, for example, Eve Kosofsky Sedgwick, *Between Men: English Literature and Male Homosocial Desire* (New York: Columbia University Press, 1985); Jim Reichert, *In the Company of Men: Representations of Male-Male Sexuality in Meiji Literature* (Stanford, CA: Stanford University Press, 2006).

79. "Arashi no bara," in *Yoshiya Nobuko zenshū*, vol. 3 (1975), 508.

80. Ibid.

81. Rich uses the term "*lesbian continuum*" to signify "a range . . . of woman-identified experience; not simply the fact that a woman has had or consciously desired genital sexual experience with another woman." In her view, "many more forms of primary intensity between and among women, including the sharing of a rich inner life, the bonding against male tyranny, the giving and receiving of practical and political support" should be considered a part of "lesbian" resistance. See "Compulsory Heterosexuality and Lesbian Existence," *Signs: Journal of Women in Culture and Society* 5, no. 4 (1980): 648–649.

Part Two: The Wife's Progress
Several paragraphs that discuss love marriage in Chapters Four and Five appeared in an earlier form in "Progress and Love Marriage: Rereading Tanizaki Jun'ichirō's *Chijin no ai*," *Journal of Japanese Studies* 31, no. 2 (2005).

Chapter Four: Love Marriage Ideology
1. For more on *katei* ideology and the idea of love within the home presented in Iwamoto's *Journal of Female Learning*, see Iwahori Yōko, "Meiji chūki ōkashugi

shisō ni miru shufu risōzō no keisei: *Jogaku zasshi* no seikatsu shisō ni tsuite," in *Jendaa no Nihonshi ge: Shutai to hyōgen, shigoto to seikatsu*, ed. Wakita Haruko and S. B. Hanley (Tokyo daigaku shuppankai, 1995), 465–467; Inoue Teruko, "'Jogaku' shisō no keisei to tenkai: Jogaku zasshisha no shisōshiteki kenkyū," *Tokyo daigaku shinbun kenkyūjo kiyō* 17 (1968): 49–60; Ken K. Ito, *An Age of Melodrama: Family, Gender, and Social Hierarchy in the Turn-of-the-Century Japanese Novel* (Stanford, CA: Stanford University Press, 2008), 52–53, 156. For more on *katei*, see Muta, *Senryaku*; Ito, *Age of Melodrama*, 52–58; Sand, 21–54.

2. "Risō no kajin," in *Jogaku zasshi Bungakkai shū*, ed. Sasabuchi Tomoichi, vol. 32 of Meiji bungaku zenshū (Chikuma shobō, 1977), 17; originally published in *Jogaku zasshi* 104–105 (1888). "Kon'in ron," in *Jogaku zasshi Bungakkai shū*, 31–39; originally published in *Jogaku zasshi* 273, 275, 277 (1891). These editorials (*shasetsu*) were published without the name of the author, but scholars are in agreement that the author is Iwamoto Yoshiharu. See Sasabuchi Tomoichi, "Kaidai," in *Jogaku zasshi Bungakkai shū*, 419–420.

3. For more on the use of these terms, see Saeki, 24–26, 104–108.

4. See Saeki, 80.

5. See Takahashi, *Kindai ren'ai*, 20, 48; Nishimura and others, 192–195.

6. Kitamura, "Ensei shika to josei," 67. Emphasis in original.

7. Harald Fuess, *Divorce in Japan: Family, Gender, and the State, 1600–2000* (Stanford, CA: Stanford University Press, 2004), 12. Fuess (177–178) cites Sepp Linhart in commenting that from 1936 to 1945, love marriages increased to 11 percent and *miai* to 51 percent while arranged marriages without any prior contact decreased to 24 percent; see Sepp Linhart, "Familie," in *Japan-Handbuch*, ed. Horst Hammitzsch (Wiesbaden: Franz Steiner, 1981), 552. As Fuess notes (177), some scholars challenge the idea that love marriages were rare, citing cases in rural communities. My project does not touch on this issue, because I am interested in understanding love marriage discourse and its recommendation as a modern ideal rather than in analyzing actual practice at different levels of class, geography, and educational status. For a discussion of rural cases of female agency with regard to marriage, see Chizuko Ueno, "The Position of Japanese Women Reconsidered," *Current Anthropology* 28, no. 4 (1987): S75–S85.

8. Yoshikawa Toyoko, for example, uses this term to mean "the idealization of love-based marriage and the couple-based family unit" in discussing the important role that Hiratsuka's translation of Key's *Love and Marriage* played in disseminating the idea of love marriage during the Taishō period; see "*Ren'ai to kekkon* (Ellen Key) to sexorojii," in Seitō o yomu, 245. As I discuss in the chapter text, my own use of the term *love marriage ideology* particularly emphasizes the validation of love marriage as a means for progress, self-development, and self-realization, as well as for the attainment of male-female equality.

9. Iwahori, 470–471; Ito, *Age of Melodrama*, 156.

10. "Yo no fujintachi e," in *Hiratsuka Raichō chosakushū*, vol. 1, 221; originally published in *Seitō* 3, no. 4 (1913). For an introduction to and translation of this essay, see Bardsley, *Bluestockings of Japan*, 91–92, 103–107.

11. "Dokuritsu suru ni tsuite ryōshin ni," in *Hiratsuka Raichō chosakushū*, vol. 1, 292–293.

12. Key, *Love and Marriage; Ren'ai to kekkon*.

13. Her son's "illegitimate" status would have been detrimental to his military service. Suzuki Yūko, *Haha to onna: Hiratsuka Raichō, Ichikawa Fusae o jiku ni*, vol. 1 of Joseishi o hiraku (Miraisha, 1994), 45–46.

14. For more on the difficulty in determining the precise notion of marriage during this period, see Fuess, *Divorce in Japan*, 11–15. Fuess also points out that during the Taishō period, legalization of marriage through registration was "frequently delayed until the relationship had matured" (11).

15. Hiratsuka, "Sabetsuteki seidōtoku ni tsuite," in *Hiratsuka Raichō chosakushū*, vol. 2, 191; originally published as "Danjo seiteki dōtokuron" in *Fujin kōron* (1916).

16. "Kekkon no dōtokuteki kiso," in *Hiratsuka Raichō chosakushū*, vol. 3 (1983), 15–16; original date and place of publication unknown. This version of the essay reprinted from *Josei no kotoba* (1918).

17. Yamamoto Takeshi, *Kindai Nihon no shinbun dokushasō* (Hōsei daigaku shuppankyoku, 2006), 410.

18. Kano, *Kindai Nihon shisō*, 180.

19. Kuriyagawa Hakuson, "Kindai no ren'aikan," in *Ren'aikan oyobi zassan*, vol. 5 of Kuriyagawa Hakuson zenshū (Kaizōsha, 1929), 18–19, 24, 25–26.

20. See Kano, *Kindai Nihon shisō*, 180.

21. See Barbara Sato's discussion of love marriage and self-cultivation in *New Japanese Woman*, 141–148.

22. Yoshiya Nobuko, "Junketsu no igi ni tsukite Hakuson shi no ren'aikan o bakusu," *Kuroshōbi* 1: 48–49.

23. *Views of Love in the Modern Era*, along with works by Carpenter, Ellis, and Key, also played an important role in shaping ideas about love in China. See Haiyan Lee, *Revolution of the Heart: A Genealogy of Love in China, 1900–1950* (Stanford, CA: Stanford University Press, 2007), 172–178.

24. She is also called by her married name, Itō Akiko, as well as Itō Byakuren. For works on Byakuren, see Nagahata Michiko, *Koi no hana: Byakuren jiken* (Shinhyōron, 1982); Hayashi Mariko, *Byakuren renren* (Chūō kōronsha, 1998); Senda Minoru, *Meiji Taishō Shōwa Kazoku jikenroku* (Shin jinbutsu ōraisha, 2003), 88–99; Hasegawa Shigure, "Yanagihara Akiko (Byakuren)," in *Shinpen Kindai bijinden*, vol. 2, ed. Sugimoto Sonoko (Iwanami shoten, 1993), 9–37. In English, see Phyllis Birnbaum's biography of Byakuren in *Modern Girls, Shining Stars, the Skies of Tokyo: Five Japanese Women* (New York: Columbia University Press, 1999), 102–162. Also see Byakuren's fictionalized autobiography: Yanagihara Akiko, *Ibara no mi: Jijoden* (Shinchōsha, 1928). The names of the people in this book have been changed, but it covers the story of her life up to the 1921 Byakuren incident.

25. "Tsukushi no joō Akiko 1–10," *Osaka Asahi shinbun*, April 11, 13–21, 1918. For discussion of this series, see Nagahata, 167–171; Hayashi, *Byakuren*, 153. *Osaka Asahi shinbun* had higher circulation numbers than *Tokyo Asahi shinbun* since the

late Meiji period; in 1918 it was printing about 341,000 copies per day. Yamamoto, 284, 410–412.

26. "Moyuru hana," in *Yoshiya Nobuko zenshū*, vol. 1, 141–158.

27. "Shinju fujin," in *Kikuchi Kan zenshū*, vol. 5 (Takamatsu: Takamatsu-shi Kikuchi Kan kinenkan, 1994), 5–300; originally serialized June 9–December 22, 1920. *Osaka Mainichi shinbun* and *Tokyo Nichi Nichi shinbun* had both been published by the Mainichi shinbunsha since 1911. In 1920, they were printing approximately 622,000 and 358,000 copies, respectively; see Mainichi shinbun hyakunenshi kankō iinkai, ed., *Mainichi shinbun hyakunenshi 1872–1972* (Mainichi shinbunsha, 1972), 359–360, 363.

28. Takagi Takeo, *Shinbun shōsetsushi: Taishō hen* (Kokusho kankōkai, 1976), 214; Kawakami Minako, "Kikuchi Kan *Shinju fujin*: Taishōki besuto seraa shōsetsu no jendaa ideorogii," in *20 seiki no besuto seraa o yomitoku: Josei, dokusha, shakai no 100 nen*, ed. Egusa Mitsuko and Inoue Yoshie (Gakugei shorin, 2001), 66–67.

29. In a 1921 essay, Kikuchi rejects the idea that the protagonist of *Madame Pearl* was modeled on Byakuren. At this juncture, he probably wanted to distance himself from the controversial Byakuren scandal. See *"Shinju fujin* no moderu to jinin seshi Byakuren joshi," in *Kikuchi Kan zenshū*, vol. 21 (1995), 350–351; first published in *Fujokai* (1921). For a reprint of the 1920 newspaper advertisement that prompted Byakuren's query to Kikuchi, see Katayama Hiroyuki, *Kikuchi Kan no kōseki: Shoki bungaku seishin no tenkai* (Osaka: Izumi shoin, 1997), 102.

30. See Maeda Ai, *Kindai dokusha*, 261; Takagi, 214.

31. "Den'emon shi e Akiko saigo no tegami," *Tokyo Asahi shinbun*, October 23, 1921. The letter as well as other major newspaper articles on this incident are reprinted in Asahi shinbunsha, ed., *Asahi shinbun no kiji ni miru ren'ai to kekkon (Meiji, Taishō)* (Asahi shinbunsha, 1997), 293–324; Meiji Taishō Shōwa shinbun kenkyūkai, "Hoi," in *Shinbun shūsei Taishō hennenshi Taishō jūnendohan gekan* (Meiji Taishō Shōwa shinbun kenkyūkai, 1983), 1125–1155. For more on the Byakuren incident, see Nagahata; Hayashi, *Byakuren*; Birnbaum, 102–162; Hasegawa, "Yanagihara," 9–37; Sato, *New Japanese Woman*, 110–111; Senda, 88–99; Takahashi, *Kindai ren'ai*, 96–97, 116–117.

32. *Tokyo Asahi shinbun*, October 21–31, November 3–4, November 6, 1921.

33. "Hakuson to Byakuren," *Tokyo Asahi shinbun*, October 25, 1921. Also published in Asahi shinbunsha, 319; Meiji Taishō Shōwa shinbun kenkyūkai, "Hoi," 1145.

34. Kuriyagawa Hakuson, "Akiko mondai ni tsuite: Ren'ai to kekkon no koto (jō)," *Tokyo Asahi shinbun*, October 30, 1921. Also published in Asahi shinbunsha, 321.

35. "Yanagihara Akiko san," in *Hiratsuka Raichō chosakushū* vol. 3, 241–246; original date and place of publication unknown. This version of the essay reprinted from *Kumo, kusa, hito* (1933).

36. "Akiko mondai ni tsuite." Also published in Asahi shinbunsha, 321–322.

37. "Yanagihara Akiko san," 246.

38. Kuriyagawa, "Kindai no ren'aikan," 58.

39. The letter was serialized October 24–27, 1921. See Meiji Taishō Shōwa shinbun kenkyūkai, "Hoi," 1142–1143, 1146–1147, 1149–1150.

40. "Akiko jiken no hankyō: Dokusha kara tōsho 412 tsū," *Tokyo Asahi shinbun*, October 31, 1921.

41. For information on Uno's life and publications, see Rebecca L. Copeland, *The Sound of the Wind: The Life and Works of Uno Chiyo* (Honolulu: University of Hawai'i Press, 1992); "Uno Chiyo," in *Japanese Women Writers*, 440–448.

42. "Kanojo no seikatsu," in *Tamura Toshiko sakuhinshū*, vol. 2 (1988), 237–268; originally published in *Chūō kōron* (July 1915). "Kurenai," in *Sata Ineko shū*, 35–136; originally serialized in *Fujin kōron* (January-May 1936) and *Chūō kōron* (August 1938). For a translation of an excerpt from "Kurenai," see Sata Ineko, "Crimson," trans. Yukiko Tanaka, in *To Live and to Write: Selections by Japanese Women Writers 1913–1938*, ed. Yukiko Tanaka (Seattle, WA: Seal Press, 1987), 167–180. Sata was legally married to Kubokawa Tsurujirō from 1929 to 1945. For her chronology, see "Nenpu," in *Sata Ineko shū*.

43. "Nagesuteyo!" in *Hirabayashi Taiko zenshū*, vol. 1 (Ushio shuppan, 1979), 75, 78; originally published in *Kaihō* (March 1927). The female character calls herself a "wife," but Hirabayashi was not legally married to the man who was the model for the husband character. For the official chronology, see "Hirabayashi Taiko Nenpu," in *Hirabayashi Taiko zenshū*, vol. 12 (Ushio shuppan, 1997), 335–399.

44. "Machiko," in *Nogami Yaeko zenshū*, vol. 7 (Iwanami shoten, 1981), 3–382. First serialized in *Kaizō* (August-September 1928; January, March, and October 1929; January and May 1930) and *Chūō kōron* (December 1930). For analyses of this novel, see Eleanor Joan Hogan, "When Art Does *Not* Represent Life: Nogami Yaeko and the Marriage Question," *Women's Studies: An Interdisciplinary Journal* 33, no. 4 (2004): 381–398; Watanabe Sumiko, "Kimyō na genkaku: Nogami Yaeko *Machiko*," in *Feminizumu hihyō e no shōtai*, 201–225. Nogami was listed as a Bluestocking member only for the first month of the journal's existence. Although she contributed to *Bluestocking*, she claims she was never a member; see Raichō kenkyūkai, 132. For more on her connection to the Bluestocking Society, see Raichō kenkyūkai, 132–133; Bardsley, *Bluestockings of Japan*, 204–208. For a translation of Nogami's "Atarashiki inochi" (New Life, 1914), a story published in *Bluestocking*, see *Bluestockings of Japan*, 208–221.

45. "Sōban kōnatte iku ano fujin no unmei to Byakuren fujin ni dōjōsuru Chūjō Yuriko fujin kataru," reprinted in Meiji Taishō Shōwa shinbun kenkyūkai, "Hoi," 1142. Miyamoto was known by her maiden name, Chūjō, at this time.

46. See, for example, *Miyamoto Yuriko zenshū*, vol. 26 (Shin Nihon shuppansha, 2003), 294–295, 350, 390; *Miyamoto Yuriko zenshū*, vol. 27 (2003), 36, 40, 46–47, 49, 53, 107–109, 124, 169–172, 181. *The Renaissance of Motherhood* was translated from English into Japanese and published in book form by Shinchōsha in 1919. According to Hiratsuka, the work was only partially translated by her (although it was published under her name); the remainder of the translation was completed by Katō Asadori, husband of Katō Midori (1888–1922), who wrote for *Bluestocking*; see *Hiratsuka Raichō jiden*, vol. 2, 593; *In the Beginning*, 278. Bardsley briefly comments

on this in *Bluestockings of Japan*, 17. *The Renaissance of Motherhood* essentially argues for the importance of motherhood in society, positing that women who become mothers should be given special education and be compensated for their work. With regard to marriage, it treats issues such as female labor within the home, love and equality, and differences between men and women. Ellen Key, *The Renaissance of Motherhood*, trans. Anna E. B. Fries (New York: G. P. Putnam's Sons, 1914).

Chapter Five: Miyamoto Yuriko and the Nobuko Narratives

1. The serialization was published in ten installments in the following issues of *Kaizō*: vol. 6, nos. 9 and 11 (1924); vol. 7, nos. 1, 4, 6, and 10 (1925); vol. 8, nos. 1, 2, 4, and 10 (1926). All installments have different titles and are published under Miyamoto's maiden name, Chūjō Yuriko. The book version was published in March 1928. For the official chronology, see "Nenpu" and "Zenkankōsho mokuroku," in *Miyamoto Yuriko zenshū*, vol. bessatsu (2004), 9–100, 101–181. For more on Miyamoto and *Nobuko* in English, see Noriko Mizuta Lippit, *Reality and Fiction in Modern Japanese Literature* (White Plains: M. E. Sharpe, 1980), 146–162; Michiko Niikuni Wilson, "Misreading and Un-Reading the Male Text, Finding the Female Text: Miyamoto Yuriko's Autobiographical Fiction," *U.S.-Japan Women's Journal English Supplement* 13 (1997): 26–55; Masao Miyoshi, *Off Center: Power and Culture Relations Between Japan and the United States* (Cambridge, MA: Harvard University Press, 1991), 197–206; James R. Morita, "Miyamoto Yuriko," in *Japanese Women Writers*, 221–228; Tanaka, "Miyamoto Yuriko," in Tanaka, *To Live and to Write*, 39–45; Anne Sokolsky, "Miyamoto Yuriko and Socialist Writers," in *Columbia Companion*, 164–169. A brief excerpt from *Nobuko* is translated by Yukiko Tanaka as "Nobuko," in *To Live and to Write*, 47–64.

2. Mizuno Akiyoshi, *Kindai bungaku no seiritsu to Miyamoto Yuriko* (Shin Nihonsha, 1980), 135. Honda Shūgo notes that the novel did not receive its due praise until after the war; see "Miyamoto Yuriko: Sono shōgai to sakuhin," in *Miyamoto Yuriko: Sakuhin to shōgai*, ed. Takiji Yuriko kenkyūkai (Shin Nihon shuppansha, 1976), 30.

3. "Atogaki," in *Miyamoto Yuriko zenshū*, vol. 18 (2002), 138; originally published in *Miyamoto Yuriko senshū*, vol. 6 (Aki shobō, 1948).

4. "Nobuko," in *Miyamoto Yuriko zenshū*, vol. 3 (2001), 230. Subsequent quotes from this edition are noted parenthetically in the text.

5. YMCA is Young Men's Christian Association; C University refers to Columbia University.

6. Yoshimi is modeled on Yuasa Yoshiko (1896–1990), a translator of Russian literature. Yuasa and Miyamoto first met at the home of Nogami Yaeko in 1924; they started living together from 1925 while Miyamoto was finalizing her divorce. They lived together in Moscow from 1927 to 1930 and continued cohabiting after returning to Japan in 1930. Miyamoto met Miyamoto Kenji in 1931; she married and started living with him in 1932. There has been much speculation about whether or not the Yuasa-Miyamoto relationship was a sexual same-sex love relationship. Although Miyamoto erases this aspect of her life in her autobiographical works,

maintaining that it was a platonic relationship, Yuasa's assertion is different. Regardless of whether or not it was a physical relationship, their letters and diaries show that both women viewed this as a relationship based on love. Until recently, the only sources for interpreting the relationship were Miyamoto's diaries collected in *Miyamoto Yuriko zenshū* vols. 26–29; her selected letters in vols. 30–31; *The Two Gardens* (vol. 6) and *Signpost* (vols. 7–8), Miyamoto's I-novels that focus on their life together in Japan and Moscow; 118 of Miyamoto's letters to Yuasa published in Yuasa Yoshiko, ed., *Yuriko no tegami* (Chikuma shobō, 1978); and a biography of Yuasa that focuses on the women's relationship: Sawabe Hitomi, *Yuriko, dasuvidaaniya: Yuasa Yoshiko no seishun* (Gakuyō shobō, 1996). The publication in 2008 of the Miyamoto-Yuasa correspondence (247 letters sent between 1924 and 1931) and selections from Yuasa's diaries, however, provides valuable, fresh insight into the relationship and its dissolution. See Kurosawa Ariko, ed., *Ōfuku shokan Miyamoto Yuriko to Yuasa Yoshiko* (Kanrin shobō, 2008).

7. Iwabuchi Hiroko uses love marriage in interpreting *Nobuko* as a work that expresses the importance of both love and work in human development; see *Miyamoto Yuriko: Kazoku, seiji, soshite feminizumu* (Kanrin shobō, 1996), 40–67. She defines "love marriage ideology" (*ren'ai kekkon ideorogii*), however, as the validation of sex through love and the legitimization of love through marriage (46). This definition of love marriage ideology as well as Iwabuchi's approach are different from mine. Mizuta Noriko also underscores the importance of love marriage in this novel. Although she does not discuss love marriage ideology and related discourses as such, she comments thus: "For Nobuko, just as for all women during the prewar period who desired freedom, love marriage was a ritual to gain spiritual independence." Mizuta also adds that "marriage" for Nobuko was "a heightening of love, [an indication of] love's eternal continuation, a place in which one developed the self, where the self opened up toward the husband's self"; see *Hiroin kara hiirō e: Josei no jiga to hyōgen* (Tabata shoten, 1982), 91–92.

8. For a brief, general summary of the differences between the versions, see *Miyamoto Yuriko zenshū*, vol. 3, 589–592. The second installment of *Nobuko*, titled "Tōmin," *Kaizō* 6, no. 11 (1924): 57–89, is reprinted as "Shiryō" in *Miyamoto Yuriko zenshū*, vol. 3, 599–622. For criticism that discusses the two versions, see, for example, Numazawa Kazuko, *Miyamoto Yuriko ron* (Musashino shobō, 1993), 213–231; Nagami Megumi, "Futatsu no Nobuko: Gensaku to kaisaku ni tsuite," in *Miyamoto Yuriko: Sakuhin to shōgai*, ed. Takiji Yuriko kenkyūkai (Shin Nihon shuppansha, 1976), 125–130, originally published in *Takiji to Yuriko* 7 (December 1954); Ōmori Sueko, *Wakaki hi no Miyamoto Yuriko: Sōshun no sudachi zōhoban* (Shin Nihon shuppansha, 1993), 195–369; Tsuda Takashi, "Rekishi no naka no Nobuko: *Nobuko* no kaisaku mondai o kangaeru," *Minshu bungaku* 400 (February 1999): 156–174.

9. The 1928 text used is "Nobuko," in *Miyamoto Yuriko zenshū*, vol. 3, 5–358. It is based on the 1953 edition published by Kawade shobō, which is essentially the same as the 1928 version with only minor postwar changes such as *kanji* usage.

10. Chūjō Yuriko, "Kikiwakerarenu ashioto," *Kaizō* 6, no. 9 (1924): 49–50.

11. This kiss scene that marks the beginning of their romance is censored in the original 1924 text, but readers can guess that Tsukuda has kissed her and that the kiss has been reciprocated. "Kikiwakerarenu ashioto," 72.

12. Chūjō, "Tōmin," 70, 71.

13. Chūjō Yuriko, "Chiisai kumo," *Kaizō* 7, no. 4 (1925): 173.

14. Chūjō Yuriko, "Yureru kigi," *Kaizō* 7, no. 1 (1925): 70, 84–86. For the 1928 version, see *Miyamoto Yuriko zenshū*, vol. 3, 77–78. Tsukuda's Japanese phrases noted in my discussion are the same in both versions. In the *Kaizō* version, the dotted ellipses vary in length from between six to twelve dots. In the 1928 version, these have been made uniform as six-dot ellipses, and there are fewer ellipses and dashes. The ellipses and dashes in both versions are predominantly used in dialogue, to signify actual pauses between words.

15. This aspect of the names has been noted by Ogata Akiko, *Sakuhin no naka no onnatachi: Meiji, Taishō bungaku o yomu* (Domesu shuppan, 1997), 214. Wilson (36) develops this argument further.

16. "Ai no kunren," in *Yosano Akiko hyōron chosakushū*, vol. 5 (2001), 328, 331; facsimile edition of *Ai, risei oyobi yūki* (Oranda shobō, 1917).

17. "Chijin no ai," in *Tanizaki Jun'ichirō zenshū*, vol. 10 (Chūō kōronsha, 1973), 15, 40, 48; originally serialized March-June 1924 in *Osaka Asahi shinbun* and November 1924–July 1925 in *Josei*. The book version was published in 1925 by Kaizōsha. For the English translation of the novel, see Tanizaki, *Naomi*, trans. Anthony Chambers (New York: North Point Press, 1985). For a full exploration of this work in relation to love marriage discourse, see Michiko Suzuki, "Progress and Love Marriage: Rereading Tanizaki Jun'ichirō's *Chijin no ai*," *Journal of Japanese Studies* 31, no. 2 (2005): 357–384.

18. See Fujime Yuki, *Sei no rekishigaku: Kōshō seido, dataizai taisei kara baishun bōshihō, yūsei hogohō taisei e* (Fuji shuppan, 1998), 246; Ōta Tenrei, *Nihon sanji chōsetsushi: Meiji, Taishō, Shōwa shoki made* (Nihon kazoku keikaku kyōkai, 1969), 101–115.

19. "Kojin toshite no seikatsu to sei toshite no seikatsu tono aida no sōtō ni tsuite," in *Hiratsuka Raichō chosakushū*, vol. 2, 36–52; originally published in *Seitō* 5, no. 8 (1915) as "Kojin toshite no seikatsu to sei toshite no seikatsu tono aida no sōtō ni tsuite (Noe san ni)." For a discussion of this essay, particularly in relation to debates about abortion, see Bardsley, *Bluestockings of Japan*, 66–70; Orii, 287–288; Iwabuchi, "Sexuaritii," 317.

20. "Haha toshite no ichinenkan," in *Hiratsuka Raichō chosakushū*, vol. 2, 274–275; originally published in *Fujin kōron* (1917). See also Key, *Love and Marriage*, 215–217; Hiratsuka, "Kojin toshite no seikatsu," 50.

21. For example, Ubukata Tomoko reads Nobuko's rejection of pregnancy as a desire to be a resistant "writing subject." See "Chōkō toshite no shintai: *Nobuko* ni okeru 'shutai' no yōtai," *Kokubungaku kaishaku to kanshō* 71, no. 4 (2006): 98–105.

22. Chūjō Yuriko, "Gake no ue," *Kaizō* 7, no. 10 (1925): 64.

23. "Chijin no ai," 25, 39, 49, 87, 294–295. On the power dynamic in Jōji and

182 NOTES TO PAGES 89–94

Naomi's sadomasochistic relationship, see Ken K. Ito, *Visions of Desire: Tanizaki's Fictional Worlds* (Stanford, CA: Stanford University Press, 1991), 90–100.

24. *A Doll's House* (*Ningyō no ie*) was performed in September 1911, starring Matsui Sumako (1886–1919) as Nora. For more on the play, Nora, and discussions in *Bluestocking*, see Hasegawa , "Atarashii onna," 286–293; Raichō kenkyūkai, 206; Lowy, *Japanese "New Woman,"* 21–39; Ayako Kano, *Acting Like a Woman in Modern Japan: Theater, Gender and Nationalism* (New York: Palgrave, 2001), 184–199.

25. Kuriyagawa, "Kindai no ren'aikan," 28–29.

26. Mizuta, *Hiroin*, 92.

27. For more on the meaning of the two dogs, see Numazawa, 288–291.

28. Although the two terms are often conflated, "free love" is different from "free marriage" (*jiyū kekkon*), another term for a love marriage that is carried out by "free will."

29. For more on the incident, Ōsugi, and the women involved, see Raichō kenkyūkai, 40–41, 76–77, 79, 148–149, 197; *Hiratsuka Raichō jiden*, vol. 2, 605–611; *In the Beginning*, 282–286. The Ōsugi-Hori marriage was not a legal union. For an introduction to Itō Noe and translations of works she published in *Bluestocking*, see Bardsley, *Bluestockings of Japan*, 119–146.

30. *Hiratsuka Raichō jiden*, vol. 2, 611; *In the Beginning*, 286.

31. "Iwayuru jiyū ren'ai to sono seigen," in *Hiratsuka Raichō chosakushū*, vol. 2, 256, 261; originally published in *Osaka Asahi shinbun*, January 4, 1917.

32. *Love and Marriage*, 305.

33. Kurata Hyakuzō, "Ippu ippu no konkyo ni tsuite," in *Ippu ippu ka jiyū ren'ai ka* (Iwanami shoten, 1927), 13–14, 59–65; originally published in *Fuji* (1925). For more on Kurata, see Suzuki Norihisa, *Kurata Hyakuzō zōhoban* (Daimyōdō, 1980); Shōwa joshi daigaku kindai bungaku kenkyūshitsu, "Kurata Hyakuzō," in *Kindai bungaku kenkyū sōsho*, vol. 50 (Shōwa joshi daigaku kindai bunka kenkyūjo, 1980), 289–366. For the chronology, see "Nenpu," in Kurata Hyakuzō, *Kurata Hyakuzō: Hikariau inochi* (Nihon tosho sentaa, 2001), 229–243.

34. Fuess, *Divorce in Japan*, 133.

35. Kuriyagawa, "Kindai no ren'aikan," 58.

36. "Iwayuru ren'ai no sankaku kankei ni tsuite no kōsatsu," in *Hiratsuka Raichō chosakushū*, vol. 3, 359. Original place of publication unknown.

37. Fuess, *Divorce in Japan*, 2, 141–143. Kuriyagawa also notes that Japan has the highest divorce rate in the world for an advanced nation; see "Kindai no ren'aikan," 57.

38. Fuess discusses the "evolutionary theory of divorce" presented in 1885 by University of Tokyo law professor Hozumi Nobushige, who helped revise parts of the Civil Code. This theory argues that divorce has four historical stages that mirror the development of a particular country's culture: "free divorce (*jiyū rikon*), no divorce (*rikon kinshi*), restricted divorce (*seigen rikon*) and, again, free divorce." In the first free-divorce stage, only men have the right to divorce; this stage is manifest in "several East Asian countries" and considered the lowest stage. The fourth free-divorce stage is the highest stage; it is not yet practiced by any country and is

the stage in which "spouses decided together, based on equality (*byōdō*), resulting in genuinely free divorce." See Fuess, *Divorce in Japan*, 104. The original source he cites is Hozumi Nobushige, "Rikon no hikakuron," in *Hozumi Nobushige ibunshū*, ed. Hozumi shōgaku zaidan shuppan (Iwanami shoten, 1932), 389–404; originally published in *Hōritsu kyōkai zasshi* (May-July 1885).

39. Chūjō Yuriko, "Suō no hana," *Kaizō* 7, no. 6 (1925): 77.

40. The narrative depicting the vacation to the Nasu region hot spring has been considerably shortened in the 1928 version. For the longer version, see "Hakumu (Zoku)," *Kaizō* 8, no. 2 (1926): 23–48.

41. Susan Sontag, *Illness As Metaphor and AIDS and Its Metaphors* (New York: Anchor Books, 1989), 57.

42. Fukuda Mahito, *Kekkaku no bunkashi: Kindai Nihon ni okeru yamai no imeeji* (Nagoya: Nagoya daigaku shuppankai, 1995), 163.

43. Tokutomi Roka, *Hototogisu* (Iwanami shoten, 1998). For discussions on this work in relation to TB, see Karatani, 97–113; Fukuda, 119–140; William Johnston, *The Modern Epidemic: A History of Tuberculosis in Japan* (Cambridge, MA: Council on East Asian Studies, Harvard University, 1995), 23–24, 130–132. For a full discussion of this novel, including issues related to TB, see Ito, *Age of Melodrama*, 46–85.

44. See Karatani, 106; Johnston, 116–123.

45. Johnston (31) notes that even today the "exact function" of heredity for TB still remains unclear despite extensive research.

46. Hiratsuka Raichō, "Kekkon no dōtokuteki kiso," in *Hiratsuka Raichō chosakushū*, vol. 3, 18–19. The examples she gives of such diseases are alcoholism, syphilis, epilepsy, and mental illness. This essay is dated 1918, original place of publication unknown. For an extended discussion of this issue by Key, see *The Century of the Child* (New York: Arno Press, 1972), 46–51; facsimile reprint of the first English translation (G. P. Putnam's Sons, 1909). (Hiratsuka cites this work in her essay cited here.) Hiratsuka was active in the area of eugenics. In 1919 she cofounded Shin fujin kyōkai (New Ladies' Association) with suffragist Ichikawa Fusae (1893–1981). This feminist group aimed to change parts of the Police Peace Law (*chian keisatsu hō*), which forbade women from participating in political activities; the group also petitioned for premarital testing for venereal disease and for marriage restrictions on men with such diseases. The Police Peace Law was successfully revised, but the eugenics petition never made it into law. The group disbanded in 1922. For more on this group, especially on its eugenics efforts, see Sumiko Otsubo, "Engendering Eugenics: Feminists and Marriage Restriction Legislation in the 1920s," in *Gendering Modern Japanese History*, 225–256; Tomida, 263–330.

47. *Love and Marriage*, 168.

48. "Tōmin," 89.

49. Johnston, 35, 91.

50. Michael K. Bourdaghs, *The Dawn That Never Comes: Shimazaki Tōson and Japanese Nationalism* (New York: Columbia University Press, 2003), 52.

51. In the 1947–1950 sequel, *Signpost*, Nobuko finds out that Tsukuda has died from TB at age forty-five, leaving a wife and three young, delicate children.

Tsukuda, Nobuko remembers, made a point of having children so that his wife would not run away this time. The text suggests that this was an irresponsible attitude, considering the fate of the widow and the children left behind. "Dōhyō Dai sanbu," in *Miyamoto Yuriko zenshū*, vol. 8 (2002), 112–115. Araki Shigeru, the model for Tsukuda, also died of TB in 1932, several months after Miyamoto's marriage to Miyamoto Kenji.

52. See Numazawa, 296–301.

53. See diary entry for Oct. 8, 1926, in *Miyamoto Yuriko zenshū*, vol. 27, 441.

54. For more on the Kollontai boom and debates, see Koyano, *Ren'ai no Shōwashi*, 128–133; William O. Gardner, *Advertising Tower: Japanese Modernism and Modernity in the 1920s* (Cambridge, MA: Harvard University Asia Center, 2006), 150; Yamashita Etsuko, *Mazakon bungakuron: Jubaku toshite no "haha"* (Shinyōsha, 1991), 116–147; Yagi Akiko, "Ren'ai to jiyū shakai," in *Ai to sei no jiyū*, 210–212; originally published under the name Sagami Akiko, in *Jiyū rengō shinbun*, November 1, 1928. For the English translation of "The Loves of Three Generations," see Alexandra Kollontay, *A Great Love*, trans. Lily Lore (New York: Vanguard Press, 1929), 179–243. Hayashi Fusao's translation of the story was collected in *Ren'ai no michi* (1927).

55. "Ren'ai to kekkon no sho," in *Kikuchi Kan zenshū*, vol. 21, 13, 14, 17; a compilation of essays and columns published during the early to mid-1930s; originally published as a book in 1935 by Modan Nihonsha.

56. "Ren'ai kekkon seido," in *Kikuchi Kan zenshū*, vol. 3 (1994), 532–545; originally published in *Fujokai* (January-February 1930).

57. "Atogaki (*Nobuko* Dai ichibu)," in *Miyamoto Yuriko zenshū*, vol. 16 (2002), 355–356; originally published in *Nobuko* (Bungei shunjū shinsha, 1946).

58. *Fujin to bungaku: Kindai Nihon no fujin sakka*, vol. 43 of Sōsho Joseiron, ed. Yamazaki Tomoko (Ōzorasha, 1997), 153; facsimile of the 1947 book published by Jitsugyō no Nihonsha.

59. "Futatsu no niwa," in *Miyamoto Yuriko zenshū*, vol. 6 (2001), 288–290, 293, 296–298; "Dōhyō Dai ichibu," in *Miyamoto Yuriko zenshū*, vol. 7 (2002), 273; "Dōhyō Dai nibu," in *Miyamoto Yuriko zenshū*, vol. 7, 589–592. *The Two Gardens* was originally serialized in *Chūō kōron* (January-September 1947) and published in book form by Chūō kōronsha in 1948. *Signpost* was originally serialized in three parts in *Tenbō* (October 1947–December 1950). The first part ("Dai ichibu") was published in book form in 1948, the second part ("Dai nibu") in 1949, and the third part ("Dai sanbu") in 1951, all by Chikuma shobō.

60. "Dōhyō Dai sanbu," 437.

61. "*Nobuko* ni tsuite," in *Miyamoto Yuriko zenshū*, vol. 13 (2001), 82; originally published in *Chōhen shōsetsu* (May 1937).

62. "Wakaki sedai e no ren'ai ron," in *Miyamoto Yuriko zenshū*, vol. 13, 16–17; originally published in *Chūya zuihitsu* (Hakuyōsha, 1937).

63. "Ōinaru mono," in *Miyamoto Yuriko zenshū*, vol. 33 (2004), 428. This essay was not published in Miyamoto's lifetime.

64. "Atogaki (*Nobuko* Dai ichibu)," 355.

Chapter Six: Maternal Love

1. See Erizabeeto Badanteeru [Elisabeth Badinter], *Bosei to iu shinwa*, trans. Suzuki Shō (Chikuma shobō, 1998); originally published in French as *L'amour en plus: Histoire de l'amour maternel (XVIIe–XXe siècle)* (Paris: Flammarion, 1980).

2. There are various views about the exact date of the first use of *bosei*. Harald Fuess notes that it was coined in 1904 by Shimoda Jirō in *Joshi kyōiku*; see "Men's Place in the Women's Kingdom: New Middle-Class Fatherhood in Taishō Japan," in *Public Spheres, Private Lives in Modern Japan, 1600–1950: Essays in Honor of Albert M. Craig*, ed. Gail Lee Bernstein, Andrew Gordon, and Kate Wildman Nakai (Cambridge, MA: Harvard University Asia Center, 2005), 259–260. Fuess cites Ulrike Wöhr, *Frauen zwischen Rollenerwartungen und Selbstdeutung: Ehe, Mutterschaft und Liebe im Spiegel der japanischen Frauenzeitschrift, "Shin shin fujin" von 1913 bis 1916* (Wiesbaden: Harrassowitz Verlag, 1997), 284, 326–328. Sawayama Mikako suggests that this word is a translation of *"moderskap"* (motherhood), used by Ellen Key; see "Kindai Nihon ni okeru 'bosei' no kyōchō to sono imi," in *Josei to bunka*, ed. Ningen bunka kenkyūkai (Hakuba shuppan, 1979), 167–168. Kanō Mikiyo claims it was first used in a 1916 essay by Yosano Akiko, "Bosei henchō o haisu," in *Taiyō* (February 1916). Kanō Mikiyo, "Bosei fashizumu," 35; "Bosei shugi to nashonarizumu," in *"Kazoku" no shakaigaku*, vol. 19 of Iwanami kōza gendai shakaigaku, ed. Inoue Shun, Ueno Chizuko, and others (Iwanami shoten, 1999), 198; "'Bosei' no tanjō to tennōsei," in *Bosei*, ed. Inoue Teruko, Ueno Chizuko, and Ehara Yumiko, vol. 5 of Nihon no feminizumu (Iwanami shoten, 1995), 57.

3. Sawayama, 167–168; Kanō, "'Bosei' no tanjō," 57–58; Tomida, 225.

4. Kanō, "Bosei fashizumu," 35; "'Bosei' shugi," 198; "'Bosei' no tanjō," 57–58. See also Fuess, "Men's Place," 258–259. For more on the Motherhood Protection Debates, see Kōuchi; Tomida, 221–261.

5. "Bosei fashizumu," 41. See also Sawayama, 168.

6. "Kojin to shite no seikatsu," 41, 45, 49, 51. The Key quotes are from *Love and Marriage*, 216. The Browning quote is from *Renaissance of Motherhood*, 95.

7. For more on this dichotomy between "women's rights" and "mothers' rights" or "motherhood" movements within prewar Japan and on influences from Western feminism, see Miyake Yoshiko, "Kindai Nihon joseishi no saisōzō no tame ni: Tekisuto no yomikae," in *Shakai no hakken*, vol. 4 of Kanagawa daigaku hyōron sōsho, ed. Kanagawa daigaku hyōron henshū senmon iinkai (Ochanomizu shobō, 1994), 63–128. See Chapter Five, note 46, for details about Hiratsuka's establishment of the New Ladies' Association. For more on Hiratsuka's activism, see "Hiratsuka Raichō nenpu," 159–192; Ōmori, *Hiratsuka Raichō*; Yoneda; Suzuki, *Haha to onna*.

8. "Haha toshite no ichinenkan," 266, 274–275.

9. Kuriyagawa, "Kindai no ren'aikan," 24.

10. "Shakai kaizō ni taisuru fujin no shimei: Josei dōmei sōkan no ji ni kaete," in *Hiratsuka Raichō chosakushū*, vol. 3, 160–161, 165, 168; originally published in *Josei dōmei* (October 1920).

11. For more on Takamure's life, thought, and writing, see Takamure Itsue, *Takamure Itsue zenshū*, ed. Hashimoto Kenzō, 10 vols. (Rironsha, 1965–1967); *Takamure*

Itsue ronshū, ed. Takamure Itsue ronshū henshū iinkai (JCA shuppan, 1979); *Takamure Itsue goroku*, ed. Kano Masanao and Horiba Kiyoko (Iwanami shoten, 2001); *Waga michi wa tsune ni fubuki keri: 15 nen sensō zenya*, ed. Nagahata Michiko (Fujiwara shoten, 1995); Kano Masanao and Horiba Kiyoko, *Takamure Itsue* (Asahi shinbunsha, 1977); Yamashita Etsuko, *Takamure Itsue ron: "Haha" no arukeorojii* (Kawade shobō shinsha, 1988); Nishikawa Yūko, *Mori no ie no miko: Takamure Itsue* (Shinchōsha, 1982); Koyama Shizuko, "Takamure Itsue ni okeru josei kaihō shisō no keisei to tenkai," *Shakai shisōshi kenkyū* 6 (1982): 99–115; E. Patricia Tsurumi, "Visions of Women and the New Society in Conflict: Yamakawa Kikue Versus Takamure Itsue," in *Japan's Competing Modernities: Issues in Culture and Democracy, 1900–1930*, ed. Sharon A. Minichiello (Honolulu: University of Hawai'i Press, 1998), 335–357; Ronald P. Loftus, "Female Self-Writing: Takamure Itsue's *Hi no Kuni no Onna no Nikki*," *Monumenta Nipponica* 51, no. 2 (1996): 153–170; Sonia Ryang, "Love and Colonialism in Takamure Itsue's Feminism: A Postcolonial Critique," *Feminist Review* 60 (Autumn 1998): 1–32. For the chronology, see "Takamure Itsue nenpu," in *Takamure Itsue zenshū*, vol. 10, (1965), 485–491.

12. "Rojiura no ki II," in *Takamure Itsue zenshū*, vol. 9 (1966), 233–234.

13. "Takamure Itsue san," in *Hiratsuka Raichō chosakushū*, vol. 4 (1983), 221; dated 1926, original place of publication unknown. "Kakuarubeki modan gaaru," in *Hiratsuka Raichō chosakushū*, vol. 4, 297; originally published in *Fujin kōron* (June 1927). "Fujin sensen ni sanka shite," in *Hiratsuka Raichō chosakushū*, vol. 5 (1984), 182; originally published in *Fujin sensen* 1, no. 2 (1930).

14. Kano and Horiba, 161; Nishikawa, 118–119; "Takamure Itsue nenpu," 488.

15. "Fujin sensen ni sanka shite," 182.

16. "*Josei shugi*" (womanism) is the equivalent of what is commonly called *bosei shugi* or *boken shugi* (motherhood-ism or mothers' rights-ism). Takamure contrasts this belief in sexual difference with "*joken shugi*" (women's rights-ism), an ideology that promotes sexual equality and does not accept difference. According to Takamure, "women's rights-ism" is the idea behind the feminist movements in the United Kingdom and the United States, while "*shin joken shugi*" (new women's rights-ism) is found in Russia. "Womanism" developed in Germany and the Scandinavian countries. See "Ren'ai sōsei," in *Takamure Itsue zenshū*, vol. 7 (1967), 9–10. See also Tsurumi, 342.

17. See "Ren'ai sōsei," 9–10, 33, 118–119, 181, 186, 188.

18. Kano and Horiba (147–148) describe *Creation of Love* as a "work of negation" that rejects all established institutions and ideologies created by men; attacks ideas about "love, marriage, women, education"; and criticizes "modernity," "individualism," and the "West."

19. "Ren'ai sōsei," 79.

20. Kano and Horiba (148) also say that *Creation of Love* is a "work of *kaiki*" that turns away from "modernity" and "the West." It presents the "ancient period" as a "period of love [*koi*]," the only time that "Japanese women had freedom and authority." Tsurumi (342) explains that in Takamure's eyes the "survival of the fittest principle" was created by Western civilization. This is why Takamure sees "men,

modern society, and the West" as inherently evil. In contrast, Takamure lauds premodern Japanese society as an ideal space where "women were highly respected beings who received appropriate reproductive and child-care support and loved passionately without the harmful restrictions of matrimony." For more on Takamure's nativist and ethnocentrist position, see Ryang, "Love and Colonialism."

21. "Ren'ai sōsei," 99, 109, 189–190.

22. Kanō, "Bosei shugi," 201–203. It is important, however, to remember that "romantic love" is also emphasized in this text as a part of "motherhood" and "maternal love."

23. "Takamure Itsue san no *Ren'ai sōsei* o yomu," in *Hiratsuka Raichō chosakushū*, vol. 4, 223; dated 1926, original place of publication unknown.

24. Yamakawa Kikue, "Keihintsuki tokkahin toshite no onna," in *Ai to sei no jiyū*, 191–193; originally published in *Fujin kōron* (January 1928). Takamure wrote a response to this article as an anarchist, arguing that Marxian socialism would not allow women to achieve true love; see "Yamakawa Kikue shi no ren'aikan o nanzu," in *Ai to sei no jiyū*, 196–208; originally published in *Fujin kōron* (May 1928). For more on the difference between these two feminists' ideologies, see Tsurumi. Frederick discusses this *Fujin kōron* debate between the two women in *Turning Pages*, 48–53.

25. "Bosei ni sosogu namida," in *Hiratsuka Raichō chosakushū*, vol. 5, 224–225; originally published as "Haha e sosogu namida" in *Fujin kōron* (December 1930).

26. See Kano Masanao, *Senzen "ie" no shisō* (Sōbunsha, 1983), 183–187; *Fujin, josei, onna: Joseishi no toi* (Iwanami shoten, 1995), 102–104.

27. Kano, *Fujin, josei, onna*, 89–90, 104–105.

28. For examples of maternal love iconography in post-1937 wartime women's magazines, see Wakakuwa Midori, *Sensō ga tsukuru joseizō: Dai niji sekai taisenka no Nihon josei dōin no shikakuteki propaganda* (Chikuma shobō, 1997). For other examples of wartime female mobilization through motherhood identity, see Sharalyn Orbaugh, *Japanese Fiction of the Allied Occupation: Vision, Embodiment, Identity* (Leiden: Brill, 2007), 261–271.

29. For more on this "doubling expectation" placed on mothers during this time, see Miyake, "Doubling Expectations," 267–295. See also Orbaugh (340–346) for more on the mobilization of motherhood and female labor.

30. For ideas on maternal love's "purity" and "self-sacrifice" in relation to the nation, see Kano, *Senzen*, 202–203; Kawamura, *Sexuariti*, 225–226.

31. Sawayama, 179.

32. Mori Yasuko explained in 1945 that "*kokkateki bosei*" is the "actualization [*genjitsuka*] of the spirit of the nation"; see *Kokkateki bosei no kōzō*, vol. 24 of *Onna to sensō*, ed. Nakajima Kuni (Ōzorasha, 1992), 287; facsimile of the 1945 book published by Dōbunkan. See also Miyake, "Doubling Expectations," 271. I use Miyake's English translation of "*kokkateki bosei*."

33. Kawamura, *Sexuariti*, 208–209. In discussing such use of maternal love in *Friend of the Housewife*, Kawamura (224–225) says that Hiratsuka's praise of maternal love during wartime was not as nationalistic and notes that she did not publish much during this period. He does acknowledge, however, that Hiratsuka did

adopt the state policy of encouraging women to have as many children as possible, and that she endorsed the view of the emperor as a living god even before the start of the China War.

34. Yamaguchi Aisen, "Nihon no haha," in *Nihon no haha: Hoka ippen*, vol. 25 of "Teikoku" sensō to bungaku, ed. Iwabuchi Hiroko and Hasegawa Kei (Yumani shobō, 2005), 14, 363; facsimile of Yamaguchi Aisen, *Nihon no haha* (Rikugō shoin, 1943).

35. See Kubokawa, "Haha no jikaku," 216–218.

36. "Kigi shinryoku," in *Sata Ineko shū*, 137–181; originally published in *Bungei* (1938).

37. "Otto no teisō," in *Yoshiya Nobuko zenshū*, vol. 5 (1975), 3–268; originally serialized in *Osaka Mainichi shinbun* and *Tokyo Nichi Nichi shinbun*, October 6, 1936–April 15, 1937.

Chapter Seven: Okamoto Kanoko and the Mythic Mother

1. "Uta to shōsetsu to shūkyō to," in *Okamoto Kanoko zenshū*, vol. 14 (Tōjusha, 1977), 410–411; originally published in *Bungei tsūshin* (August 1936).

2. Okamoto published poetry in issues from *Seitō* 2, no. 3 (1912) to *Seitō* 5, no. 9 (1915). She also published two letters in *Bluestocking*—one written during her hospitalization and printed in "Henshūshitsu yori," *Seitō* 3, no. 12 (1913); the other, addressed to Bluestocking member Ikuta Hanayo, printed as "Byōi o nugite," *Seitō* 5, no. 8 (1915). The latter letter thanks the Society members for their support while she was ill. See Raichō kenkyūkai, 64–65.

3. For Okamoto's official chronology, I refer to both "Nenpu," in *Okamoto Kanoko zenshū*, vol. bekkan 2 (1978), 291–335; and "Okamoto Kanoko nenpu," in *Okamoto Kanoko zenshū*, vol. 12 (1994), 447–486. For biographical information about Okamoto in English, see Maryellen T. Mori, "The Splendor of Self-Exaltation: The Life and Fiction of Okamoto Kanoko," *Monumenta Nipponica* 50, no. 1 (1995): 67–102; Kazuko Sugisaki, "A Writer's Life: A Biographical Sketch," in *The House Spirit and Other Stories* (Santa Barbara, CA: Capra Press, 1995), 7–30; Copeland, "Okamoto Kanoko," in *Japanese Women Writers*, 294–302; Tanaka, "Okamoto Kanoko (1889–1939)," in *To Live and to Write*, 197–203.

4. *Kanoko ryōran* (Kōdansha, 1993), originally serialized in *Fujin gahō* (July 1962–June 1964); *Kanoko ryōran sonogo* (Kōdansha, 1994), originally published by Tōjusha (1978).

5. For more on the relationships between maternal love, Buddhism, and Kannon in Okamoto's thought, see her Buddhist poem "Boseiai," in *Okamoto Kanoko zenshū*, vol. 9 (1975), 298–302; originally published in *Bukkyō dokuhon* (Daitō shuppansha, 1934). Here Okamoto calls herself "*Haha Kanzeon*" (Mother Kannon). Kannon is often presented as a maternal female deity in popular Japanese Buddhism.

6. For essays and symposium discussion, see *Bungakkai* 9 (September 1942): 6–51; and *Bungakkai* 9 (October 1942): 44–112. For Kamei and Hayashi's essays in the October 1942 special issue of *Bungakkai*, see Kamei, "Gendai seishin ni kansuru oboegaki," 2–10; and Hayashi, "Kinnō no kokoro," 10–27. For more on the Overcoming

Modernity symposium, see Harootunian, 34–94. For more on the Japan Romantic School, see Kevin Michael Doak, *Dreams of Difference: The Japan Romantic School and the Crisis of Modernity* (Berkeley: University of California Press, 1994).

7. Okamoto's political position has been debated among Japanese critics. Due to her death in 1939, her exact political stance is difficult to determine. Kōra Rumiko, who has dealt closely with the question of Okamoto's politics, points out that her most right-wing essay, published in the feminist journal *Kagayaku* after the start of the China War, praises Japanese soldiers as gods ("Waga shōshi o omou kotoba," *Kagayaku*, October 1937). Kōra also notes, however, that although Okamoto wrote a fair number of pro-war essays and poems, nationalistic jingoism was never an element in her fiction. Kōra interprets this as a conscious strategy; by publishing such essays and poetry, Okamoto could avoid government censorship and criticism of her fiction, despite the fact that its contents were not suitably pro-war. See *Okamoto Kanoko inochi no kaiki* (Kanrin shobō, 2004), 130–148.

8. In translating the title *Shōjo ruten* as *Wheel of Life*, I have consulted Maryellen Toman Mori's work in which she translates it as *The Wheel of Life*; see "The Quest Motif in the Fiction of Okamoto Kanoko (1889–1939)" (Ph.D. diss., Harvard University, 1988).

9. "Byōi o nugite," in *Okamoto Kanoko zenshū*, vol. 14, 7–9; originally published in *Seitō* (September 1915). Tarō was Okamoto's only surviving child. The other two (born 1913 and 1915) were raised by other people and died several months after birth. Most critics speculate that these children were fathered by her lover, Horikiri Shigeo (1891–1916) and not by Ippei.

10. Kobayashi Hideo, "Bungei jihyō: Karada zentai de kaiteiru Okamoto shi no *Boshi jojō*," in *Okamoto Kanoko zenshū*, vol. bekkan 2 (1978), 71; originally published in *Yomiuri shinbun*, March 5, 1937.

11. "Boshi jojō," in *Okamoto Kanoko zenshū*, vol. 2 (1974), 228, 252. Some words are censored out of this original version. For the uncensored text, probably rewritten by Tarō, and for critical comments about this issue, see "Boshi jojō" and "Kaidai," in *Okamoto Kanoko zenshū*, vol. 3 (1993), 61–191, 448–451. A partial translation of this story is published as "A Mother's Love," in *Rabbits, Crabs, Etc.: Stories by Japanese Women*, trans. Phyllis Birnbaum (Honolulu: University of Hawai'i Press, 1982), 49–97.

12. Kōra (17–18, 24–30, 182–183) discusses the vine symbolism and the mirrored relationship between the two mothers. Junko Ikezu Williams views Kikuo as Ichirō's doppelganger; see "Visions and Narratives: Modernism in the Prose Works of Yoshiyuki Eisuke, Murayama Tomoyoshi, Yumeno Kyūsaku, and Okamoto Kanoko" (Ph.D diss., Ohio State University, 1998), 238–243.

13. Kano, *Fujin, josei, onna*, 105–106; Suzuki, *Haha to onna*, 140–157.

14. Because *Wheel of Life* was published posthumously, scholars have questioned whether Okamoto was its sole author. Setouchi Jakuchō's theory that the letter from Shijin'an to Chōko in the last part of the novel was written by Ippei from an autobiographical perspective has been accepted by most critics. See Setouchi, *Kanoko ryōran*, 526–541; "Kaidai," in *Okamoto Kanoko zenshū*, vol. 7 (1993), 514–515;

Furuya Teruko, *Okamoto Kanoko: Hanayagu inochi* (Chūsekisha, 1982), 290–296. Kōra (149–180) ascribes a greater portion of the text to Ippei than suggested by Setouchi. For another view that this novel and other works were reworked by Ippei and others after Okamoto's death, see Arai Tomiyo, *Onna shujinkō no fukigen: Higuchi Ichiyō kara Tomioka Taeko made* (Sōbunsha, 2001), 119–141. Miyauchi Junko points out the difficulty in determining authorship solely on the basis of stylistic variation; see *Okamoto Kanoko: Mujō no umi e* (Musashino shobō, 1994), 269–280.

15. "Quest Motif," 215.

16. "Shōjō ruten," in *Okamoto Kanoko zenshū*, vol. 6 (1975), 358, 361. Subsequent quotes from this work are noted directly in the text in parentheses. In working on my translations I have consulted translated passages in Mori, "Quest Motif."

17. See Mori, "Quest Motif," 239; Furuya, 280; Kamei Katsuichirō, "Kawa no yōsei," in *Okamoto Kanko zenshū*, vol. bekkan 2 (1978), 19–31; earlier version originally published as "Shogyō mujō: *Shōjō ruten* ni tsuite," in *Bungakkai* (May 1940). Using Jungian psychoanalysis and feminist critique, Mori reads the text as a quest novel of awakening; see "Quest Motif," 215–282. Williams views the work as reflecting Buddhist thought and modernist technique; see "Visions and Narratives," 256–277.

18. Tsutsumi Shigehisa, "Dazai Osamu danshō," *Dazai Osamu kenkyū* 3 (1996): 85. *Wheel of Life* is also listed as one of the seventy-eight influential works of modern Japanese literature in Ara Masahito and Hirata Jizaburō, *Nihon no kindai bungaku* (Jitsugyō no Nihonsha, 1951), 171–174.

19. Arai Tomiyo suggests that this school, called "F Gakuen," might have been modeled on Bunka Gakuen, a progressive private school; see "Kanoko ronkō: *Shōjō ruten* ni tsuite," *Ōtani gakuhō* 70, no. 1 (1990): 36. For information on Bunka Gakuen, see Hashimoto Noriko, *Danjo kyōgakusei no shiteki kenkyū* (Ōtsuki shoten, 1992), 195–220.

20. In her early Buddhist works, Okamoto often invokes the idea of the trajectory of development, in which a character attains enlightenment by moving from a narrow earthly love to a higher, expansive love. In a 1928 play, "Anan to jujutsushi no musume" (Ānanda and the witch's daughter), Buddha's disciple Ānanda and a village girl both experience enlightenment (pure, asexual love) by understanding the limitations of romantic love. In the short story "Kishimo no ai" (Love of Hārītī, 1928), the demon Hārītī, who eats other people's infants but does not eat her own brood, is taught by Buddha to transcend her selfish love and love all children as if they were her own. This awareness of a higher maternal love enables Hārītī to transform into the goddess of motherhood. Such a view of love as a process does not simply reflect a Buddhist perspective but also shows Okamoto's engagement with contemporary love discourses. "Anan to jujutsushi no musume" and "Kishimo no ai," in *Okamoto Kanoko zenshū*, vol. 1 (1974), 61–105, 106–117; originally serialized in *Yomiuri shinbun* from May 16–June 19, 1928, and July 3–12, 1928, respectively. Both were published in *Sangeshō*, a collection of writings on Buddhism, published in 1929 by Daiyūkaku. "Ānanda and the Witch's Daughter" was first performed December 2–23, 1934, at Tokyo Gekijō. For

the English translation of "Kishimo no ai," see "The Love of Kishimo," trans. Charlotte Eubanks, in *Modanizumu: Modernist Fiction from Japan 1913–1938*, ed. William J. Tyler (Honolulu: University of Hawai'i Press, 2008), 453–461.

With regard to philosophical influences, Furuya suggests that Okamoto was inspired by Henri Bergson (1859–1941), particularly his concept of "*élan vital*" (life force), considered the source of social and human development, propelled by "absolute love." She argues that Okamoto combined this philosophy with Buddhist thought; see Furuya, 194–200. Suzuki Sadami notes that the idea of "*élan vital*" was popular among intellectuals at the time and was an important component of the "Taishō life force ideology" (*Taishō seimeishugi*) boom. Such an influence on Okamoto may be considered in conjunction with her engagement with modern love ideology, particularly with the notion that the female self is completed through love, and the understanding of maternal love as an endpoint. Suzuki also comments that Ellen Key's "liberal feminism" was also a significant part of the "Taishō life force ideology" boom; see "'Taishō seimeishugi' towa nanika," in *Taishō seimeishugi to gendai*, ed. Suzuki Sadami (Kawade shobō shinsha, 1995), 5–7.

21. Mori sees Chōko as representing "'all women' or the female principle"; see "Quest Motif," 237.

22. See "Quest Motif," 238, 251.

23. Seiji M. Lippit, *Topographies of Japanese Modernism* (New York: Columbia University Press, 2002), 176–177; Gardner, *Advertising Tower*, 155. Gardner (152) describes the protagonist as a "montage of various new roles related to love and work" in the modern city.

Hayashi Fumiko, *Hōrōki*, ed. Sekii Mitsuo, vol. 12 of Shin'ei bungaku sōsho (Yumani shobō, 1998); facsimile edition of *Hōrōki* (Kaizōsha, 1930). Hayashi Fumiko's *Diary of a Vagabond* was first serialized from 1928 to 1930 in *Nyonin geijutsu*, a journal in which Okamoto also published. In 1930, the Kaizōsha book edition became a bestseller; a sequel, *Zoku Hōrōki* (Diary of a vagabond, continued) was published the same year. In 1939 a revised version was published. The third section, *Hōrōki dai sanbu* (Diary of a vagabond, part three), was serialized in *Nihon shōsetsu* from 1947 to 1948 and published in book form in 1949; see Ericson, 121–122. Also see Ericson for analyses of the work and "Diary of a Vagabond," the English translation of the 1939 version of *Hōrōki* (123–219). For other critical works, see, for example, Lippit, *Topographies*, 159–195; William O. Gardner, "Mongrel Modernism: Hayashi Fumiko's *Hōrōki* and Mass Culture," *Journal of Japanese Studies* 29, no. 1 (2003): 69–101; *Advertising Tower*, 118–168; Janice Brown, "De-siring the Center: Hayashi Fumiko's Hungry Heroines and the Male Literary Canon," in *The Father-Daughter Plot: Japanese Literary Women and the Law of the Father*, ed. Rebecca L. Copeland and Esperanza Ramirez-Christensen (Honolulu: University of Hawai'i Press, 2001), 143–166.

24. Arai, *Onna shujinkō*, 130–131. Arai also points out here that in a 1937 essay, "Hayashi san ni tsuite," Okamoto praises Hayashi and comments on *Diary of a Vagabond*. See *Okamoto Kanoko zenshū*, vol. 14, 439–441; originally published in *Hayashi Fumiko senshū geppō* 1, supplement to *Hayashi Fumiko senshū*, vol. 5 (Kaizōsha, 1937).

25. "Hōrōsha no shi" and "Iede no shi," in *Takamure Itsue zenshū*, vol. 8 (1966), 65–136, 305–320. The first work was originally published as *Hōrōsha no shi* (Shinchōsha, 1921), the second was originally published in *Tokyo wa netsubyō ni kakkate iru* (Banseikaku, 1925).

26. Kano and Horiba, 89, 93.

27. Arai, *Onna shujinkō*, 131.

28. For another view of the differences between Hayashi's vagabond, Takamure's pilgrim, and Chōko, see Arai, *Onna shujinkō*, 131–133.

29. Orikuchi first discussed this idea fully in "Tokoyo oyobi 'marebito,'" *Minzoku* (January 1929), which was later published as "Kokubungaku no hassei (dai sankō): Marebito no igi" in *Kodai kenkyū (Kokubungaku hen)* (1929); see Nishimura Tōru, ed., *Orikuchi Shinobu jiten zōhoban* (Taishūkan shoten, 1998), 19, 495. Iwabuchi Hiroko suggests the influence of *minzokugaku* on *Wheel of Life* and views the beggars in the story as "*marebito*"-type figures; see "*Shōjō ruten* no fōkuroa: Kojiki no imi," *Shōwa gakuen tanki daigaku kiyō* 26 (1989): 55–56.

30. The interpretation of "*tokoyo*" is extremely complex and Origuchi shifts his view depending on the context of the discussion. It can be roughly divided into two broad categories—"*ikyō*" (foreign land) and "*takai*" (other world)—and associated with, for example, other peoples, utopia, death, ancestors, and gods. For explanations of *marebito* and *tokoyo* that describe the shifts within Origuchi's analyses, see Nishimura, 13–44. Harootunian (350–357) discusses these issues in relation to *minzokugaku*'s "prospect of realizing a repetitive history exempt from modernity's temporalizing regime" (306).

31. "Imo no chikara," in *Yanagita Kunio zenshū*, vol. 11 (Chikuma shobō, 1998), 247–261; originally published in *Fujin kōron* (October 1925). *Imo no chikara*, a book about legends and deities connected with women, was first published in 1940 by Sōgensha.

32. D. H. Lawrence, "The Woman Who Rode Away," in *The Woman Who Rode Away and Other Stories*, ed. Dieter Mehl and Christa Jansohn (Cambridge, UK: Cambridge University Press, 1995), 39–71.

33. "Iki iki shita mono," in *Okamoto Kanoko zenshū*, vol. 12 (1976), 149–150; originally published in *Yomiuri shinbun*, November 30, 1935; later collected in *Josei no sho* (Okakura shobō, 1936).

34. *Yamahime* is commonly known as a goddess who protects the mountains. In this novel, the definition given is "a mixed-blood offspring of a god and a mountain beast" (200).

35. Rachel Blau DuPlessis, *Writing Beyond the Ending: Narrative Strategies of Twentieth-Century Women Writers* (Bloomington: Indiana University Press, 1985), 107.

36. See Kawamura, *Otome no shintai*, 48–54.

37. For more on sports as both liberating and restrictive for prewar women, see Andō Kyōko, "Okamoto Kanoko *Shōjō ruten*: Onna taiikuka Ataka sensei o chūshin ni," in *Shōwa no chōhen shōsetsu*, ed. Yasukawa Sadao (Shibundō, 1992), 75–77.

38. Nakagawa Kenjirō, *Fujin no chikara to teikoku no shōrai*, vol. 20 of Kindai

Nihon joshi kyōiku bunkenshū, ed. Nakajima Kuni (Nihon tosho sentaa, 1984), 195; facsimile of the 1925 book published by Fuzanbō.

39. Elias Lönnrot, *Kalevala*, 2 vols., trans. W. F. Kirby (London: J. M. Dent and Sons, 1956). For the most readily available current Japanese translation, see Ryonrotto [Elias Lönnrot], ed., *Finrando jojishi: Karewara*, 2 vols., trans. Koizumi Tamotsu (Iwanami shoten, 1998).

40. "Finrando no gakumon," in *Yanagita Kunio zenshū*, vol. 29 (Chikuma shobō, 2002), 276–288; originally published in *Hishika* 134 (1935). For a bibliography of *Kalevala* research in Japan, see Hagishima Takashi, "Nihon ni okeru *Karewara* kenkyū," supplement to *Karewara no oitachi*, ed. Anneri Asupurundo [Anneli Asplund] and Urra Ripponen [Ulla Lipponen], trans. Ōkura Jun'ichirō (Helsinki: Finrando bungaku kyōkai, 1985), 49–51.

41. Ryonrotto [Elias Lönnrot], *Karewara*, 2 vols., trans. Morimoto Kakutan (Kōdansha, 1983); originally published as a deluxe edition by Nihon shosō (1937).

42. Matsumura Takeo, *Finrando no shinwa densetsu*, vol. 31 of Sekai shinwa densetsu taikei (Meicho fukyūkai, 1980), 27; reprint of *Finrando shinwa densetsu shū*, vol. 12 of Shinwa densetsu taikei (Kindaisha, 1929). Although Okamoto uses phrases from Matsumura's commentary to summarize the plot, the words spoken by Lemminkainen's mother seem to be Okamoto's own.

43. Arnold van Gennep established the classic concept of rites of passage. In explaining van Gennep's definition, Victor Turner notes its three phases: "separation" (detachment from the community or one's place in the social structure), "margin" (state of liminality), and "aggregation" (reincorporation). See Victor Turner, *The Ritual Process: Structure and Anti-Structure* (Ithaca, NY: Cornell University Press, 1969), 94–95. See also Arnold van Gennep, *The Rites of Passage*, trans. Monika B. Vizedom and Gabrielle L. Caffee (Chicago: University of Chicago Press, 1960).

44. See Jacob and Wilhelm Grimm, *Deutsches Wörterbuch* (Leipzig: Verlag von S. Hirzel, 1936). In current German usage, *Urmutter* can have a range of definitions depending on context.

45. "Kōsho shushu," in *Okamoto Kanoko zenshū*, vol. 14, 403–404; originally published in *Dokusho kankyō* (July 1936).

46. Sigmund Freud, *Das Unbehagen in der Kultur* (Wien: Internationaler Psychoanalytischer Verlag, 1930), 61, 114. See also Freud, *Civilization and Its Discontents*, trans. and ed. James Strachey (New York: Norton, 1961), 46, 79. For more on the Great Mother archetype, see Erich Neumann, *The Great Mother: An Analysis of the Archetype*, trans. Ralph Manheim (Princeton, NJ: Princeton University Press, 1970).

47. Frederick Engels, *The Origin of the Family, Private Property, and the State: In the Light of the Researches of Lewis H. Morgan*, introduction and notes by Eleanor Burke Leacock (New York: International Publishers, 1972), 29, 75–76, 97, 106. According to the National Diet Library's online catalog, the earliest recorded Japanese translation of this work is *Kazoku, shiyūzaisan oyobi kokka no kigen*, trans. Naitō Kichinosuke (Reshinasō, 1922). A more widely found edition is the translation by Nishi Masao, published by Hakuyōsha (1927). A work with the same title translated

by Tanaka Kyūichi is included in the collected works of Marx and Engels in Japanese: *Marukusu Engerusu zenshū*, vol. 12 (Kaizōsha, 1928).

48. *Myth, Religion, and Mother Right: Selected Writings of J. J. Bachofen*, trans. Ralph Manheim (Princeton, NJ: Bollingen Foundation, 1967), 79. For the introduction from *Mother Right*, see *Myth, Religion, and Mother Right*, 69–120. For a brief summary and interpretation of Bachofen's ideas, see Madelon Sprengnether, *The Spectral Mother: Freud, Feminism, and Psychoanalysis* (Ithaca, NY: Cornell University Press, 1990), 101–102. According to Sprengnether, Bachofen argues that after "hetaerism" and the matrilineal stage, there is "Demetrian matriarchy," agricultural societies based on monogamy, "in which women dominate and the principle of maternity is honored by the worship of a female deity." Both matrilineality and "the mother goddess" are later overthrown by "the modern form of patriarchy, which includes a recognition of paternity." Sprengnether's work is also helpful for examining the relationship between discussions of evolutionary sociohistorical development and the works of Freud and Jung. As she shows, Freud strongly resisted the idea of an originary Great Mother, while Jung embraced this figure over paternal authority (86–119). For other brief summaries and interpretations, see *Myth, Religion, and Mother Right*, xix; Engels, 75–76.

Leacock notes that matriarchy "as accompanying matrilineal descent is specifically contradicted by Engels," who suggests that in primitive societies there was no sense of "'right' in the legal sense"; see Engels, 266. This does not seem, however, to contradict Bachofen's argument that matriarchy and mother veneration emerged from primitive matrilineal societies.

49. Bahaōfen [Johann Jakob Bachofen], *Bokenron*, trans. Tomino Yoshiteru (Hakuyōsha, 1938). This volume includes Bachofen's autobiography, the introductory chapter of *Mutterrecht*, and a commentary on Bachofen's works by Erich Fromm.

50. "Senkuteki na koten to shite: Bahaōfen, *Bokenron*, Tomino Yoshiteru shi yaku," in *Miyamoto Yuriko zenshū*, vol. 13, 371.

51. "Bokeisei no kenkyū," in *Takamure Itsue zenshū*, vol. 1, ed. Hashimoto Kenzō (Rironsha, 1966), 1–633; the earlier version was originally published as the first volume of a planned five-volume work: *Dai Nihon joseishi* (Kōseikaku, 1938).

52. "Takamure Itsue joshi cho *Dai Nihon joseishi: Bokeisei no kenkyū*," in *Okamoto Kanoko zenshū*, vol. hokan (1977), 111–112; originally published in *Osaka Asahi shinbun*, July 25, 1938. Okamoto is listed as a member of this association in *Bokeisei no kenkyū* (Dai Nihon yūbenkai kōdansha, 1954), batsu 3. Her name is not listed in the original Kōseikaku editions, which suggests that she was not a founding member. "Bokeisei no kenkyū," in *Takamure Itsue zenshū*, vol. 1, does not provide a list of association members, but the official chronology notes that Hiratsuka Raichō was the central figure in establishing this association; see "Takamure Itsue nenpu," 489.

53. This entry into the ocean (*mer* / *mère*) may prompt a psychoanalytic reading based on French feminism in which this escape becomes a performative act of entry into *jouissance* or an expression of *parler-femme* / *écriture féminine*. Chōko's becoming one with the ocean can be read as a reclaiming of the mother, the breaking of

the taboo that Luce Irigaray calls *"le désir de'elle, son désir à elle"* (her desire, the desire she has); see "Le Corps-à-Corps avec la Mère," in *Sexes Et Parentés* (Paris: Les Éditions de Minuit, 1987), 23. English translation from "Body Against Body: In Relation to the Mother," in *Sexes and Genealogies,* trans. Gillian C. Gill (New York: Columbia University Press, 1993), 11. Although I do not use psychoanalysis in my approach, the affirmation of female self as a kind of self-reflexive maternal love can be a part of such an interpretive strategy.

For another example of Okamoto's fiction in which the main female character enters the ocean, see Okamoto Kanoko, "Konton mibun," in *Okamoto Kanoko zenshū,* vol. 2 (1974), 54–78; originally published in *Bungei* (September 1936). The English translation is "The Unordered World," trans. Michiko Suzuki, *Manoa: A Pacific Journal of International Writing* 8 (Summer 1996): 158–171. For an analysis of this text (referred to as "Primeval Chaos"), see Maryellen T. Mori, "Cross-Cultural Patterns in the Quest Fiction of Okamoto Kanoko," *The Comparatist* 20 (1996): 153–178.

54. See Sakamoto Yukio and Iwamoto Yutaka, trans. and eds., *Hokkekyō,* vol. 2 (Iwanami shoten, 2000), 204–225, 374, 379. In Japanese, Sagara's daughter is usually referred to as Ryūnyo. For more on this figure, see Bernard Faure, *The Power of Denial: Buddhism, Purity, and Gender* (Princeton, NJ: Princeton University Press, 2003), 91–118; Yoshida Kazuhiko, "The Enlightenment of the Dragon King's Daughter in the Lotus Sutra," trans. and adapt. Margaret H. Childs, in *Engendering Faith: Women and Buddhism in Premodern Japan,* ed. Barbara Ruch (Ann Arbor: Center for Japanese Studies, University of Michigan, 2002), 297–324.

55. "Bukkyō dokuhon," in *Okamoto Kanoko zenshū,* vol. 9 (1975), 271–272. Originally published in book form by Daitō shuppan (1934).

56. D. Max Moerman, *Localizing Paradise: Kumano Pilgrimage and the Religious Landscape of Premodern Japan* (Cambridge, MA: Harvard University Asia Center, 2005), 109–111.

57. *Takamure Itsue zenshū,* vol. 1, reigen 2.

58. *Dai Nihon joseishi,* 637.

59. Ibid. For discussions of this "matrilineal self-sacrifice," see Kano and Horiba, 219–220; and Yamashita, *Takamure Itsue ron,* 162–163.

60. "Takumashiki dōjo: Okamoto Kanoko to watashi," in *Yoshiya Nobuko zenshū,* vol. 11 (1975), 346–347, 350; originally printed in *Shōsetsu Chūō kōron* (1961); later collected in *Jidenteki joryū bundanshi* (Chūō kōronsha, 1962); also reprinted in *Okamoto Kanoko zenshū,* vol. bekkan 1 (1978), 430–441. Setouchi notes that Yoshiya was the only woman writer to come to the 1962 unveiling of the Okamoto Kanoko, a memorial sculpture by Okamoto Tarō; see *Kanoko ryōran sonogo,* 205.

61. Miyamoto, *Fujin to bungaku,* 205–210.

62. Kamei, 24. This idea of the "eternal mother" continues to be important in the Japanese postwar cultural and psychic imaginary. The essentialist association of this figure with "Eastern" mentality can be found, for example, in the ideas of Zen master Suzuki Daisetsu, who explained in 1958 that such a mother is at the basis of the "Oriental nature": "The mother . . . enfolds everything in an unconditional love. There is no question of right or wrong. Everything is accepted without difficulties

or questioning. Love in the West always contains a residue of power. Love in the East is all-embracing. It is open to all sides. One can enter from any direction": "Tōyō bunmei no kontei ni aru mono," *Asahi shinbun*, December 22, 1958; quoted in Takeo Doi, *The Anatomy of Dependence*, trans. John Bester (Tokyo: Kodansha International, 1973), 77.

63. Hayashi Fusao, "Nihon bungaku no fukkatsu: Okamoto Kanoko ron sono ichi," in *Okamoto Kanoko zenshū*, vol. bekkan 2 (1978), 32–33; originally published in *Bungakkai* (June 1938).

64. For the basic ideas of linear time and monumental time within French psychoanalysis and feminism, see Julia Kristeva, "Women's Time," trans. Alice Jardine and Harry Blake, in *The Kristeva Reader*, ed. Toril Moi (New York: Columbia University Press, 1986), 187–213.

65. For a different reading of the "female first-person narration" and its meaning in *Wheel of Life*, see Seki Reiko, "*Shōjō ruten* ni okeru josei ichininshō," in *Shōwa bungaku ronkō: Machi to mura to*, ed. Odagiri Susumu (Yagi shoten, 1990), 323–338.

66. Ariyoshi Sawako, "Issatsu no hon," quoted in Komiya Tadahiko, "Kaidai," in *Okamoto Kanoko zenshū*, vol. 7 (1993), 501; originally published in *Asahi shinbun*, May 3, 1964.

67. Tsushima Yūko, "Ōonna no imeeji," in *Okamoto Kanoko kenkyū: Okamoto Kanoko zenshū dai ni kan furoku* 3 (Tōjusha, 1974), 14; also quoted in Komiya, 502.

Conclusion

1. Denise Riley, *"Am I That Name?": Feminism and the Category of "Women" in History* (Minneapolis: University of Minnesota Press, 1988), 47. Emphasis added.

Bibliography

Unless otherwise noted, all Japanese works are published in Tokyo.

Andō Kyōko. "Okamoto Kanoko *Shōjō ruten*: Onna taiikuka Ataka sensei o chūshin ni." In *Shōwa no chōhen shōsetsu*. Ed. Yasukawa Sadao, 64–84. Shibundō, 1992.

Ara Masahito and Hirata Jizaburō. *Nihon no kindai bungaku*. Jitsugyō no Nihonsha, 1951.

Arai Tomiyo. "Kanoko ronkō: *Shōjō ruten* ni tsuite." *Ōtani gakuhō* 70, no. 1 (1990): 34–46.

———. *Onna shujinkō no fukigen: Higuchi Ichiyō kara Tomioka Taeko made*. Sōbunsha, 2001.

Asahi shinbunsha, ed. *Asahi shinbun no kiji ni miru ren'ai to kekkon (Meiji, Taishō)*. Asahi shinbunsha, 1997.

Bachofen, Johann Jakob. *Myth, Religion, and Mother Right: Selected Writings of J. J. Bachofen*. Trans. Ralph Manheim. Princeton, NJ: Bollingen Foundation, 1967.

Badanteeru, Erizabeeto [Elisabeth Badinter]. *Bosei to iu shinwa*. Trans. Suzuki Shō. Chikuma shobō, 1998. Originally published as *L'amour en plus: Histoire de l'amour maternel (XVIIe–XXe siècle)*. Paris: Flammarion, 1980.

Bahaōfen [Johann Jakob Bachofen]. *Bokenron*. Trans. Tomino Yoshiteru. Hakuyōsha, 1938.

Bardsley, Jan. *The Bluestockings of Japan: New Woman Essays and Fiction from* Seitō, *1911–1916*. Ann Arbor: Center for Japanese Studies, University of Michigan, 2007.

———. "*Seitō* and the Resurgence of Writing by Women." In *The Columbia Companion to Modern East Asian Literature*. Ed. Joshua S. Mostow, Kirk A. Denton, Bruce Fulton, and Sharalyn Orbaugh, 93–98. New York: Columbia University Press, 2003.

Beichman, Janine. *Embracing the Firebird: Yosano Akiko and the Birth of the Female Voice in Modern Japanese Poetry*. Honolulu: University of Hawai'i Press, 2002.

Bhabha, Homi K. "Postcolonial Authority and Postmodern Guilt." In *Cultural Studies*. Ed. Lawrence Grossberg, Cary Nelson, and Paula A. Treichler, 56–68. New York: Routledge, 1992.

Birnbaum, Phyllis. *Modern Girls, Shining Stars, the Skies of Tokyo: Five Japanese Women*. New York: Columbia University Press, 1999.

Bourdaghs, Michael K. *The Dawn That Never Comes: Shimazaki Tōson and Japanese Nationalism*. New York: Columbia University Press, 2003.

Brown, Janice. "De-siring the Center: Hayashi Fumiko's Hungry Heroines and the Male Literary Canon." In *The Father-Daughter Plot: Japanese Literary Women and the Law of the Father*. Ed. Rebecca L. Copeland and Esperanza Ramirez-Christensen, 143–166. Honolulu: University of Hawai'i Press, 2001.

Bungakkai 9 (September and October, 1942).

Burnett, Frances Hodgson. *A Little Princess*. New York: Bantam Books, 1987.

Butler, Judith. *Gender Trouble: Feminism and the Subversion of Identity*. New York: Routledge, 1990.

———. *The Psychic Life of Power: Theories in Subjection*. Stanford, CA: Stanford University Press, 1997.

Carpenter, Edward. *The Intermediate Sex: A Study of Some Transitional Types of Men and Women*. London: George Allen and Unwin, 1930.

Castle, Terry. *The Apparitional Lesbian: Female Homosexuality and Modern Culture*. New York: Columbia University Press, 1993.

Chow, Rey. *Woman and Chinese Modernity: The Politics of Reading Between West and East*. Minneapolis: University of Minnesota Press, 1991.

Chūjō Yuriko. "Chiisai kumo." *Kaizō* 7, no. 4 (1925): 147–173.

———. "Kikiwakerarenu ashioto." *Kaizō* 6, no. 9 (1924): 1–72.

———. "Gake no ue." *Kaizō* 7, no. 10 (1925): 1–64.

———. "Hakumu." *Kaizō* 8, no. 1 (1926): 271–324.

———. "Hakumu (Zoku)." *Kaizō* 8, no. 2 (1926): 23–48.

———. "Koke." *Kaizō* 8, no. 4 (1926): 55–112.

———. "Suō no hana." *Kaizō* 7, no. 6 (1925): 40–77.

———. "Tōmin." *Kaizō* 6, no. 11 (1924): 57–89.

———. "Ugo." *Kaizō* 8, no. 10 (1926): 113–170.

———. "Yureru kigi." *Kaizō* 7, no. 1 (1925): 56–107.

Copeland, Rebecca L. "Hiratsuka Raichō." In *Japanese Women Writers: A Bio-Critical Sourcebook*. Ed. Chieko I. Mulhern, 132–143. Westport, CT: Greenwood Press, 1994.

———. "Introduction: Meiji Women Writers." In *The Modern Murasaki: Writing by Women of Meiji Japan*. Ed. Rebecca L. Copeland and Melek Ortabasi, 1–28. New York: Columbia University Press, 2006.

———. *Lost Leaves: Women Writers of Meiji Japan*. Honolulu: University of Hawai'i Press, 2000.

———. "Okamoto Kanoko." In *Japanese Women Writers: A Bio-Critical Sourcebook*. Ed. Chieko I. Mulhern, 294–302. Westport, CT: Greenwood Press, 1994.

———. *The Sound of the Wind: The Life and Works of Uno Chiyo*. Honolulu: University of Hawai'i Press, 1992.

———. "Uno Chiyo." In *Japanese Women Writers: A Bio-Critical Sourcebook*. Ed. Chieko I. Mulhern, 440–448. Westport, CT: Greenwood Press, 1994.

———, ed. *Woman Critiqued: Translated Essays on Japanese Women's Writing*. Honolulu: University of Hawai'i Press, 2006.

Copeland, Rebecca L., and Melek Ortabasi, eds. *The Modern Murasaki: Writing by Women of Meiji Japan*. New York: Columbia University Press, 2006.

De Angelis, Ronald William. "Ellen Key: A Biography of the Swedish Reformer." Ph.D. diss., University of Connecticut, 1978.

Deleuze, Gilles. *Essays Critical and Clinical*. Trans. Daniel W. Smith and Michael A. Greco. Minneapolis: University of Minnesota Press, 1997.

Doak, Kevin Michael. *Dreams of Difference: The Japan Romantic School and the Crisis of Modernity*. Berkeley: University of California Press, 1994.

Doi, Takeo. *The Anatomy of Dependence*. Trans. John Bester. Tokyo: Kodansha International, 1973.

Dollase, Hitomi Tsuchiya. "Early Twentieth Century Japanese Girls' Magazine Stories: Examining Shōjo Voice in *Hanamonogatari* (Flower Tales)." *Journal of Popular Culture* 36, no. 4 (2003): 724–755.

———. "Yoshiya Nobuko's 'Yaneura no nishojo': In Search of Literary Possibilities in *Shōjo* Narratives." *U.S.-Japan Women's Journal English Supplement* 20 (2001): 151–178.

DuPlessis, Rachel Blau. *Writing Beyond the Ending: Narrative Strategies of Twentieth-Century Women Writers*. Bloomington: Indiana University Press, 1985.

Ellis, Havelock. *Studies in the Psychology of Sex*. 2 vols. New York: Random House, 1942.

Engels, Frederick. *The Origin of the Family, Private Property, and the State: In the Light of the Researches of Lewis H. Morgan*. Introduction and notes by Eleanor Burke Leacock. New York: International Publishers, 1972.

Ericson, Joan E. *Be a Woman: Hayashi Fumiko and Modern Japanese Women's Literature*. Honolulu: University of Hawai'i Press, 1997.

Esashi Akiko, ed. *Ai to sei no jiyū: "Ie" kara no kaihō*. Shakai hyōronsha, 1989.

Faderman, Lillian. *Odd Girls and Twilight Lovers: A History of Lesbian Life in Twentieth-Century America*. New York: Penguin Books, 1992.

Faison, Elyssa. *Managing Women: Disciplining Labor in Modern Japan*. Berkeley: University of California Press, 2007.

Faure, Bernard. *The Power of Denial: Buddhism, Purity, and Gender*. Princeton, NJ: Princeton University Press, 2003.

Felski, Rita. *The Gender of Modernity*. Cambridge, MA: Harvard University Press, 1995.

Foucault, Michel. *Technologies of the Self: A Seminar with Michel Foucault*. Ed. Luther H. Martin, Huck Gutman, and Patrick H. Hutton. Amherst: University of Massachusetts Press, 1988.

Fowler, Edward. "Tamura Toshiko (1884–1945)." In *The Modern Murasaki: Writing by Women of Meiji Japan*. Ed. Rebecca L. Copeland and Melek Ortabasi, 339–347. New York: Columbia University Press, 2006.

Frederick, Sarah. "Aposiopesis and Completion: Yoshiya Nobuko's Typographic Melodrama." *Proceedings of the Association for Japanese Literary Studies* 7 (2006): 70–77.

————. "Not That Innocent: Yoshiya Nobuko's Good Girls." In *Bad Girls of Japan*. Ed. Laura Miller and Jan Bardsley, 65–79. New York: Palgrave MacMillan, 2005.

————. *Turning Pages: Reading and Writing Women's Magazines in Interwar Japan*. Honolulu: University of Hawai'i Press, 2006.

Freud, Sigmund. *Civilization and Its Discontents*. Trans. and Ed. James Strachey. New York: Norton, 1961.

————. *Das Unbehagen in der Kultur*. Wien: Internationaler Psychoanalytischer Verlag, 1930.

Frühstück, Sabine. *Colonizing Sex: Sexology and Social Control in Modern Japan*. Berkeley: University of California Press, 2003.

Fuess, Harald. *Divorce in Japan: Family, Gender, and the State, 1600–2000*. Stanford, CA: Stanford University Press, 2004.

————. "Men's Place in the Women's Kingdom: New Middle-Class Fatherhood in Taishō Japan." In *Public Spheres, Private Lives in Modern Japan, 1600–1950: Essays in Honor of Albert M. Craig*. Ed. Gail Lee Bernstein, Andrew Gordon, and Kate Wildman Nakai, 259–292. Cambridge, MA: Harvard University Asia Center, 2005.

Fujime Yuki. *Sei no rekishigaku: Kōshō seido, dataizai taisei kara baishun bōshihō, yūsei hogohō taisei e*. Fuji shuppan, 1998.

Fukuda Mahito. *Kekkaku no bunkashi: Kindai Nihon ni okeru yamai no imeeji*. Nagoya: Nagoya daigaku shuppankai, 1995.

Furukawa Makoto. "Dōsei 'ai' kō." *Imago* 6, no. 12 (1995): 201–207.

————. "Sexuaritii no henyō: Kindai Nihon no dōseiai o meguru mittsu no kōdo." *Nichibei josei jaanaru* 17 (1994): 29–55.

Furukawa Makoto and Akaeda Kanako, eds. *Senzenki Dōseiai kanren bunken shūsei*, vol. 3. Fuji shuppan, 2006.

Furuya Teruko. *Okamoto Kanoko: Hanayagu inochi*. Chūsekisha, 1982.

Gardner, William O. *Advertising Tower: Japanese Modernism and Modernity in the 1920s*. Cambridge, MA: Harvard University Asia Center, 2006.

————. "Mongrel Modernism: Hayashi Fumiko's *Hōrōki* and Mass Culture." *Journal of Japanese Studies* 29, no. 1 (2003): 69–101.

Gennep, Arnold van. *The Rites of Passage*. Trans. Monika B. Vizedom and Gabrielle L. Caffee. Chicago: University of Chicago Press, 1960.

Grimm, Jacob, and Wilhelm Grimm. *Deutsches Wörterbuch*. Leipzig: Verlag von S. Hirzel, 1936.

Gulick, Sidney L. *The Evolution of the Japanese*. New York: Fleming H. Revell, 1903.

Habuto Eiji. *Kyōiku shiryō: Ippan seiyokugaku*. Jitsugyō no Nippon sha, 1921.

Haeberle, Erwin J. *The Birth of Sexology: A Brief History in Documents*. Pamphlet published for the Sixth World Congress of Sexology, Washington, DC, 1983.

Hagishima Takashi. "Nihon ni okeru *Karewara* kenkyū." Supplement to *Karewara no oitachi*. Ed. Anneri Asupurundo [Anneli Asplund] and Urra Ripponen [Ulla Lipponen]. Trans. Ōkura Jun'ichirō, 49–51. Helsinki: Finrando bungaku kyōkai, 1985.

Halberstam, Judith. *Female Masculinity*. Durham, NC: Duke University Press, 1998.

Hall, Radclyffe. *The Well of Loneliness*. New York: Anchor Books, 1990.

Hane, Mikiso, trans. and ed. *Reflections on the Way to the Gallows: Rebel Women in Prewar Japan*. Berkeley: University of California Press, 1988.

Harootunian, Harry. *Overcome by Modernity: History, Culture, and Community in Interwar Japan*. Princeton, NJ: Princeton University Press, 2000.

Hasegawa Kei. "Atarashii onna no tankyū: Furoku 'Nora,' 'Magda,' 'Atarashii onna, sonota fujin mondai ni tsuite.'" In Seitō o yomu. Ed. Shin feminizumu hihyō no kai, 285–304. Gakugei shorin, 1998.

Hasegawa Shigure. "Yanagihara Akiko (Byakuren)." In *Shinpen Kindai bijinden*, vol. 2. Ed. Sugimoto Sonoko, 9–37. Iwanami shoten, 1993.

Hashimoto Noriko. *Danjo kyōgakusei no shiteki kenkyū*. Ōtsuki shoten, 1992.

Hayashi Fumiko. *Hōrōki*. Ed. Sekii Mitsuo. Vol. 12 of Shin'ei bungaku sōsho. Yumani shobō, 1998. Facsimile edition of *Hōrōki* (Kaizōsha, 1930).

Hayashi Fusao. "Nihon bungaku no fukkatsu: Okamoto Kanoko ron sono ichi." In *Okamoto Kanoko zenshū*, vol. bekkan 2, 32–38. Tōjusha, 1978.

Hayashi Mariko. *Byakuren renren*. Chūō kōronsha, 1998.

Hirabayashi Taiko. *Hirabayashi Taiko zenshū*, vol. 1. Ushio shuppan, 1979.

———. *Hirabayashi Taiko zenshū*, vol. 12. Ushio shuppan, 1997.

Hirakawa Keiko. "Kokumin kokka keiseiki ni okeru shojokai: Joshi seinendan no soshikika." In *Sei gensō o kataru*. Ed. Kondō Kazuko. Vol. 2 of Kindai o yomikaeru, 111–145. San'ichi shobō, 1998.

Hiratsuka Raichō. *Hiratsuka Raichō chosakushū*. Ed. Hiratsuka Raichō chosakushū henshū iinkai. 7 vols. Ōtsuki shoten, 1983–1984.

———. *Hiratsuka Raichō chosakushū ho: Shashin, shokan, nenpu, shosaku mokuroku*. Ed. Hiratsuka Raichō chosakushū henshū iinkai. Ōtsuki shoten, 1984.

———. *Hiratsuka Raichō jiden: Genshi josei wa taiyō de atta*. 2 vols. Ōtsuki shoten, 1971.

———. *In the Beginning, Woman Was the Sun: The Autobiography of a Japanese Feminist*. Trans. Teruko Craig. New York: Columbia University Press, 2006.

Hogan, Eleanor Joan. "When Art Does *Not* Represent Life: Nogami Yaeko and the Marriage Question." *Women's Studies: An Interdisciplinary Journal* 33, no. 4 (2004): 381–398.

Honda Masuko. *Ibunka to shite no kodomo*. Chikuma shobō, 1992.

———. *Jogakusei no keifu: Saishoku sareru Meiji*. Seidosha, 1990.

Honda Shūgo. "Miyamoto Yuriko: Sono shōgai to sakuhin." In *Miyamoto Yuriko: Sakuhin to shōgai*. Ed. Takiji Yuriko kenkyūkai, 15–45. Shin Nihon shuppansha, 1976.

Horiba Kiyoko, ed. *Seitō josei kaihō ronshū*. Iwanami shoten, 1999.

Hunter, Janet. "Gendering the Labor Market: Evidence from the Interwar Textile Industry." In *Gendering Modern Japanese History*. Ed. Barbara Molony and Kathleen Uno, 359–383. Cambridge, MA: Harvard University Asia Center, 2005.

Ichikawa Genzō. *Josei bunka kōwa*. Vol. 27 of Kindai Nihon joshi kyōiku bunkenshū. Ed. Nakajima Kuni. Nihon tosho sentaa, 1984. Facsimile edition of the 1935 book published by Meiji tosho.

Ide Fumiko. *Seitō kaisetsu, sōmokuji, sakuin*. Fuji shuppan, 1983.

Iida Yūko, ed. *Seitō to iu ba: Bungaku, jendaa, "atarashii onna."* Shinwasha, 2002.

Ikuta Hanayo. "Taberu koto to teisō to." In *Shiryō sei to ai o meguru ronsō*. Ed. Orii Miyako. Vol. 5 of Ronsō shiriizu, 13–18. Domesu shuppan, 1991.

Imada Erika. *"Shōjo" no shakaishi*. Keisō shobō, 2007.

Inagaki Kyōko. *Jogakkō to jogakusei: Kyōyō, tashinami, modan bunka*. Chūōkōron shinsha, 2007.

Inoue, Kyoko. *Individual Dignity in Modern Japanese Thought: The Evolution of the Concept of Jinkaku in Moral and Educational Discourse*. Ann Arbor: Center for Japanese Studies, University of Michigan, 2001.

Inoue, Miyako. *Vicarious Language: Gender and Linguistic Modernity in Japan*. Berkeley: University of California Press, 2006.

Inoue Teruko. "'Jogaku' shisō no keisei to tenkai: Jogaku zasshisha no shisōshiteki kenkyū." *Tokyo daigaku shinbun kenkyūjo kiyō* 17 (1968): 35–62.

Inoue Teruko, Ueno Chizuko, and Ehara Yumiko, eds. *Bosei*. Vol. 5 of Nihon no feminizumu. Iwanami shoten, 1995.

Irigaray, Luce. "Body Against Body: In Relation to the Mother." In *Sexes and Genealogies*. Trans. Gillian C. Gill, 7–21. New York: Columbia University Press, 1993.

———. "Le Corps-à-Corps avec la Mère." In *Sexes Et Parentés*, 19–33. Paris: Les Éditions de Minuit, 1987.

Ito, Ken K. *An Age of Melodrama: Family, Gender, and Social Hierarchy in the Turn-of-the-Century Japanese Novel*. Stanford, CA: Stanford University Press, 2008.

———. *Visions of Desire: Tanizaki's Fictional Worlds*. Stanford, CA: Stanford University Press, 1991.

Ito, Ruri. "The 'Modern Girl' Question in the Periphery of Empire: Colonial Modernity and Mobility Among Okinawan Women in the 1920s and 1930s." In *The Modern Girl Around the World: Consumption, Modernity, and Globalization*. Ed. The Modern Girl Around the World Research Group, 240–262. Durham, NC: Duke University Press, 2008.

Ivy, Marilyn. *Discourses of the Vanishing: Modernity, Phantasm, Japan*. Chicago: University of Chicago Press, 1995.

Iwabuchi Hiroko. *Miyamoto Yuriko: Kazoku, seiji, soshite feminizumu*. Kanrin shobō, 1996.

———. "Sexuaritii no seijigaku e no chōsen: Teisō, datai, haishō ronsō." In *Seitō o yomu*. Ed. Shin feminizumu hihyō no kai, 305–331. Gakugei shorin, 1998.

———. *"Shōjo ruten* no fōkuroa: Kojiki no imi." *Shōwa gakuen tanki daigaku kiyō* 26 (1989): 43–57.

Iwahori Yōko. "Meiji chūki ōkashugi shisō ni miru shufu risōzō no keisei: *Jogaku zasshi* no seikatsu shisō ni tsuite." In *Jendaa no Nihonshi ge: Shutai to hyōgen, shigoto to seikatsu*. Ed. Wakita Haruko and S. B. Hanley, 459–486. Tokyo daigaku shuppankai, 1995.

Iwata Nanatsu. *Bungaku to shite no* Seitō. Fuji shuppan, 2003.

Iwaya Daishi. *Bundan monoshiri chō*. Kawade shobō, 1981.

Jameson, Fredric. *The Political Unconscious: Narrative as a Socially Symbolic Act.* Ithaca, NY: Cornell University Press, 1981.

Jennison, Rebecca. "Shimizu Shikin (1868–1933)." In *The Modern Murasaki: Writing by Women of Meiji Japan.* Ed. Rebecca L. Copeland and Melek Ortabasi, 222–227. New York: Columbia University Press, 2006.

Johnston, William. *The Modern Epidemic: A History of Tuberculosis in Japan.* Cambridge, MA: Council on East Asian Studies, Harvard University, 1995.

Kamei Katsuichirō. "Kawa no yōsei." In *Okamoto Kanko zenshū*, vol. bekkan 2, 19–31. Tōjusha, 1978.

Kami Shōichirō. "Kaisetsu *Kuroshōbi* to Yoshiya Nobuko." In *Fukkokuban Kuroshōbi*, 3–14. Fuji shuppan, 2001.

———. *Nihon jidō bungaku no shisō*. Kokudosha, 1976.

Kanai Harumi. "Yoshiya Nobuko no shōjo shōsetsu ni okeru shōjozō: *Hanamonogatari* no shōjozō." *Yamaguchi kokugo kyōiku kenkyū* 5 (1995): 12–19.

Kaneko Sachiko. *Kindai Nihon joseiron no keifu*. Fuji shuppan, 1999.

Kanno Satomi. *Shōhisareru ren'ai ron: Taishō chishikijin to sei*. Seikyūsha, 2001.

Kano, Ayako. *Acting Like a Woman in Modern Japan: Theater, Gender, and Nationalism.* New York: Palgrave, 2001.

Kano Masanao. *Fujin, josei, onna: Joseishi no toi*. Iwanami shoten, 1995.

———. *Kindai Nihon shisō annai*. Iwanami shoten, 2000.

———. *Senzen "ie" no shisō*. Sōbunsha, 1983.

———. *Taishō demokurashii*. Vol. 27 of Nihon no rekishi. Ed. Kodama Kōta, Inoue Mitsusada, and Nagahara Keiji. Shōgakkan, 1976.

Kano Masanao and Horiba Kiyoko. *Takamure Itsue*. Asahi shinbunsha, 1977.

Kanō Mikiyo. "Bosei fashizumu no fūkei." In *Bosei fashizumu*. Ed. Kanō Mikiyo. Vol. 6 of Nyū feminizumu rebyū [New Feminism Review], 30–52. Gakuyō shobō, 1995.

———. "'Bosei' no tanjō to tennōsei." In *Bosei*. Ed. Inoue Teruko, Ueno Chizuko, and Ehara Yumiko. Vol. 5 of Nihon no feminizumu, 56–61. Iwanami shoten, 1995.

———. "Bosei shugi to nashonarizumu." In *"Kazoku" no shakaigaku*. Vol. 19 of Iwanami kōza gendai shakaigaku. Ed. Inoue Shun, Ueno Chizuko, and others, 189–215. Iwanami shoten, 1999.

———, ed. *Jiga no kanata e: Kindai o koeru feminizumu*. Shakai hyōron sha, 1990.

Karatani Kōjin. *Origins of Modern Japanese Literature*. Trans. and ed. Brett de Bary. Durham, NC: Duke University Press, 1993.

Katayama Hiroyuki. *Kikuchi Kan no kōseki: Shoki bungaku seishin no tenkai.* Osaka: Izumi shoin, 1997.

Kawakami Minako. "Kikuchi Kan *Shinju fujin*: Taishōki besuto seraa shōsetsu no jendaa ideorogi." In *20 seiki no besuto seraa o yomitoku: Josei, dokusha, shakai no 100 nen*. Ed. Egusa Mitsuko and Inoue Yoshie, 65–86. Gakugei shorin, 2001.

Kawamura Kunimitsu. *Otome no inori: Kindai josei imeeji no tanjō*. Kinokuniya shoten, 1993.

————. *Otome no shintai: Onna no kindai to sexuariti.* Kinokuniya shoten, 1994.

————. *Sexuariti no kindai.* Kōdansha, 1996.

————. "'Shojo' no kindai: Fūin sareta nikutai." In *Sexuariti no shakaigaku.* Vol. 10 of Iwanami kōza gendai shakaigaku. Ed. Inoue Shun, Ueno Chizuko, and others, 131–147. Iwanami shoten, 1999.

Kawasaki Kenko. *Shōjo biyori.* Seikyūsha, 1990.

Key, Ellen. *The Century of the Child.* New York: Arno Press, 1972. Facsimile edition of the 1909 book published by G. P. Putnam's Sons.

————. *Love and Marriage.* Trans. Arthur G. Chater. New York: G. P. Putnam's Sons, 1911.

————. *Ren'ai to kekkon.* 2 vols. Trans. Onodera Makoto and Onodera Yuriko. Iwanami shoten, 1975–1976.

————. *The Renaissance of Motherhood.* Trans. Anna E. B. Fries. New York: G. P. Putnam's Sons, 1914.

Kikuchi Kan [Hiroshi]. *Kikuchi Kan zenshū.* 24 vols. Takamatsu: Takamatsu-shi Kikuchi Kan kinenkan, 1993–1995.

————. *Kikuchi Kan zenshū hokan.* 5 vols. Musashino shobō, 1999–2003.

Kimura Ryōko. "Jogakusei to jokō: 'Shisō' to no deai." In *Onna no bunka.* Vol. 8 of Kindai Nihon bunkaron. Ed. Aoki Tamotsu and others, 73–95. Iwanami shoten, 2000.

Kitamura Tōkoku. *Kitamura Tōkoku shū.* Ed. Odagiri Hideo. Vol. 29 of Meiji bungaku zenshū. Chikuma shobō, 1976.

Kobayashi Tomie. *Hiratsuka Raichō.* Vol. 71 of Hito to shisō. Shimizu shoin, 2001.

Kollontay, Alexandra. *A Great Love.* Trans. Lily Lore. New York: Vanguard Press, 1929.

Komashaku Kimi. *Yoshiya Nobuko kakure feminisuto.* Libroporto, 1994.

Komatsu Satoko. "Yoshiya Nobuko *Hanamonogatari* no buntai." *Ochanomizu joshi daigaku ningen bunka kenkyū nenpō* 18 (1994): 2-48–2-54.

Komiya Tadahiko. "Kaidai." In *Okamoto Kanoko zenshū,* vol. 7, 497–518. Chikuma shobō, 1993.

Komori Yōichi. *Buntai to shite no monogatari.* Chikuma shobō, 1994.

Kōra Rumiko. *Okamoto Kanoko inochi no kaiki.* Kanrin shobō, 2004.

Kōtō jogakkō kenkyūkai, ed. *Kōtō jogakkō kenkyū: Seidoteki enkaku to setsuritsu katei.* Ōzorasha, 1994.

Kōuchi Nobuko, ed. *Shiryō bosei hogo ronsō.* Vol. 1 of Ronsō shiriizu. Domesu shuppan, 1988.

Koyama Shizuko. *Ryōsai kenbo to iu kihan.* Keisō shobō, 1992.

————. "Takamure Itsue ni okeru josei kaihō shisō no keisei to tenkai." *Shakai shisōshi kenkyū* 6 (1982): 99–115.

Koyano Atsushi. *"Otoko no koi" no bungakushi.* Asahi shinbunsha, 1997.

————. *Ren'ai no Shōwashi.* Bungei shunjū, 2005.

————. *Sei to ai no Nihongo kōza.* Chikuma shobō, 2003.

Kristeva, Julia. "Women's Time." Trans. Alice Jardine and Harry Blake. In *The Kristeva Reader.* Ed. Toril Moi, 187–213. New York: Columbia University Press, 1986.

Kubokawa Ineko. "Haha no jikaku to konran." In *Jiga no kanata e: Kindai o koeru feminizumu*. Ed. Kanō Mikiyo, 216–223. Shakai hyōronsha, 1990.

Kume Yoriko. "Esu: Yoshiya Nobuko *Hana monogatari, Yaneura no nishojo*." *Kokubungaku kaishaku to kyōzai no kenkyū* 46, no. 3 (2001): 152–154.

———. "Kōseisareru 'shōjo': Meijiki 'shōjo shōsetsu' no janru keisei." *Nihon kindai bungaku* 68 (2003): 1–15.

———. "Shōjo shōsetsu: Sai to kihan no gensetsu sōchi." In *Media, hyōshō, ideorogii: Meiji 30 nendai no bunka kenkyū*. Ed. Komori Yōichi, Kōno Kensuke, and Takahashi Osamu, 195–222. Ozawa shoten, 1997.

Kurata Hyakuzō. *Ippu ippu ka jiyū ren'ai ka*. Iwanami shoten, 1927.

———. *Kurata Hyakuzō: Hikariau inochi*. Nihon tosho sentaa, 2001.

Kuriyagawa Hakuson. *Ren'aikan oyobi zassan*. Vol. 5 of Kuriyagawa Hakuson zenshū. Kaizōsha, 1929.

Kurosawa Ariko, ed. *Ōfuku shokan Miyamoto Yuriko to Yuasa Yoshiko*. Kanrin shobō, 2008.

———. "1912 nen no Raichō to Kōkichi: 'Josei kaihō' to lezubianizumu o megutte." In *Bungaku shakai e chikyū e*. Ed. Nishida Masaru tainin taishoku kinen bunshū henshū iinkai, 309–327. San'ichi shobō, 1996.

———. "Shōjotachi no chikadōmei: Yoshiya Nobuko no *Onna no yūjō* o megutte." In *Onna to hyōgen: Feminizumu hihyō no genzai*. Ed. Mizuta Noriko. Vol. 2 of Nyū feminizumu rebyū [New Feminism Review], 81–95. Gakuyō shobō, 1991.

Lawrence, D. H. "The Woman Who Rode Away." In *The Woman Who Rode Away and Other Stories*. Ed. Dieter Mehl and Christa Jansohn, 39–71. Cambridge, UK: Cambridge University Press, 1995.

Lee, Haiyan. *Revolution of the Heart: A Genealogy of Love in China, 1900–1950*. Stanford, CA: Stanford University Press, 2007.

Levy, Indra. *Sirens of the Western Shore: The Westernesque Femme Fatale, Translation, and Vernacular Style in Modern Japanese Literature*. New York: Columbia University Press, 2006.

Lippit, Noriko Mizuta. *Reality and Fiction in Modern Japanese Literature*. White Plains: M. E. Sharpe, 1980.

Lippit, Seiji M. *Topographies of Japanese Modernism*. New York: Columbia University Press, 2002.

Loftus, Ronald P. "Female Self-Writing: Takamure Itsue's *Hi no Kuni no Onna no Nikki*." *Monumenta Nipponica* 51, no. 2 (1996): 153–170.

———. *Telling Lives: Women's Self-Writing in Modern Japan*. Honolulu: University of Hawai'i Press, 2004.

Lönnrot, Elias. *Kalevala*. 2 vols. Trans. W. F. Kirby. London: J. M. Dent and Sons, 1956.

Lowy, Dina. *The Japanese "New Woman": Images of Gender and Modernity*. New Brunswick: Rutgers University Press, 2007.

———. "Love and Marriage: Ellen Key and Hiratsuka Raichō Explore Alternatives." *Women's Studies* 33 (2004): 361–380.

Mackie, Vera. *Creating Socialist Women in Japan: Gender, Labour and Activism, 1900–1937.* Cambridge, UK: Cambridge University Press, 1997.

Maeda Ai. *Kindai dokusha no seiritsu.* Iwanami shoten, 1993.

Maeda Ai and Hasegawa Izumi, eds. *Nihon bungaku shinshi: Kindai.* Shibundō, 1990.

Mainichi shinbun hyakunenshi kankō iinkai, ed. *Mainichi shinbun hyakunenshi 1872–1972.* Mainichi shinbunsha, 1972.

Matsumura Takeo. *Finrando no shinwa densetsu.* Vol. 31 of Sekai shinwa densetsu taikei. Meicho fukyūkai, 1980.

Matsuzaki Tenmin. "Shakai kansatsu mannenhitsu." In *Ningen seken.* Ed. Minami Hiroshi, Namase Katsumi, and Sakata Minoru. Vol. 1 of Kindai shomin seikatsushi. Ed. Minami Hiroshi, 10–58. San'ichi shobō, 1991.

Meiji Taishō Shōwa shinbun kenkyūkai. *Shinbun shūsei Taishō hennenshi Taishō jūnendohan gekan.* Meiji Taishō Shōwa shinbun kenkyūkai, 1983.

Minami Hiroshi and Shakai shinri kenkyūjo, eds. *Shōwa bunka 1925–1945.* Keisō shobō, 1992.

———. *Taishō bunka.* Keisō shobō, 1977.

Miyake, Yoshiko. "Doubling Expectations: Motherhood and Women's Factory Work Under State Management in Japan in the 1930s and 1940s." In *Recreating Japanese Women, 1600–1945.* Ed. Gail Lee Bernstein, 267–295. Berkeley: University of California Press, 1991.

———. "Kindai Nihon joseishi no saisōzō no tame ni: Tekisuto no yomikae." In *Shakai no hakken.* Vol. 4 of Kanagawa daigaku hyōron sōsho. Ed. Kanagawa daigaku hyōron henshū senmon iinkai, 63–128. Ochanomizu shobō, 1994.

Miyamoto Yuriko. *Fujin to bungaku: Kindai Nihon no fujin sakka.* Vol. 43 of Sōsho Joseiron. Ed. Yamazaki Tomoko. Ōzorasha, 1997. Facsimile edition of the 1947 book published by Jitsugyō no Nihonsha.

———. *Miyamoto Yuriko zenshū.* 34 vols. Shin Nihon shuppansha, 2000–2004.

———. "Nobuko." Trans. Yukiko Tanaka. In *To Live and to Write: Selections by Japanese Women Writers 1913–1938.* Ed. Yukiko Tanaka, 47–64. Seattle, WA: Seal Press, 1987.

Miyauchi Junko. *Okamoto Kanoko: Mujō no umi e.* Musashino shobō, 1994.

Miyoshi, Masao. *Off Center: Power and Culture Relations Between Japan and the United States.* Cambridge, MA: Harvard University Press, 1991.

Mizuno Akiyoshi. *Kindai bungaku no seiritsu to Miyamoto Yuriko.* Shin Nihonsha, 1980.

Mizuta Noriko. *Hiroin kara hiirō e: Josei no jiga to hyōgen.* Tabata shoten, 1982.

Moerman, D. Max. *Localizing Paradise: Kumano Pilgrimage and the Religious Landscape of Premodern Japan.* Cambridge, MA: Harvard University Asia Center, 2005.

Molony, Barbara. "Activism Among Women in the Taishō Cotton Textile Industry." In *Recreating Japanese Women, 1600–1945.* Ed. Gail Lee Bernstein, 217–238. Berkeley: University of California Press, 1991.

Moretti, Franco. *The Way of the World: The* Bildungsroman *in European Culture.* London: Verso, 1987.

Mori, Maryellen Toman. "Cross-Cultural Patterns in the Quest Fiction of Oka-
moto Kanoko." *The Comparatist* 20 (1996): 153–178.
————. "The Quest Motif in the Fiction of Okamoto Kanoko (1889–1939)."
Ph.D. diss., Harvard University, 1988.
————. "The Splendor of Self-Exaltation: The Life and Fiction of Okamoto
Kanoko." *Monumenta Nipponica* 50, no. 1 (1995): 67–102.
Mori Yasuko. *Kokkateki bosei no kōzō.* Vol. 24 of Onna to sensō. Ed. Naka-
jima Kuni. Ōzorasha, 1992. Facsimile edition of the 1945 book published by
Dōbunkan.
Morita, James R. "Miyamoto Yuriko." In *Japanese Women Writers: A Bio-Critical
Sourcebook.* Ed. Chieko I. Mulhern, 221–228. Westport, CT: Greenwood Press,
1994.
Morita Sōhei. *Baien.* Iwanami shoten, 1940.
Muta Kazue. "'Ryōsai kenbo' shisō no omoteura: Kindai Nihon no katei bunka to
feminizumu." In *Onna no bunka.* Vol. 8 of Kindai Nihon bunkaron. Ed. Aoki
Tamotsu and others, 23–46. Iwanami shoten, 2000.
————. *Senryaku to shite no kazoku: Kindai Nihon no kokumin kokka keisei to
josei.* Shinyōsha, 1998.
Muta Kazue and Shin Chi Won. "Kindai no sexuaritii no sōzō to 'atarashii onna':
Hikaku bunseki no kokoromi." *Shisō* 886 (April 1998): 89–115.
Nagahata Michiko. *Koi no hana: Byakuren jiken.* Shinhyōron, 1982.
Nagai Kiyoko. "Tanjō shōjotachi no kaihōku: *Shōjo sekai* to 'shōjo dokushakai.'"
In *Semegiau onna to otoko: Kindai.* Ed. Okuda Akiko. Vol. 5 of Onna to otoko
no jikū: Nihon joseishi saikō. Ed. Tsurumi Kazuko, Kōno Nobuko, and others,
278–311. Fujiwara shoten, 1995.
Nagamatsu, Kyoko. "Tamura Toshiko." In *Japanese Women Writers: A Bio-Critical
Sourcebook.* Ed. Chieko I. Mulhern, 389–397. Westport, CT: Greenwood Press,
1994.
Nagami Megumi. "Futatsu no Nobuko: Gensaku to kaisaku ni tsuite." In *Miya-
moto Yuriko: Sakuhin to shōgai.* Ed. Takiji Yuriko kenkyūkai, 125–130. Shin
Nihon shuppansha, 1976.
Nagy, Margit. "Middle-Class Working Women During the Interwar Years." In
Recreating Japanese Women, 1600–1945. Ed. Gail Lee Bernstein, 199–216. Berke-
ley: University of California Press, 1991.
Nakagawa Kenjirō. *Fujin no chikara to teikoku no shōrai.* Vol. 20 of Kindai Nihon
joshi kyōiku bunkenshū. Ed. Nakajima Kuni. Nihon tosho sentaa, 1984. Facsimile
edition of the 1925 book published by Fuzanbō.
Narita Ryūichi. *Taishō demokurashii.* Vol. 4 of Shiriizu Nihon kingendaishi.
Iwanami shoten, 2007.
Neumann, Erich. *The Great Mother: An Analysis of the Archetype.* Trans. Ralph
Manheim. Princeton, NJ: Princeton University Press, 1970.
Nishikawa Yūko. *Mori no ie no miko: Takamure Itsue.* Shinchōsha, 1982.
Nishimura Hiroko, Sekiguchi Hiroko, Sugano Noriko, and Esashi Akiko, eds.
Bungaku ni miru Nihon josei no rekishi. Yoshikawa kōbunkan, 2000.

Nishimura Tōru, ed. *Orikuchi Shinobu jiten zōhoban.* Taishūkan shoten, 1998.

Nogami Yaeko. *Nogami Yaeko zenshū,* vol. 7. Iwanami shoten, 1981.

Numata Rippō. *Gendai shōjo to sono kyōiku.* Vol. 15 of Kindai Nihon joshi kyōiku bunkenshū. Ed. Nakajima Kuni. Nihon tosho sentaa, 1984. Facsimile edition of the 1916 book published by Dōbunsha.

Numazawa Kazuko. *Miyamoto Yuriko ron.* Musashino shobō, 1993.

Ogata Akiko. *Sakuhin no naka no onnatachi: Meiji, Taishō bungaku o yomu.* Domesu shuppan, 1997.

Okamoto Kanoko. "The Love of Kishimo." Trans. Charlotte Eubanks. In *Modanizumu: Modernist Fiction from Japan 1913–1938.* Ed. William J. Tyler, 453–461. Honolulu: University of Hawai'i Press, 2008.

———. "A Mother's Love." In *Rabbits, Crabs, Etc.: Stories by Japanese Women.* Trans. Phyllis Birnbaum, 49–97. Honolulu: University of Hawai'i Press, 1982.

———. *Okamoto Kanoko zenshū.* 18 vols. Tōjusha, 1974–1978.

———. *Okamoto Kanoko zenshū.* 12 vols. Chikuma shobō, 1993–1994.

———. "The Unordered World." Trans. Michiko Suzuki. *Manoa: A Pacific Journal of International Writing* 8 (Summer 1996): 158–171.

Ōmori Kaoru. *Hiratsuka Raichō no hikari to kage.* Daiichi shorin, 1997.

Ōmori Sueko. *Wakaki hi no Miyamoto Yuriko: Sōshun no sudachi zōhoban.* Shin Nihon shuppansha, 1993.

Orbaugh, Sharalyn. *Japanese Fiction of the Allied Occupation: Vision, Embodiment, Identity.* Leiden: Brill, 2007.

Orii Miyako, ed. *Shiryō sei to ai o meguru ronsō.* Vol. 5 of Ronsō shiriizu. Domesu shuppan, 1991.

Osaka Asahi shinbun. (1918, 1921).

Ōta Tenrei. *Nihon sanji chōsetsushi: Meiji, Taishō, Shōwa shoki made.* Nihon kazoku keikaku kyōkai, 1969.

Otsubo, Sumiko. "Engendering Eugenics: Feminists and Marriage Restriction Legislation in the 1920s." In *Gendering Modern Japanese History.* Ed. Barbara Molony and Kathleen Uno, 225–256. Cambridge, MA: Harvard University Asia Center, 2005.

Ōtsuka Eiji. *Shōjo minzokugaku: Seikimatsu no shinwa o tsumugu "miko no matsuei."* Kōbunsha, 1997.

Ōya Sōichi. *Ōya Sōichi senshū,* vol. 2. Chikuma shobō, 1959.

Pettis, Ruth M. "Ellis, Havelock." *glbtq: An Encyclopedia of Gay, Lesbian, Bisexual, Transgender, and Queer Culture.* http://www.glbtq.com/social-sciences/ellis_h .html.

Pflugfelder, Gregory M. *Cartographies of Desire: Male-Male Sexuality in Japanese Discourse, 1600–1950.* Berkeley: University of California Press, 1999.

———. "'S' Is for Sister: Schoolgirl Intimacy and 'Same-Sex Love' in Early Twentieth-Century Japan." In *Gendering Modern Japanese History.* Ed. Barbara Molony and Kathleen Uno, 133–190. Cambridge, MA: Harvard University Asia Center, 2005.

Raichō kenkyūkai, ed. Seitō *jinbutsu jiten: 110 nin no gunzō*. Taishūkan shoten, 2001.

Reichert, Jim. *In the Company of Men: Representations of Male-Male Sexuality in Meiji Literature*. Stanford, CA: Stanford University Press, 2006.

Rich, Adrienne. "Compulsory Heterosexuality and Lesbian Existence." *Signs: Journal of Women in Culture and Society* 5, no. 4 (1980): 631–660.

Riley, Denise. *"Am I That Name?": Feminism and the Category of "Women" in History*. Minneapolis: University of Minnesota Press, 1988.

Robertson, Jennifer. "Dying to Tell: Sexuality and Suicide in Imperial Japan." *Signs: Journal of Women in Culture and Society* 25, no. 1 (1999): 1–35.

———. *Takarazuka: Sexual Politics and Popular Culture in Modern Japan*. Berkeley: University of California Press, 1998.

———. "Yoshiya Nobuko: Out and Outspoken in Practice and Prose." In *The Human Tradition in Modern Japan*. Ed. Anne Walthall, 155–174. Wilmington, DE: Scholarly Resources, 2002.

Rodd, Laurel Rasplica. "Yosano Akiko and the Taishō Debate Over the 'New Woman.'" In *Recreating Japanese Women, 1600–1945*. Ed. Gail Lee Bernstein, 175–198. Berkeley: University of California Press, 1991.

———, ed. "Yosano Akiko (1878–1942)." *Journal of the Association of Teachers of Japanese* 25, no. 1, Special issue (1991).

Roden, Donald. "Taishō Culture and the Problem of Gender Ambivalence." In *Culture and Identity: Japanese Intellectuals During the Interwar Years*. Ed. J. Thomas Rimer, 37–55. Princeton, NJ: Princeton University Press, 1990.

Ryang, Sonia. "Love and Colonialism in Takamure Itsue's Feminism: A Postcolonial Critique." *Feminist Review* 60 (Autumn 1998): 1–32.

———. *Love in Modern Japan: Its Estrangement from Self, Sex, and Society*. London: Routledge, 2006.

Ryonrotto [Elias Lönnrot], ed. *Finrando jojishi: Karewara*. 2 vols. Trans. Koizumi Tamotsu. Iwanami shoten, 1998.

———. *Karewara*. 2 vols. Trans. Morimoto Kakutan. Kōdansha, 1983.

Saeki Junko. *"Iro" to "ai" no hikaku bunkashi*. Iwanami shoten, 1999.

Sakamoto Yukio and Iwamoto Yutaka, trans. and eds. *Hokkekyō*. 3 vols. Iwanami shoten, 2000.

Sakurai Mamoru, *Joshi kyōikushi*. Osaka: Zōshindō, 1943.

Sand, Jordan. *House and Home in Modern Japan: Architecture, Domestic Space, and Bourgeois Culture, 1880–1930*. Cambridge, MA: Harvard University Asia Center, 2003.

Sasabuchi Tomoichi, ed. *Jogaku zasshi Bungakkai shū*. Vol. 32 of Meiji bungaku zenshū. Chikuma shobō, 1977.

Sasaki Hideaki. *"Atarashii onna" no tōrai: Hiratsuka Raichō to Sōseki*. Nagoya: Nagoya daigaku shuppankai, 1994.

Sata Ineko. "Crimson." Trans. Yukiko Tanaka. In *To Live and to Write: Selections by Japanese Women Writers 1913–1938*. Ed. Yukiko Tanaka, 167–180. Seattle, WA: Seal Press, 1987.

————. *Sata Ineko shū.* Ed. Sasaki Kiichi. Vol. 39 of Nihon bungaku zenshū. Shinchōsha, 1965.

Sato, Barbara. "Commodifying and Engendering Morality: Self-Cultivation and the Construction of the 'Ideal Woman' in 1920s Mass Women's Magazines." In *Gendering Modern Japanese History.* Ed. Barbara Molony and Kathleen Uno, 99–130. Cambridge, MA: Harvard University Asia Center, 2005.

————. "Contesting Consumerisms in Mass Women's Magazines." In *The Modern Girl Around the World: Consumption, Modernity, and Globalization.* Ed. The Modern Girl Around the World Research Group, 263–287. Durham, NC: Duke University Press, 2008.

————. *The New Japanese Woman: Modernity, Media, and Women in Interwar Japan.* Durham, NC: Duke University Press, 2003.

Sato, Barbara Hamill. "Japanese Women and Modanizumu: The Emergence of a New Women's Culture in the 1920s." Ph.D. diss., Columbia University, 1994.

————. "Josei: Modanizumu to kenri ishiki." In *Shōwa bunka 1925–1945.* Ed. Minami Hiroshi and Shakai shinri kenkyūjo, 198–231. Keisō shobō, 1992.

Sawabe Hitomi. *Yuriko, dasuvidaaniya: Yuasa Yoshiko no seishun.* Gakuyō shobō, 1996.

Sawayama Mikako. "Kindai Nihon ni okeru 'bosei' no kyōchō to sono imi." In *Josei to bunka.* Ed. Ningen bunka kenkyūkai, 164–180. Hakuba shuppan, 1979.

Sedgwick, Eve Kosofsky. *Between Men: English Literature and Male Homosocial Desire.* New York: Columbia University Press, 1985.

Seitō. (1911–1916).

Seki Reiko. "Shōjō ruten ni okeru josei ichininshō." In *Shōwa bungaku ronkō: Machi to mura to.* Ed. Odagiri Susumu, 323–338. Yagi shoten, 1990.

Senda Minoru. *Meiji Taishō Shōwa Kazoku jikenroku.* Shin jinbutsu ōraisha, 2003.

Setouchi Harumi [Jakuchō]. *Kanoko ryōran.* Kōdansha, 1993.

————. *Kanoko ryōran sonogo.* Kōdansha, 1994.

————. *Seitō.* Chūō kōronsha, 1987.

Shimizu Shikin. "The Broken Ring." Trans. Rebecca Jennison. In *The Modern Murasaki: Writing by Women of Meiji Japan.* Ed. Rebecca L. Copeland and Melek Ortabasi, 232–239. New York: Columbia University Press, 2006.

————. "Koware yubiwa." In *Ai to sei no jiyū: "Ie" kara no kaihō.* Ed. Esashi Akiko, 22–33. Shakai hyōronsha, 1989.

Shin feminizumu hihyō no kai, ed. *Seitō o yomu.* Gakugei shorin, 1998.

Shōwa joshi daigaku kindai bungaku kenkyūshitsu. "Kurata Hyakuzō." In *Kindai bungaku kenkyū sōsho,* vol. 50, 289–366. Shōwa joshi daigaku kindai bunka kenkyūjo, 1980.

Sievers, Sharon L. *Flowers in Salt: The Beginnings of Feminist Consciousness in Modern Japan.* Stanford, CA: Stanford University Press, 1983.

Silverberg, Miriam. "After the Grand Tour: The Modern Girl, the New Woman, and the Colonial Maiden." In *The Modern Girl Around the World: Consumption, Modernity, and Globalization.* Ed. The Modern Girl Around the World Research Group, 354–361. Durham, NC: Duke University Press, 2008.

———. "The Café Waitress Serving Modern Japan." In *Mirror of Modernity: Invented Traditions of Modern Japan*. Ed. Stephen Vlastos, 208–225. Berkeley: University of California Press, 1998.

———. "Constructing a New Cultural History of Prewar Japan." In *Japan in the World*. Ed. Masao Miyoshi and H. D. Harootunian, 115–143. Durham, NC: Duke University Press, 1993.

———. *Erotic Grotesque Nonsense: The Mass Culture of Japanese Modern Times*. Berkeley: University of California Press, 2006.

———. "The Modern Girl as Militant." In *Recreating Japanese Women, 1600–1945*. Ed. Gail Lee Bernstein, 239–266. Berkeley: University of California Press, 1991.

Smith, Paul. *Discerning the Subject*. Minneapolis: University of Minnesota Press, 1988.

Smith-Rosenberg, Carroll. *Disorderly Conduct: Visions of Gender in Victorian America*. Oxford, UK: Oxford University Press, 1985.

Sōgō Masaaki and Hida Yoshifumi, eds. *Meiji no kotoba jiten*. Tokyodō shuppan, 1998.

Sokolsky, Anne. "Miyamoto Yuriko and Socialist Writers." In *Columbia Companion to Modern East Asian Literature*. Ed. Joshua S. Mostow, Kirk A. Denton, Bruce Fulton, and Sharalyn Orbaugh, 164–169. New York: Columbia University Press, 2003.

Sontag, Susan. *Illness As Metaphor and AIDS and Its Metaphors*. New York: Anchor Books, 1989.

Sprengnether, Madelon. *The Spectral Mother: Freud, Feminism, and Psychoanalysis*. Ithaca, NY: Cornell University Press, 1990.

Strong, Sarah M. "Passion and Patience: Aspects of Feminine Poetic Heritage in Yosano Akiko's *Midaregami* and Tawara Machi's *Salad kinenbi*." *Journal of the Association of Teachers of Japanese* 25, no. 2 (1991): 177–194.

Suga Hidemi. *Nihon kindai bungaku no "tanjō": Genbun-itchi undō to nashonari-zumu*. Ōta shuppan, 1995.

Sugisaki, Kazuko. "A Writer's Life: A Biographical Sketch." In *The House Spirit and Other Stories*, 7–30. Santa Barbara, CA: Capra Press, 1995.

Suzuki, Michiko. "Becoming a Virgin: Female Growth and Sexuality in *Yaneura no nishojo*." In *Across Time and Genre: Reading and Writing Japanese Women's Texts*. Ed. Janice Brown and Sonja Arntzen, 52–56. Edmonton: Department of East Asian Studies, University of Alberta, 2002.

———. "Kindaiteki shutai tankyū: Female Bildungsroman to shite no *Yaneura no nishojo* ni okeru sōzō to kotoba." In *Kotoba to sōzōryoku*. Ed. Kaneko Yūji and Ōnishi Naoki, 198–214. Kaibunsha, 2001.

———. "Progress and Love Marriage: Rereading Tanizaki Jun'ichirō's *Chijin no ai*." *Journal of Japanese Studies* 31, no. 2 (2005): 357–384.

———. "Writing Same-Sex Love: Sexology and Literary Representation in Yoshiya Nobuko's Early Fiction." *Journal of Asian Studies* 65, no. 3 (2006): 575–599.

Suzuki Norihisa. *Kurata Hyakuzō zōhoban*. Daimyōdō, 1980.

Suzuki Sadami. "'Taishō seimeishugi' towa nanika." In *Taishō seimeishugi to gendai*. Ed. Suzuki Sadami, 2–15. Kawade shobō shinsha, 1995.

Suzuki, Tomi. *Narrating the Self: Fictions of Japanese Modernity*. Stanford, CA: Stanford University Press, 1996.

Suzuki Yūko. *Haha to onna: Hiratsuka Raichō, Ichikawa Fusae o jiku ni*. Vol. 1 of Joseishi o hiraku. Miraisha, 1994.

Takagi Takeo, *Shinbun shōsetsushi: Taishō hen*. Kokusho kankōkai, 1976.

Takahashi Jukei. *Joji no seikyōiku*. Vol. 21 of Kindai Nihon joshi kyōiku bunkenshū. Ed. Nakajima Kuni. Nihon tosho sentaa, 1984. Facsimile edition of the 1925 book published by Meiji tosho.

Takahashi Yōji, ed. *Kindai ren'ai monogatari 50*. Vol. 26 of Bessatsu Taiyō. Heibonsha, 1997.

Takamure Itsue. *Bokeisei no kenkyū*. Dai Nihon yūbenkai kōdansha, 1954.

———. *Dai Nihon joseishi*. Kōseikaku, 1938.

———. *Takamure Itsue goroku*. Ed. Kano Masanao and Horiba Kiyoko. Iwanami shoten, 2001.

———. *Takamure Itsue ronshū*. Ed. Takamure Itsue ronshū henshū iinkai. JCA shuppan, 1979.

———. *Takamure Itsue zenshū*. 10 vols. Ed. Hashimoto Kenzō. Rironsha, 1965–1967.

———. *Waga michi wa tsune ni fubuki keri: 15 nen sensō zenya*. Ed. Nagahata Michiko. Fujiwara shoten, 1995.

———. "Yamakawa Kikue shi no ren'aikan o nanzu." In *Ai to sei no jiyū: "Ie" kara no kaihō*. Ed. Esashi Akiko, 196–203. Shakai hyōronsha, 1989.

Tamura Toshiko. "Lifeblood." Trans. Edward Fowler. In *The Modern Murasaki: Writing by Women of Meiji Japan*. Ed. Rebecca L. Copeland and Melek Ortabasi, 348–357. New York: Columbia University Press, 2006.

———. *Tamura Toshiko sakuhinshū*. 3 vols. Orijin shuppan sentaa, 1987–1988.

Tanabe Seiko. *Yume haruka Yoshiya Nobuko: Aki tomoshi tsukue no ue no ikusanga*. 2 vols. Asahi shinbunsha, 1999.

Tanaka, Yukiko, ed. *To Live and to Write: Selections by Japanese Women Writers 1913–1938*. Seattle, WA: Seal Press, 1987.

Tanizaki Jun'ichirō. *Naomi*. Trans. Anthony Chambers. New York: North Point Press, 1985.

———. *Tanizaki Jun'ichirō zenshū*, vol. 10. Chūō kōronsha, 1973.

Tatsuko. "Jogakusei dōshi no aijin: 'Omesan' no ryūkō." *Murasaki* 6, no. 10 (1910). Reprinted in *Ansorojii onna to seikatsu*. Ed. Okano Yukie. Vol. 22 of Josei no mita kindai, 69–71. Yumani shobō, 2001.

Taylor, Sandra C. *Advocate of Understanding: Sidney Gulick and the Search for Peace with Japan*. Kent, OH: Kent State University Press, 1984.

Tipton, Elise K. "The Café: Contested Space of Modernity in Interwar Japan." In *Being Modern in Japan: Culture and Society from the 1910s to the 1930s*. Ed. Elise K. Tipton and John Clark, 119–136. Honolulu: University of Hawai'i Press, 2000.

Tokutomi Roka. *Hototogisu*. Iwanami shoten, 1998.

Tokyo Asahi shinbun. (1921).

Tomida, Hiroko. *Hiratsuka Raichō and Early Japanese Feminism*. Leiden: Brill, 2004.

Tsuda Takashi. "Rekishi no naka no Nobuko: *Nobuko* no kaisaku mondai o kangaeru." *Minshu bungaku* 400 (February 1999): 156–174.

Tsurumi, E. Patricia. "Visions of Women and the New Society in Conflict: Yamakawa Kikue Versus Takamure Itsue." In *Japan's Competing Modernities: Issues in Culture and Democracy, 1900–1930*. Ed. Sharon A. Minichiello, 335–357. Honolulu: University of Hawai'i Press, 1998.

Tsushima Yūko. "Ōonna no imeeji." In *Okamoto Kanoko kenkyū: Okamoto Kanoko zenshū dai ni kan furoku* 3, 12–16. Tōjusha, 1974.

Tsutsui Kiyotada. "Kindai Nihon no kyōyō shugi to shūyō shugi." *Shisō* 812 (February 1992): 151–174.

Tsutsumi Shigehisa. "Dazai Osamu danshō." *Dazai Osamu kenkyū* 3 (1996): 80–90.

Turner, Victor. *The Ritual Process: Structure and Anti-Structure*. Ithaca, NY: Cornell University Press, 1969.

Ubukata Tomoko. "Chōkō toshite no shintai: *Nobuko* ni okeru 'shutai' no yōtai." *Kokubungaku kaishaku to kanshō* 71, no. 4 (2006): 98–105.

Ubukata Toshirō. *Meiji Taishō kenbunshi*. Chūō kōronsha, 1995.

Ueno Chizuko. "The Position of Japanese Women Reconsidered." *Current Anthropology* 28, no. 4 (1987): S75–S85.

Uno, Kathleen S. "The Death of 'Good Wife, Wise Mother'?" In *Postwar Japan as History*. Ed. Andrew Gordon, 293–322. Berkeley: University of California Press, 1993.

———. "Womanhood, War and Empire: Transmutations of 'Good Wife, Wise Mother' Before 1931." In *Gendering Modern Japanese History*. Ed. Barbara Molony and Kathleen Uno, 493–519. Cambridge: Harvard University Asia Center, 2005.

Vicinus, Martha. "Distance and Desire: English Boarding-School Friendships." *Signs: Journal of Women in Culture and Society* 9, no. 4 (1984): 600–622.

———. "'They Wonder to Which Sex I Belong': The Historical Roots of the Modern Lesbian Identity." In *Lesbian and Gay Studies Reader*. Ed. Henry Abelove, Michèle Aina Barale, and David M. Halperin, 432–454. New York: Routledge, 1993.

Wakakuwa Midori. *Sensō ga tsukuru joseizō: Dai niji sekai taisenka no Nihon josei dōin no shikakuteki propaganda*. Chikuma shobō, 1997.

Watanabe, Mieko. "*Seitō* ni okeru lezubianizumu." In *Seitō o yomu*. Ed. Shin feminizumu hihyō no kai, 269–284. Gakugei shorin, 1998.

Watanabe Shūko. *"Shōjo" zō no tanjō: Kindai Nihon ni okeru "shōjo" kihan no keisei*. Shinsensha, 2007.

Watanabe Sumiko. "Kimyō na genkaku: Nogami Yaeko *Machiko*." In *Feminizumu hihyō e no shōtai: Kindai josei bungaku o yomu*. Ed. Iwabuchi Hiroko, Kitada Sachie, and Kōra Rumiko, 201–225. Gakugei shorin, 1995.

Watanabe Yōko. *Kindai Nihon joshi shakai kyōiku seiritsu shi: Shojokai no zenkoku soshikika to shidō shisō*. Akashi shoten, 1997.

Williams, Junko Ikezu. "Visions and Narratives: Modernism in the Prose Works of Yoshiyuki Eisuke, Murayama Tomoyoshi, Yumeno Kūsaku and Okamoto Kanoko." Ph.D. diss., Ohio State University, 1998.

Wilson, Michiko Niikuni. "Misreading and Un-Reading the Male Text, Finding the Female Text: Miyamoto Yuriko's Autobiographical Fiction." *U.S.-Japan Women's Journal English Supplement* 13 (1997): 26–55.

Wōdo, Resutaa [Lester Ward] and Edowaado Kaapentaa [Edward Carpenter]. *Josei chūshinsetsu to Dōseiai*. Trans. Sakai Toshihiko and Yamakawa Kikue. Arususha, 1919.

Wu, Peichen. "Performing Gender Along the Lesbian Continuum: The Politics of Sexual Identity in the Seitō Society." *U.S.-Japan Women's Journal English Supplement* 22 (2002): 64–86.

Yagi Akiko. "Ren'ai to jiyū shakai." In *Ai to sei no jiyū: "Ie" kara no kaihō*. Ed. Esashi Akiko, 209–213. Shakai hyōronsha, 1989.

Yamaguchi Aisen. "Nihon no haha." In *Nihon no haha: Hoka ippen*. Vol. 25 of "Teikoku" sensō to bungaku. Ed. Iwabuchi Hiroko and Hasegawa Kei, 1–365. Yumani shobō, 2005. Facsimile of Yamaguchi Aisen, *Nihon no haha* (Rikugō shoin, 1943).

Yamakawa Kikue. "Keihintsuki tokkahin toshite no onna." In *Ai to sei no jiyū: "Ie" kara no kaihō*. Ed. Esashi Akiko, 190–195. Shakai hyōronsha, 1989.

Yamamoto Takeshi. *Kindai Nihon no shinbun dokushasō*. Hōsei daigaku shuppan-kyoku, 2006.

Yamashita Etsuko. *Mazakon bungakuron: Jubaku toshite no "haha."* Shinyōsha, 1991.

———. *Takamure Itsue ron: "Haha" no arukeorojii*. Kawade shobō shinsha, 1988.

Yanabu Akira. *Honyakugo seiritsu jijō*. Iwanami shoten, 1982.

Yanagihara Akiko. *Ibara no mi: Jijoden*. Shinchōsha, 1928.

Yanagita Kunio. "Finrando no gakumon." In *Yanagita Kunio zenshū*, vol. 29, 276–288. Chikuma shobō, 2002.

———. "Imo no chikara." In *Yanagita Kunio zenshū*, vol. 11, 247–261. Chikuma shobō, 1998.

Yasuda Satsuki, "Ikiru koto to teisō to: *Hankyō* 9 gatsu gō 'Taberu koto to teisō to' o yonde." In *Shiryō sei to ai o meguru ronsō*. Ed. Orii Miyako. Vol. 5 of Ronsō shiriizu, 18–24. Domesu shuppan, 1991.

Yasuda Tokutarō. "Dōseiai no rekishikan." *Chūō kōron* 50, no. 3 (1935): 146–152.

Yoneda Sayoko. *Hiratsuka Raichō: Kindai Nihon no demokurashii to jendaa*. Yoshikawa kōbunkan, 2002.

Yoneda Sayoko and Ikeda Emiko, eds. *Seitō o manabu hito no tame ni*. Kyoto: Sekai shisōsha, 1999.

Yosano Akiko. "Midaregami." In *Ai to sei no jiyū: "Ie" kara no kaihō*. Ed. Esashi Akiko, 52–72. Shakai hyōronsha, 1989.

———. *Yosano Akiko hyōron chosakushū*. 22 vols. Ryūkei shosha, 2001–2002.

Yoshida Kazuhiko. "The Enlightenment of the Dragon King's Daughter in the Lotus Sutra." Trans. and adapt. Margaret H. Childs. In *Engendering Faith: Women and Buddhism in Premodern Japan*. Ed. Barbara Ruch, 297–324. Ann Arbor: Center for Japanese Studies, University of Michigan, 2002.

Yoshikawa Toyoko. "'Josei dōseiai' toiu 'yamai' to jendaa." In *Jendaa no Nihon kindai bungaku*. Ed. Nakayama Kazuko, Egusa Mitsuko and Fujimori Kiyoshi, 111–117. Kanrin shobō, 1998.

———. "Kindai Nihon no 'lezubianizumu': 1910 nendai no shōsetsu ni egakareta lezubiantachi." In *Sei gensō o kataru*. Ed. Kondō Kazuko. Vol. 2 of Kindai o yomikaeru, 75–110. San'ichi shobō, 1998.

———. "*Ren'ai to kekkon* (Ellen Key) to sexorojii." In *Seitō o yomu*. Ed. Shin feminizumu hihyō no kai, 243–268. Gakugei shorin, 1998.

———. "*Seitō* kara 'taishū shōsetsu' sakka e no michi: Yoshiya Nobuko *Yaneura no nishojo*." In *Feminizumu hihyō e no shōtai: Kindai josei bungaku o yomu*. Ed. Iwabuchi Hiroko, Kitada Sachie, and Kōra Rumiko, 121–147. Gakugei shorin, 1995.

Yoshitake Teruko. *Nyonin Yoshiya Nobuko*. Bungei shunjū, 1982.

Yoshiya Nobuko. *Akogare shiru koro*. Kōransha, 1923.

———. *Fukkokuban Kuroshōbi*. Fuji shuppan, 2001. Reissued facsimile collected edition of *Kuroshōbi* (January-August 1925) with critical introduction and table of contents.

———. *Mittsu no hana*. Kateisha, 1947.

———. *Safuran*. Hōbunkan, 1928.

———. *Shojo dokuhon*. Vol. 35 of Sōsho Joseiron. Ed. Yamazaki Tomoko. Ōzorasha, 1997. Facsimile edition of the 1936 book published by Kenbunsha.

———. *Yoshiya Nobuko zenshū*. 12 vols. Asahi shinbunsha, 1975–1976.

———. *Yoshiya Nobuko zenshū geppō* 6 and 7. Shinchōsha, 1935.

Yuasa Yoshiko, ed. *Yuriko no tegami*. Chikuma shobō, 1978.

Index

"Ānanda and the witch's daughter"
(Anan to jujutsushi no musume)
(Okamoto), 190*n*20
Abnormal sexuality, 24–31, 35, 47–48,
55–61, 102, 164*n*13, 173*n*64. *See also*
Inversion, sexual; *Ome*
"About Survival and Chastity" (Taberu
koto to teisō to) (Ikuta), 52
After Kanoko in Bloom (Kanoko ryōran
sonogo) (Setouchi), 119
Aijō (love), 36, 168*n*12
Ai (love), 9, 157*n*24. *See also* Het-
erosexual love; Love; Romantic
friendship
"Akiko, Queen of Tsukushi" (Tsukushi
no joō Akiko) (newspaper series),
72–73
Akirame (Giving up) (Tamura), 29,
165*n*28
Akutagawa Ryūnosuke, 118
Alcott, Louisa May, 44
Altruism, 87, 109. *See also* Selflessness;
Self-sacrifice
"Anan to jujutsushi no musume"
(Ānanda and the witch's daughter)
(Okamoto), 190*n*20
Anarchism, 111
Arai Tomiyo, 126
Araki Shigeru, 78, 80
Arashi no bara (The rose in the storm)
(Yoshiya), 60–62
Ariyoshi Sawako: *Ki no kawa* (The

River Ki), 144; *Kōkotsu no hito* (The
Twilight Years), 144
Arranged marriage (*miai*), 65–68, 70,
74, 75, 93
"Aru orokashiki mono no hanashi"
(A tale of a certain foolish person)
(Yoshiya), 54–59
Association to Support the Works of
Takamure Itsue (Takamure Itsue
chosaku kōenkai), 137
Atarashii onna (New Woman/New
Women), 6, 11, 12, 89, 159*n*35
Athletics, 130–31
Autobiography: I-novels, 2, 15, 43,
59–60, 75–76, 79–81, 116, 119; traces
of, in fiction, 15–16, 59–60, 75–76,
78–81, 117, 119, 122, 123, 136, 169*n*27

Baba Kochō, 19
Bachofen, Johann Jakob, 139, 194*n*48;
Mutterrecht (Mother right), 136; *Bo-
kenron* (The theory of mother right),
136–37
Badinter, Elisabeth, 107–8
Baien (Cinder and smoke) (Morita), 12
Becoming, 4–8, 41, 129–41, 149.
See also Development; Linearity;
Maturity; Modernity; Progress; Self-
development
Becoming-one ideology (*ittai shugi*), 111
Before the Dawn (Yoakemae) (Shi-
mazaki), 124

Beggar, 123, 125–29, 135, 138, 139, 192*n*29

Bergson, Henri, 191*n*20

Bhabha, Homi, 39

Bibunchō (ornate style), 39

Bildungsroman, 2, 123

Birth control, 87–88

Black Rose (Kuroshōbi) (magazine), 54–55, 59–60, 72, 173*n*59

Bluestocking (Seitō) (journal): feminism and, 10–11; Hiratsuka and, 5, 7, 8, 10–13, 69–70, 92, 109, 156*n*19; Miyamoto and, 103–4; Nogami and, 77, 178*n*44; Okamoto and, 19, 116–18, 120, 188*n*2; and same-sex love, 12, 29–32, 165*n*28; and sexology, 26; Tamura and, 29, 165*n*28; and Virginity/Chastity Debates, 52; writings in, 5, 8, 10–14, 16, 17, 19, 26, 29–31, 52–53, 69–70, 77, 103–4, 109, 117, 118, 120, 160*n*43, 164*n*15, 173*n*64, 188*n*2; Yosano and, 158*n*32; Yoshiya and, 17, 32–33, 166*n*41

Bluestocking Society (Seitōsha), 10, 12, 18, 19, 29–30, 32, 50, 52, 89, 92, 103, 110, 117, 118, 120, 159*n*35

Bokeisei no kenkyū (The study of the matrilineal system) (Takamure), 137, 142

Boken (mother right), 136–37. *See also* Matrilineality*Boken* (mothers' rights), 109, 137

Bokenron (The theory of mother right) (Bachofen), 136–37

Boken shugi (mothers' rights-ism), 186*n*16

Bolshevism, 101. *See also* Marxism; Proletarian movement; Socialism

Bosei. See Motherhood

Boseiai. See Maternal love

Boseiga (maternal self), 114

Bosei no fukkō (The renaissance of motherhood) (Key), 78, 109, 178*n*46

Bosei shugi (motherhood-ism), 186*n*16

"Boshi jojō" (Mother and child) (Okamoto), 119–22

Boston marriage, 30

Botticelli, Sandro, "Birth of Venus," 134

Bourdaghs, Michael, 98

"The Broken Ring" (Koware yubiwa) (Shimizu), 10

Browning, Robert, 109

Buddhism, 15, 118, 123, 125, 140, 190*n*20

Bungakkai. See Literary World

Burnett, Frances Hodgson, *A Little Princess*, 44, 170*n*34

"Burning Flowers" (Moyuru hana) (Yoshiya), 73

Butler, Judith, 58

Byakuren incident, 68, 72–75, 77–78

Byakuren (writing name of Yanagihara Akiko), 72–75, 77–78; *Fumie* (Icon), 72

Café waitress (*jokyū*), 6

Carpenter, Edward, 71; *The Intermediate Sex*, 26, 37, 57, 164*n*16

Castle, Terry, 38

Central Review (Chūō Kōron) (magazine), 79

Character (*jinkaku*), 37, 72, 75

Chastity Debates (*teisō ronsō*), 52–53

Chijin no ai (A fool's love) (Tanizaki), 86, 89–90

China War, 114, 115, 121

Chi no hate made (To the ends of the earth) (Yoshiya), 43

Christianity: and love, 3, 8–9, 14, 66; and marriage, 66; and same-sex love, 46–47

Chronicles of Japan (Nihon shoki), 141

Chūjō Yuriko. *See* Miyamoto Yuriko

Chūō Kōron (Central review) (magazine), 79

Cinder and Smoke (Baien) (Morita), 12

Civil Code (1898), 6

Civilization, origins of, 136–37

Collected Works of Kuriyagawa Haku-son (Kuriyagawa Hakuson zenshū) (Kuriyagawa), 70–71

Collected Works of Yoshiyo Nobuko (Yoshiya Nobuko zenshū) (Yoshiya), 54

Communist Party, 79

Confucianism, 3, 9

"The Crane Is Sick" (Tsuru wa yamiki) (Okamoto), 118

Creation of Love (Ren'ai sōsei) (Taka-mure), 111–12, 142, 186*n*18, 186*n*20

Crimson (Kurenai) (Sata), 76

Critical mythopoesis, 130, 134, 142

The Cuckoo (Hototogisu) (Tokutomi), 96–97

Culturalism (*kyōyō shugi*), 7, 72

Culture (*kyōyō*), 72

Dai Nihon kokubō fujinkai (Greater Japan National Defense Women's Association), 114, 139

Dazai Osamu, 124

Deleuze, Gilles, 41

Democracy, 7, 71

Development: gendered childhood, 44; of human civilization, 136–37; of identity, 3; love and, 3–4, 7–8, 11–14, 109–10, 129–37, 190*n*20; national, 1–2, 71, 112, 137–38, 142, 182*n*38; same-sex love and, 3, 24, 27, 30–32, 35–39, 42, 48–51, 54, 165*n*22; wom-en's, 3, 5–8, 13–14, 27, 30–32, 35–39, 42–45, 48–54, 60–62, 81–82, 86–88, 103, 109, 122, 129–35, 142, 172*n*46. *See also* Becoming; Evolution; Linearity; Maturity; Progress; Self-development

"Diary" (Nikki) (Tamura), 171*n*42

Diary of a Vagabond (Hōrōki) (Hayashi), 125–27

Disease, 91, 94–99

"Disillusioned Poets and Women" (Ensei shika to josei) (Kitamura), 9–11, 67

Divorce, 91–94, 182*n*38

Dōhyō (Signpost) (Miyamoto), 80, 82, 102–3, 183*n*51, 184*n*59

Dōseiai. See Same-sex love

"Dōsei o aisuru saiwai" (The happi-ness of loving one of the same sex) (Yoshiya), 36–37

"Dokuritsu suru ni tsuite ryōshin ni" (To my parents on becoming inde-pendent) (Hiratsuka), 8, 69

Dollase, Hiromi Tsuchiya, 40

A Doll's House (Ibsen), 89, 128

Élan vital (life force), 191*n*20

Ellis, Havelock, 57; "Joseikan no dōsei ren'ai" (Same-sex love between women), 30–31, 164*n*15, 173*n*64; "Sexual Inversion in Women," 30, 56, 164*n*15, 173*n*64; *Studies in the Psychology of Sex*, 26, 30, 164*n*13

Engels, Frederick, *The Origin of the Family, Private Property, and the State*, 136, 193*n*47

"Ensei shika to josei" (Disillusioned poets and women) (Kitamura), 9–11, 67

Equality: gender, 14, 30, 72, 80, 111; in marriage, 67–69, 71, 89–90

Establish the self, rise in the world (*ris-shin shusse*), 130

Esu (female same-sex love), 24, 163*n*5

Eternal mother, 143, 195*n*62. *See also* Great Mother; *Ur Mutter*

Eugenics, 130, 183*n*46

Evolution, 1–3, 5, 7, 37, 69, 71–72, 110, 112–13, 132, 138, 149, 182*n*38. *See also* Development; Linearity; Progress

The Evolution of the Japanese (Gulick), 1–2

Factory worker (*jokō*), 6

Faderman, Lillian, 56

Father right, 136. *See also* Patrilineality

Felski, Rita, 12

Female Friendship Continued (Zoku onna no yūjō) (Yoshiya), 60

Female Friendship (Onna no yūjō) (Yoshiya), 60

"Female friends" (Onna tomodachi) (Kawada), 29

Feminism: *Bluestocking* and, 10–11; and identity, 3; and love, 3; and love marriage ideology, 68–70; and maternal love, 108–15; and motherhood, 109–10, 112–13, 122, 143; nationalism and, 114, 143; and sexual difference, 109, 111; Takamure's notions of, 111; women writers and, 5, 10–13, 15–18, 26, 32, 34, 43, 68, 79, 80, 94, 100, 104, 110–15, 116, 119, 122, 137–38, 147–48, 169*n*27, 183*n*46, 186*n*16, 189*n*7

Fifteen-Year War, 79, 113, 115

Finland, 129, 133–34

"The Flocks of the Poor" (Mazushiki hitobito no mure) (Miyamoto), 79

Flower Tales (Hanamonogatari) (Yoshiya), 17, 33–42, 167*n*4

A Fool's Love (Chijin no ai) (Tanizaki), 86, 89–90

Foucault, Michel, 7

Frederick, Sarah, 170*n*37

Free love (*jiyū ren'ai*), 92

Free sex, 100

Freud, Sigmund, 136, 165*n*22, 194*n*48

"A Friend for Ten Days" (Junjitsu no tomo) (Sugawara), 29

Friend of the Housewife (Shufu no tomo) (magazine), 53, 61, 114

Friendships: female adult, 60–62; romantic, 24–28, 29, 35–39, 42. *See also* Sisterhood

"From the Round Window" (Marumado yori) (Hiratsuka), 30

Fuess, Harald, 67–68, 94, 182*n*38

Fujin sensen (Women's battlefront) (journal), 111

Fujin to bungaku (Women and literature) (Miyamoto), 102, 143

Fujo shinbun (Women's newspaper), 24

Fumie (Icon) (Byakuren), 72

Furukawa Makoto, 157*n*29

Furuya Teruko, 191*n*20

Futatsu no niwa (The two gardens) (Miyamoto), 80, 82, 102–3, 184*n*59

Gardner, William O., 126

Genbun itchi (unification of written and spoken language), 7, 39–41

Gender: childhood development and, 44; and equality, 14, 30, 72, 80, 100–4; language and, 58; same-sex love and, 157*n*29; sexual difference, 14, 37, 67, 109, 111, 160*n*49

General Sexology (Ippan seiyokugaku) (Habuto), 27, 165*n*21

"Genshi josei wa taiyō de atta" (In the beginning, woman was the sun) (Hiratsuka), 103–4

Girls' culture (*shōjo bunka*), 16, 32–33, 44

Girls' fiction (*shōjo shōsetsu*), 15, 32–35, 43, 44, 47

Girls' Graphic (Shōjo gahō) (magazine), 33, 35

Girls' magazines (*shōjo zasshi*), 26, 32–33, 39, 44

Girls' Realm (Shōjokai) (magazine), 32

Girls (*shōjo*): characteristics of, 44–45; development of, 27, 30–32, 35–39, 42–45, 50–51, 172*n*46; same-sex love among, 23–24, 26–28, 32–33, 35–45, 162*n*5. *See also* Girls' culture; Girls' fiction; Girls' magazines; Girls' writing style; Modern Girl; Schoolgirl

Girls' writing style, 39–43, 45–47, 54

Giving Up (Akirame) (Tamura), 29, 165*n*28

Good Wife, Wise Mother (*ryōsai kenbo*), 3, 121, 155*n*12, 168*n*12

Greater Japan National Defense Women's Association (Dai Nihon kokubō fujinkai), 114, 139

Great Mother, 136, 194*n*48. *See also* Eternal mother; *Ur Mutter*

Gulick, Sidney, 1–2, 9; *The Evolution of the Japanese*, 1

Habuto Eiji, 26, 165*n*21; *Hentai seiyoku ron* (Psychology of abnormal sexual desires), 164*n*13; *Ippan seiyokugaku* (General sexology), 27, 165*n*21

Hall, Radclyffe, *The Well of Loneliness*, 56, 57

"Hamanadeshiko" (Japanese pink) (Yoshiya), 39–40

Hanamonogatari (Flower tales) (Yoshiya), 17, 33–42, 167*n*4

"The Happiness of Loving One of the Same Sex" (Dōsei o aisuru saiwai) (Yoshiya), 36–37

Harootunian, H. D., 154*n*11

Hayashi Fumiko, *Hōrōki* (Diary of a Vagabond), 125–27, 191*n*23

Hayashi Fusao, 119, 143

Health, 48, 130. *See also* Disease

Hentai seiyoku ron (Psychology of abnormal sexual desires) (Habuto and Sawada), 164*n*13

"Her Life" (Kanojo no seikatsu) (Tamura), 76

Heterosexual love (*ai*): critiques of, 38–39, 46–47, 50–51, 53, 61–62; etymology of, 9, 157*n*27; Hiratsuka and, 8, 11–12, 31; modernity and, 2–4 (*see also* Modern love ideology); as normative, 3, 27, 30–32, 37, 56–57; women's development and, 3–4, 8, 13. *See also* Ai (love); Love; Romantic love

Higher Girls' School Act (1899), 23

Hikagejaya incident, 92

Hirabayashi Taiko, "Nagesuteyo!" (Throw them away!), 76

Hiratsuka Raichō: and birth control, 87; and *Bluestocking*, 5, 7, 8, 10–13, 69–70, 92, 109, 156*n*19; on Byakuren

incident, 74–75; characteristics of, 50, 171*n*42; and childbirth, 87; and divorce, 92–93; "Dokuritsu suru ni tsuite ryōshin ni" (To my parents on becoming independent), 8, 69; and eugenics, 183*n*46; "Genshi josei wa taiyō de atta" (In the beginning, woman was the sun), 11, 103–4, 158*n*33; "Ichinenkan" (One year), 30; and Key, 13–14, 31, 69, 78, 178*n*46; and Kuriyagawa, 71–72, 74–75; and love, 8, 11–14, 30–31, 68–70, 92–93, 100; and love marriage, 12, 69–70, 74–75; "Marumado yori" (From the round window), 30; and maternal love, 12, 87, 104, 108–11, 113, 187*n*33; Miyamoto and, 18, 78; and modern love ideology, 31; and motherhood, 78, 108–14; and nationalism, 12, 187*n*33; Okamoto and, 19, 116–17; preface to "Joseikan no dōsei ren'ai" (Same-sex love between women) (Ellis), written by, 26, 30–31; and same-sex love, 12, 30–31; as schoolgirl, 171*n*41; and sexology, 26, 30–31; significance of, 11–12; and Takamure, 110–11, 126, 137; and Virginity/Chastity Debates, 53; on women's development, 5–8; "Yo no fujintachi e" (To the Women of the World), 69; Yoshiya and, 17, 32, 50, 166*n*41, 171*n*41

Hōrōki (Diary of a Vagabond) (Hayashi), 125–27

Hōrōsha no shi (Wanderer's poems) (Takamure), 126

Home (*katei*), 66, 68

Homosexuality. *See* Same-sex love

Horiba Kiyoko, 186*n*18, 186*n*20

Horikiri Shigeo, 189*n*9

Hori Yasuko, 92

Hototogisu (The cuckoo) (Tokutomi), 96–97

Housewife (*shufu*), 6

Hozumi Nobushige, 182*n*38
The Husband's Chastity (Otto no teisō) (Yoshiya), 116

Ibsen, Henrik, *A Doll's House*, 89, 128
Ichikawa Fusae, 122, 183*n*46
Ichikawa Genzō, 172*n*46
"Ichinenkan" (One year) (Hiratsuka), 30
Icon (Fumie) (Byakuren), 72
Identity: constructing, 7–8, 16, 17; as developmental process, 3; innate/natural, 57, 112; maternal love/motherhood and, 18–19, 87, 104, 107–10, 112–17, 122, 134, 135–59, 143–45; modernity and, 2, 5–6; national, 18–19, 115, 127–35; same-sex love and, 31, 32, 35, 39, 48, 49, 51, 60, 61; sexual, 25, 31, 57, 102; true, 14, 51, 82, 123, 126, 128–29, 133, 141; virginity and, 52–53; as wife, 82, 94, 101. *See also* Self and selfhood; *specific female identities such as* Girls
Ideologemes, 8
"Iede no shi" (Poem of running away) (Takamure), 126
Ikuta Hanayo, 188*n*2; "Taberu koto to teisō to" (About survival and chastity), 52
Illness. *See* Disease
"Imo no chikara" (Power of women) (Yanagita), 128
I-novels (*watakushi shōsetsu; shishōsetsu*), 2, 15, 43, 59–60, 75–76, 79–81, 116, 119, 122
"The Institution of Love Marriage" (Ren'ai kekkon seido) (Kikuchi), 101
The Intermediate Sex (Carpenter), 26, 37, 57, 164*n*16
"In the Beginning, Woman Was the Sun" (Genshi josei wa taiyō de atta) (Hiratsuka), 11, 103–4, 158*n*33
Inversion, sexual, 24–25, 27, 31, 56–59, 173*n*64. *See also* Abnormal sexuality

Ippan seiyokugaku (General sexology) (Habuto), 27, 165*n*21
Iro (love), 8, 157*n*24
Ishizaka Minako, 67
Itō Den'emon, 72–75, 78
Itō Noe, 92
Ittai shugi (becoming-one ideology), 111
Iwabuchi Hiroko, 180*n*7
Iwamoto Yoshiharu, 9, 66, 69, 161*n*54, 175*n*2; "Kon'in ron" (Theories of marriage), 66, 175*n*2
Iwaya Daishi, 169*n*23

Jameson, Fredric, 7–8
The Japanese Mother (Nihon no haha) (Yamaguchi), 114, 115
"Japanese Pink" (Hamanadeshiko) (Yoshiya), 39–40
Japan Romantic School (*Nihon roman ha*), 15, 119, 143
Japan Women's University, 23, 29
Jiga. See Self and selfhood
Jinkaku (character), 37, 72, 75
Jinkaku shugi (personalism), 7
Jiyū ren'ai (free love), 92
Jōshi (love suicide), 24–25, 28, 75
Jogakusei (schoolgirl), 23–24, 155*n*12, 162*n*5. *See also* Girls
Jogaku zasshi (Journal of female learning), 9, 10, 66, 175*n*2
Joken (women's rights), 109, 186*n*16
Jokō (factory worker), 6
Jokyū (café waitress), 6
"Joseikan no dōsei ren'ai" (Same-sex love between women) (Ellis), 30–31, 164*n*15, 173*n*64
Josei shugi (womanism), 111, 186*n*16
Josei (woman/female), 114*Journal of Female Learning* (Jogaku zasshi), 9, 10, 66, 175*n*2
Junbungaku (pure literature), 60, 80, 116, 122
Jung, C. G., 136, 194*n*48

"Junjitsu no tomo" (A friend for ten days) (Sugawara), 29

Junrei pilgrimage, 126–27

Kaiki. See Return (*kaiki/kangen*)

Kaizō (re-creation), 130–31

Kaizō (Re-creation) (journal), 80

Kaizōsha, 71, 80, 87, 122

Kalevala, 129, 133–34

Kamei Katsuichirō, 119

Kamichika Ichiko, 92

Kangen. See Return (*kaiki/kangen*)

Kannon (Goddess of Mercy), 119, 188n5

Kanō Mikiyo, 108, 112

"Kanojo no seikatsu" (Her life) (Tamura), 76

Kanoko in Bloom (Kanoko ryōran) (Setouchi), 119

Kanoko ryōran (Kanoko in bloom) (Setouchi), 119

Kanoko ryōran sonogo (After Kanoko in bloom) (Setouchi), 119

Kano Masanao, 71, 113, 186n18, 186n20

Karatani Kōjin, 7, 156n24

Karoki netami (Light jealousy) (Okamoto), 118

Katei (home), 66, 68

Kawada Yoshi, "Onna tomodachi" (Female friends), 29

Kawamura Kunimitsu, 52, 187n33

Key, Ellen, 18, 191n20; *Bosei no fukkō* (The renaissance of motherhood), 78, 109, 178n46; on divorce, 93; Hiratsuka and, 13–14, 31, 69, 78, 178n46; on love, 13–14, 31; *Love and Marriage* (Ren'ai to kekkon), 13–14, 17, 31, 32, 69, 93, 109, 160n43; on love marriage, 68–71; and maternal love, 87, 108–9; Miyamoto and, 18, 78; and modern love ideology, 13–14; and motherhood, 78, 108–9; and progress, 14, 112; Takamure on, 111; Yoshiya and, 32, 72

"Kibara" (Yellow rose) (Yoshiya), 40–42, 55

Kigi shinryoku (The new green of the trees) (Sata), 116

Kikuchi Kan (Hiroshi): on love marriage, 100–1; "Ren'ai kekkon seido" (The institution of love marriage), 101; *Ren'ai to kekkon no sho* (Writings about love and marriage), 100; *Shinju fujin* (Madame Pearl), 73

Kikuchi Yukie, 169n27

Kindai no chōkoku (Overcoming modernity) symposium, 119

Kindai no ren'ai kan (Views of love in the modern era) (Kuriyagawa), 17, 68, 70–71, 74, 89–90, 93, 110

Kindai ren'ai ideorogii. See Modern love ideology

Ki no kawa (The River Ki) (Ariyoshi), 144

"Kishimo no ai" (Love of Hārītī) (Okamoto), 190n20

Kitamura Tōkoku, "Ensei shika to josei" (Disillusioned poets and women), 9–11, 67

Kōkotsu no hito (The Twilight Years) (Ariyoshi), 144

Kōra Rumiko, 121, 143, 190n14

Kobayashi Hideo, 120

Koi (love), 8, 156n24. *See also* Ai; Heterosexual love; Love; Romantic love

Kojiki (Records of Ancient Matters), 112, 141

Kokkateki bosei (motherhood-in-the-interest-of-the-state), 114

Kokumin seishin sōdōin (National Spiritual Mobilization), 114

Kokumin shinbun (People's newspaper), 96

Kollontai, Alexandra, "The Loves of Three Generations" (Sandai no koi), 100

"Koware yubiwa" (The broken ring) (Shimizu), 10

Krafft-Ebing, Richard von, *Psycho-pathia Sexualis*, 26, 57–58, 164*n*13
Kristeva, Julia, 40
Kubokawa Ineko. *See* Sata Ineko
Kurata Hyakuzō, 93
Kurenai (Crimson) (Sata), 76
Kuriyagawa Hakuson, 70–72, 74–76, 78, 100, 109–10; *Kindai no ren'ai kan* (Views of love in the modern era), 17, 68, 70–71, 74, 89–90, 93, 110; *Kuriyagawa Hakuson zenshū (Collected works of Kuriyagawa Hakuson)*, 70–71
Kurosawa Ariko, 31
Kuroshōbi (magazine). *See Black Rose*
Kyōyō (culture), 72
Kyōyō shugi (culturalism), 7, 72

Language: gender and, 58; unification of written and spoken, 7, 39–41
Lawrence, D. H., "The Woman Who Rode Away," 128
Lesbianism. *See* Same-sex love
Liberal humanism, 7, 18, 68
Light Jealousy (Karoki netami) (Okamoto), 118
Linearity, of time/development/modernity, 18, 123, 125, 127, 138, 140–42, 147, 149. *See also* Becoming; Development; Evolution; Modernity
Lippit, Seiji M., 126
Literary World (Bungakkai) (journal), 118–20, 122
Literature. *See* Women's literature
A Little Princess (Burnett), 44, 170*n*34
Lönnrot, Elias, 133. *See also Kalevala*
Lotus Sutra, 140
Love: Christianity and, 3, 8–9, 14, 66; concepts of, 8–9; as cultural concept, 7–8; and development, 3–4, 7–8, 11–14, 109–10, 129–37, 190*n*20; free, 92; history of, 8–10, 66–67; ideals of, 3, 8–9, 14, 67; men and, 10–12, 14, 37, 67, 160*n*49; moder-

nity and, 2–4 (*see also* Modern love ideology); new Western concept of, 3, 8–9; pilgrim's, 126; and progress, 14; self-, 123, 133, 140; selfhood and, 7–8, 9–10; spiritual and sexual, 13, 14, 37, 43, 48–49, 53, 69, 71, 83–84, 111. *See also* Heterosexual love; Love marriage; Maternal love; Romantic love; Same-sex love
Love and Marriage (Ren'ai to kekkon) (Key), 13–14, 17, 31, 69, 93, 109, 160*n*43
Love marriage ideology (*ren'ai kekkon ideorogii*): and Byakuren incident, 72–75; culturalism movement and, 72; definitions of, 17, 65, 175*n*8, 180*n*7; difference between modern love ideology and, 160*n*41; difference between *katei* ideology and, 66, 68–69; emergence of, 68; Hiratsuka and Key and, 68–70; Kuriyagawa and, 70–72; self-development and, 72; women writers and, 75–78. *See also* Love marriage; Modern love ideology
Love marriage (*ren'ai kekkon*): benefits of, 66, 71, 100; as bourgeois, 101; Christianity on, 66; critiques of and questions about, 86–104; definition and overview of, 17, 65–68; divorce and, 92–93; equality in, 68–69, 71, 89–90; Hiratsuka and, 12, 69–70, 74–75; in Key's thought, 68–71; Kikuchi's ideas about, 100–1; Kurata's view on, 93; in Meiji period, 66–67; in Miyamoto's works, 16, 18, 77–104; Okamoto and, 120; parodied in Tanizaki's *A Fool's Love*, 86, 89–90; and progress, 69–72, 82, 85–86, 93–95, 102; public opinion on, 75; and racial improvement, 97; self-development and, 68, 72, 74–75, 82, 84–86, 89–91, 94–99; women's development and, 3; women writers

and, 75–78. *See also* Love marriage
ideology
"Love of Hārītī" (Kishimo no ai)
(Okamoto), 190n20
"The Loves of Three Generations"
(Sandai no koi) (Kollontai), 100
Love suicide (*shinjū, jōshi*), 24–25, 28,
75
Love treatises, 3, 17, 68, 70–72, 93, 100
Lung disease, 96. *See also* Tuberculosis

Machiko (Nogami), 77
Madame Pearl (Shinju fujin) (Ki-
kuchi), 73
Man'yōshū (Ten Thousand Leaves), 112
Marebito (visiting gods), 127, 141
Marriage: arranged, 65–68, 70, 75, 77,
86, 93, 96, 102, 148, 175n7; Christianity on, 66; critiques of, 14, 30, 53,
61, 67, 69, 74–75, 101. *See also* Love
marriage; Love marriage ideology
"Marumado yori" (From the round
window) (Hiratsuka), 30
Marxism, 76, 101, 103–4, 136. *See also*
Bolshevism; Proletarian movement;
Socialism
Maternal love (*boseiai*): critique of,
133–44; etymology of, 9, 108; family bonding through, 113; feminism
and, 108–15; Hiratsuka and, 12, 87,
104, 108–11, 113, 187n33; historical
construction of, 107–8; identity
and, 112–17; Key and, 87, 108–9;
in modern love ideology, 109–10,
113; nationalism and, 113–15; in
Okamoto's works, 16, 18–19, 116–45;
and origins of civilization, 136–37;
overview of, 18, 108; and racial improvement, 110; and romantic love,
112, 116, 187n22; self-development
and, 109–10, 112–13, 123, 133–35; as
self-love, 123, 133, 140; Takamure
and, 110, 112–13, 142; women's development and, 3; women writers

and, 115–16. *See also* Motherhood;
Ur Mutter
Maternal self (*boseiga*), 114
Matriarchy, 136–38, 194n48
Matrilineality, 136–37, 142, 194n48
Matsuzaki Tenmin, 32
Maturity, 19, 27, 31, 39, 43, 47, 52, 54,
57, 109, 147, 155n14. *See also* Devel-
opment; Progress; Self-development
"Mazushiki hitobito no mure" (The
flocks of the poor) (Miyamoto), 79
Meiji period, 4, 8, 10, 23, 35, 51, 66–67,
129, 130–32, 148
Men: and love, 10, 14, 67, 160n49; as
norm, 5; patriarchy, 53, 55, 113, 121,
138
Miai (arranged marriage), 65–68, 70,
75, 93
Midaregami (Tangled hair) (Yosano), 10
Minzokugaku (native ethnology/folk-
lore), 127, 130, 134
Miyamoto Kenji, 79, 179n6
Miyamoto Yuriko: autobiographical
traces of, 78–80, 81; background
on, 15, 79–80, 165n28, 179n6; and
Bluestocking, 103–4; on Byakuren
incident, 77–78; commentary and
afterword to Bachofen's *Bokenron*
(The theory of mother right) by,
137; *Dōhyō* (Signpost), 80, 82, 102–3,
183n51, 184n59; *Fujin to bungaku*
(Women and literature), 102, 143;
Futatsu no niwa (The two gardens),
80, 82, 102–3, 184n59; and Hiratsuka, 18, 78, 103–4; and Key, 18,
78; and love marriage, 16, 77–104,
147; "Mazushiki hitobito no mure"
(The flocks of the poor), 79; and
modern love ideology, 15, 18, 81, 99,
104; and motherhood, 88; *Nobuko*,
18, 77–104, 124; and Okamoto,
143; "Wakaki sedai e no ren'ai ron"
(Theories on love for the young generation), 103

Miyazaki Ryūsuke, 73–75, 78
Miyazaki Tōten, 73
Mizuta Noriko, 90, 180*n*7
Modern Girl (*modan gaaru, moga*), 6
Modernism, 123
Modernity: as constructionist, 5; Japanese, 6, 131, 154*n*11; literature and, 2; love and, 2–4; resistance to or questioning of, 112, 119, 123–25, 138, 186*n*18, 186*n*20; self and, 7, 141–42; women and, 2, 4–7, 12, 19, 128–35, 141–43, 147–49. *See also* Overcoming; Overcoming Modernity symposium; Progress; West
Modern love ideology (*kindai ren'ai ideorogii*): and birth control, 87; central aspects of, 14; critiques of, 112, 144; defined, 13, 160*n*41; difference between love marriage ideology and, 160*n*41; Hiratsuka and, 31; Key and, 13–14; love marriage and, 17, 81; maternal love and, 18, 108, 113, 115, 116, 123; Miyamoto and, 15, 18, 81, 99, 104; Okamoto and, 15, 18, 117, 123–24, 143, 144; in present-day Japan, 148–49; same-sex love and, 17, 35, 43, 48–49, 53, 57, 62; Takamure and, 110–12; women writers and, 15, 104, 148; Yoshiya and, 15, 17, 33, 35, 42–43, 48–49, 53–54, 57, 62. *See also* Love marriage ideology
Moga (Modern Girl), 6
Monma Chiyo, 35
Mori, Maryellen Toman, 123
Mori Ōgai, 143, 157*n*27
Morita Sōhei, *Baien* (Cinder and smoke), 12
Morning Star (Myōjō) (journal), 118
"Mother and Child" (Boshi jojō) (Okamoto), 119–22
Mother-Child Protection Act (*Boshi hogo hō*) (1937), 122
Motherhood (*bosei*): emergence of term of, 108, 185*n*2; feminism and,

109–10, 112–13, 122, 143; Hiratsuka and, 78, 108–14; identity and, 107–10, 112–17, 122; Key and, 78, 108–9; Miyamoto and, 88; and nationalism, 113–15; Okamoto and, 16, 18–19, 116–45; Takamure and, 110–14; women writers and, 115–17. *See also* Eternal mother; Great Mother; Maternal love; *Ur Mutter*
Motherhood-ism (*bosei shugi*), 186*n*16
Motherhood Protection Debates (1918–1919), 108
Mother right (*boken*), 136–37. *See also* Matrilineality
Mother Right (Mutterrecht) (Bachofen), 136
Mothers' rights (*boken*), 109, 137, 186*n*16
Mothers' rights-ism (*boken shugi*), 186*n*16
"Moyuru hana" (Burning flowers) (Yoshiya), 73
Musan fujin geijutsu renmei (Proletarian Women Artists' League), 111
Muta Kazue, 52
Mutterrecht (Mother right) (Bachofen), 136
Myōjō (Morning star) (journal), 118
Myth, 125, 128–35, 141, 143–45
Mythic narrative, 125, 129, 130, 134–35, 142

Naganuma Chieko, 165*n*28
"Nagesuteyo!" (Throw them away!) (Hirabayashi), 76
Nationalism, 12, 19, 113–15, 117, 119, 134, 143, 148, 189*n*7. *See also* Race, improvement of
National Spiritual Mobilization (*kokumin seishin sōdōin*), 114
Native ethnology/folklore (*minzoku-gaku*), 127, 130, 134
Nativism, 115, 127
Natsume Sōseki, 143

Ne no kuni (land of the root), 141. *See also Tokoyo*

The New Green of the Trees (Kigi shin-ryoku) (Sata), 116

New Ladies' Association (Shin fujin kyōkai), 183*n*46

New womanism (*shin josei shugi*), 111

New Woman/New Women (*atarashii onna*), 6, 11, 12, 29, 30, 89, 159*n*35

New women's rights-ism (*shin joken shugi*), 186*n*16

Nihon no haha (The Japanese mother) (Yamaguchi), 114, 115

Nihon roman ha. See Japan Romantic School

Nihon shoki (Chronicles of Japan), 141

"Nikki" (Diary) (Tamura), 171*n*42

Nobuko (Miyamoto), 18, 77–104, 124

Nogami Yaeko, 178*n*44; *Machiko*, 77

Normal sexuality, 24–31, 38–39, 173*n*64. *See also* Romantic friendship

Numata Rippō, 26

Ōsugi Sakae, 92

Ohenro pilgrimage, 126–27

Ohenro (Pilgrim) (Takamure), 126

Okamoto Ippei, 118–20, 122, 189*n*14

Okamoto Kanoko: "Anan to jujutsu-shi no musume" (Ānanda and the witch's daughter), 190*n*20; auto-biographical traces of, 117, 119, 122, 123, 136; background on, 15, 118–20, 189*n*9, 191*n*20; and *Bluestocking*, 19, 116–18, 120, 188*n*2; "Boshi jojō" (Mother and child), 119–22; and Hiratsuka, 19, 116–17; *Karoki netami* (Light jealousy), 118; "Kishimo no ai" (Love of Hārītī), 190*n*20; and love marriage, 120; and maternal love, 16, 18–19, 116–45, 147–48; Mi-yamoto on, 143; and modern love ideology, 15, 18, 117, 123–24, 143, 144; and motherhood, 16, 18–19, 116–45; and nationalism, 19, 119, 143,

189*n*7; self-development in works of, 125–41, 190*n*20; *Shōjō ruten* (Wheel of life), 18–19, 119, 122–45, 189*n*14; and Takamure, 126, 137; "Tsuru wa yamiki" (The crane is sick), 118; and Yoshiya, 142, 195*n*60

Okamoto Tarō, 19, 118–20, 122

Okumura Hiroshi, 8, 12, 13, 30, 69–70, 109, 126

Ome (female same-sex love), 24–25, 27, 162*n*5

"One Year" (Ichinenkan) (Hiratsuka), 30

Onna no yūjō (Female friendship) (Yoshiya), 60

"Onna tomodachi" (Female friends) (Kawada), 29

The Origin of the Family, Private Property, and the State (Engels), 136, 193*n*47

Orikuchi Shinobu, 127

Ornate style (*bibunchō*), 39

Osaka Asahi shinbun award, 29, 43

Osaka Asahi shinbun (newspaper), 68, 70, 72–74, 137

Osaka Mainichi shinbun (newspaper), 73, 75

Otake Kōkichi (Tomimoto Kazue), 12, 30–31, 164*n*16

Otherworld (*tokoyo*), 127, 134, 141–42, 192*n*30

Otto no teisō (The husband's chastity) (Yoshiya), 116

Overcoming: in individual develop-ment, 129–30, 140, 149; modernity/the West, 115, 119, 124, 138

Overcoming Modernity (*Kindai no chōkoku*) symposium, 119

Pacific War, 115, 119

Patriarchy, 53, 55, 113, 121, 138

Patrilineality, 136, 142

People's Newspaper (Kokumin shin-bun), 96

Personalism (*jinkaku shugi*), 7

Pflugfelder, Gregory, 31, 163*n*5, 165*n*22

Pilgrim (Ohenro) (Takamure), 126

Pilgrims, 126

"Poem of Running Away" (Iede no shi) (Takamure), 126

Police Peace Law, 183*n*46

Popular fiction (*tsūzoku shōsetsu*), 15, 50, 60–62, 116, 139

"Power of women" (Imo no chikara) (Yanagita), 128

Premodernity: advocacy of return to, 112–13, 127–28; divorce and, 94; women and, 4, 127–28, 138, 187*n*20

Primal mother. *See* Ur Mutter

Progress: critiques of, 112–13, 138, 141–43; love and, 14; love marriage and, 69–72, 82, 85–86, 93–95, 102; national, 1–3, 6, 18, 98, 100, 112–13, 129–35; social, 77, 103; women's, 2–3, 5–8, 12, 14, 18, 49, 76, 78, 82, 85–87, 93–95, 102, 103, 109–13, 124–25, 149. *See also* Becoming; Development; Evolution; Linearity; Modernity

Proletarian literature, 15, 76–77, 79, 80

Proletarian movement, 6, 77, 101–3. *See also* Bolshevism; Marxism; Socialism

Proletarian Women Artists' League (Musan fujin geijutsu renmei), 111

Psychology of Abnormal Sexual Desires (Hentai seiyoku ron) (Habuto and Sawada), 164*n*13

Psychopathia Sexualis (Krafft-Ebing), 26, 57–58, 164*n*13

Punctuation. *See* Textual symbols

Pure literature (*junbungaku*), 60, 80, 116, 122

Rabu (love), 8

Race, improvement of: love marriage and, 97; maternal love and, 110

Racial hygiene, 130

Records of Ancient Matters (Kojiki), 112, 141

Re-creation (*kaizō*), 130–31, 134

Re-creation (Kaizō) (journal), 80

Rei-niku itchi (unification of spirit and flesh), 14, 69, 111

Ren'ai. See Romantic love

Ren'ai kekkon. See Love marriage

Ren'ai kekkon ideorogii. See Love marriage ideology

"Ren'ai kekkon seido" (The institution of love marriage) (Kikuchi), 101

Ren'ai sōsei (Creation of love) (Takamure), 111–12, 142, 186*n*18, 186*n*20

The Renaissance of Motherhood (Bosei no fukkō) (Key), 78, 109, 178*n*46

Ren'ai to kekkon (Love and Marriage) (Key), 13–14, 17, 31, 69, 93, 109, 160*n*43

Ren'ai to kekkon no sho (Writings about love and marriage) (Kikuchi), 100

Reproduction: becoming-one and, 111; and birth control, 87–88; female power of, 137–38; women's physical health and, 130–31

Return (*kaiki/kangen*), 112, 115, 119, 127–28, 133, 137–38, 141–42, 186*n*20

Rich, Adrienne, 62, 174*n*81

Risshin shusse (establish the self, rise in the world), 130

Rites of passage, 193*n*43

The River Ki (Ki no kawa) (Ariyoshi), 144

Robertson, Jennifer, 27

Romantic friendship, 24–28, 29, 35–39, 42. *See also* Same-sex love

Romantic love (*ren'ai*): etymology of, 9; maternal love and, 112, 187*n*22; modernity and, 3; same-sex love and, 35, 36–37; significance of, 9–10; women's development and, 8, 13–14, 53. *See also* Ai; Heterosexual love; Koi; Love; Love marriage

The Rose in the Storm (Arashi no bara) (Yoshiya), 60–62
Ryōsai kenbo. See Good Wife, Wise Mother
Ryūnyo (Dragon Girl), 129, 130, 134, 140

S (female same-sex love), 24, 163*n*5
Saeki Junko, 8, 157*n*24
Safuran (Saffron) (magazine), 164*n*16
Sagara (Dragon King of the Ocean), 140
Saikoku risshi hen (Success stories of the West) (Smiles), 131
"Same-Sex Love Between Women" (Joseikan no dōsei ren'ai) (Ellis), 30–31, 164*n*15, 173*n*64
Same-sex love (*dōseiai*): adolescent, 26–28, 32–33, 35–46, 162*n*5; adult, 27, 47–49, 54–62; *Bluestocking* and, 12, 29–32; dualistic conception of, 24, 162*n*5; etymology of, 9, 23–24; gender and, 37, 157*n*29; girls and, 23–24, 32–33, 35–45, 162*n*5; Hiratsuka and, 12, 30–31; and identity, 31, 32, 35, 39, 48, 49, 51, 60, 61; as innate, 56; masculinity in, 24–25, 27–28, 57–58, 102, 162*n*5; Miyamoto and, 102–3, 179*n*6; in Okamoto's *Wheel of Life*, 124, 132; overview of, 16–17; self and, 29, 49, 51, 61; sexology and, 25–28, 30–31, 56–57; women's development and, 3, 24, 27, 30–32, 35–39, 42–45, 48–51, 54, 165*n*22; Yosano's discussions of, 35; in Yoshiya's works, 16, 17, 32–62. *See also* Inversion, sexual; Romantic friendship
"Sandai no koi" (The Loves of Three Generations) (Kollontai), 100
Sanger, Margaret, 87
Sata Ineko (Kubokawa Ineko), 18, 115, 161*n*54; *Kigi shinryoku* (The new green of the trees), 116; *Kurenai* (Crimson), 76

Sawada Junjirō, *Hentai seiyoku ron* (Psychology of abnormal sexual desires), 164*n*13
Schoolgirl (*jogakusei*), 23–24, 155*n*12, 162*n*5. *See also* Girls
Seitō (journal). *See Bluestocking*
Seitōsha. *See* Bluestocking Society
Self and selfhood (*jiga*): beyond, 99–104, 109–10, 115, 128; concepts of, 155*n*15; love and, 7, 9–10; love marriage and, 68; maternal self, 114; modernity and, 7; same-sex love and, 29, 49, 51, 61; technologies of the self, 7, 149; true, 7, 9–10, 13, 45–46, 49–50, 58, 68, 89–90, 94, 99, 102, 104, 110, 112–13, 115, 119, 121, 123, 125, 130, 144; virginity and, 52–53; women's development and, 5, 7, 42–43. *See also* Identity; *terms beginning with* Self-
Self-completion, 103–4, 113, 133, 140
Self-construction, 131. *See also* Self-development
Self-cultivation (*shūyō*), 7, 72, 156*n*17
Self-development: love and, 13, 51, 129–35; love marriage and, 68, 72, 74–75, 82, 84–86, 89–91, 94–99; maternal love and, 109–10, 112–13, 123, 133–35; in Okamoto's works, 125–41, 190*n*20. *See also* Becoming; Development; Maturity; Self and selfhood
Self-discovery, 81, 125
Self-erasure, 128, 142, 144. *See also* Self-lessness; Self-sacrifice
Self-Help (Smiles), 131
Self-identity, 44, 61, 84, 101, 126, 143. *See also* Identity; Self and selfhood
Selflessness, 90, 114, 116, 121. *See also* Altruism; Self-erasure; Self-sacrifice
Self-love, 123, 133, 140
Self-sacrifice, 89–90, 121–22, 133, 142. *See also* Altruism; Self-erasure; Self-lessness

Setouchi Harumi (Jakuchō): *Kanoko ryōran* (Kanoko in bloom), 119; *Kanoko ryōran sonogo* (After Kanoko in bloom), 119; theory about authorship of *Wheel of Life* held by, 189n14

Sexology, 25–28, 30, 51–52, 56–57

Sexual difference, 109, 111, 137–38, 186n16

"Sexual Inversion in Women" (Ellis), 30, 56, 164n15, 173n64

Sexuality: abnormal, 24–31, 35, 47–48, 55–61, 102, 164n13, 173n64; normal, 24–31, 38–39, 173n64; rejection of, 125; virginity and, 51–52. *See also* Same-sex love

Sexual love, 13, 14, 37, 43, 48–49, 53, 69, 71, 83–84, 111

Shimazaki Tōson, *Yoakemae* (Before the dawn), 124

Shimizu Shikin, "Koware yubiwa" (The broken ring), 10

Shin fujin kyōkai (New Ladies' Association), 183n46

Shin joken shugi (new women's rightsism), 186n16

Shin josei shugi (new womanism), 111

Shinjū (love suicide), 24–25, 28, 75

Shinju fujin (Madame Pearl) (Kikuchi), 73

Shirakaba ha (White Birch School), 7

Shirakaba (White Birch) (journal), 7, 156n19

"Shirayuri" (White lily) (Yoshiya), 36

"Shiro mokuren" (White magnolia) (Yoshiya), 38

Shishōsetsu. See I-novels

Shōjō ruten (Wheel of life) (Okamoto), 18–19, 119, 122–45, 189n14

Shōjo bunka (Girls' culture), 16, 32–33, 44

Shōjo gahō (Girls' graphic) (magazine), 33, 35

Shōjokai (Girls' realm) (magazine), 32

Shōjo. See Girls

Shōjo shōsetsu (Girls' fiction), 15, 32–35, 43, 44, 47

Shōjo zasshi (Girls' magazines), 26, 32–33, 39, 44

Shōwa period, 4, 67–68, 130

Shojo. See Virgin

Shojo ronsō (Virginity Debates), 52–53

Shokugyō fujin (working woman), 6

Shūyō (self-cultivation), 7, 72, 156n17

Shufu (housewife), 6

Shufu no tomo (magazine). *See Friend of the Housewife*

Sickness. *See* Disease

Signpost (Dōhyō) (Miyamoto), 80, 82, 102–3, 183n51

Silverberg, Miriam, 5

Sisterhood, 24, 34, 60–62, 73, 116. *See also* Romantic friendship

Smiles, Samuel, *Self-Help*, 131; *Saikoku risshi hen* (Success stories of the West), 131

Social Darwinism, 1, 130–32

Socialism, 18, 76, 101. *See also* Bolshevism; Marxism; Proletarian movement

Sontag, Susan, 96

Spiritual love, 13, 14, 37, 43, 48–49, 53, 69, 71, 83–84, 111. *See also* Aijō

Studies in the Psychology of Sex (Ellis), 26, 30, 164n13

The Study of the Matrilineal System (Bokeisei no kenkyū) (Takamure), 137, 142

Stuttering language, 41–42, 45–47

Style: Hayashi and, 125–26; Okamoto and, 123; Takamure and, 112; Yoshiya and, 39–43, 45–47, 60, 169n23

Subjectivity, 155n15. *See also* Self and selfhood

Success Stories of the West (Saikoku risshi hen) (Smiles), 131

Suga Hidemi, 41

Sugawara Hatsu, "Junjitsu no tomo" (A friend for ten days), 29

Suicide. *See* Love suicide
Suzuki Daisetsu, 195*n*62
Suzuki Sadami, 191*n*20
Suzuki, Tomi, 15, 155*n*15

"Taberu koto to teisō to" (About survival and chastity) (Ikuta), 52
Taishō life force ideology (*Taishō seimeishugi*), 191*n*20
Taishō period, 4, 7, 35, 67–68, 130
Takamure Itsue, 18, 100, 110–13, 186*n*16, 187*n*24; *Bokeisei no kenkyū* (The study of the matrilineal system), 137, 142; and Hiratsuka, 110–11, 126, 137; *Hōrōsha no shi* (Wanderer's poems), 126; "Iede no shi" (Poem of running away), 126; and maternal love, 110, 112–13, 142; and modern love ideology, 110–12; motherhood and, 110–14; and Okamoto, 126, 137; *Ohenro* (Pilgrim), 126; *Ren'ai sōsei* (Creation of love), 111–12, 142, 186*n*18, 186*n*20
Takamure Itsue chosaku kōenkai (Association to Support the Works of Takamure Itsue), 137
"A Tale of a Certain Foolish Person" (Aru orokashiki mono no hanashi) (Yoshiya), 54–59
Tamura Toshiko: *Akirame* (Giving up), 29, 165*n*28; "Kanojo no seikatsu" (Her life), 76; "Nikki" (Diary), 171*n*42
Tangled hair (Midaregami) (Yosano), 10
Tanizaki Jun'ichirō, *Chijin no ai* (A fool's love), 86, 89–90
Tanka poetry, 15, 19, 117, 118, 120
TB (Tuberculosis), 96–98, 131
Technologies of the self, 7, 149
Teisō ronsō (Chastity Debates), 52–53
Ten Thousand Leaves (Man'yōshū), 112
Textual symbols, 39–42, 45–47, 169*n*23, 170*n*37, 181*n*14
"Theories on Love for the Young Generation" (Wakaki sedai e no ren'ai ron) (Miyamoto), 103
The Theory of Mother Right (Bokenron) (Bachofen), 136, 137
"Throw them away!" (Nagesuteyo!) (Hirabayashi), 76
Tokoyo (Otherworld), 127, 134, 141–42, 192*n*30
Tokutomi Roka, *Hototogisu* (The cuckoo), 96–97
Tokyo Asahi shinbun (newspaper), 68, 70, 73–75
Tokyo Nichi Nichi shinbun (newspaper), 73, 75
Tomimoto Kazue. *See* Otake Kōkichi
"To My Parents on Becoming Independent" (Dokuritsu suru ni tsuite ryōshin ni) (Hiratsuka), 8, 69
To the Ends of the Earth (Chi no hate made) (Yoshiya), 43
"To the Women of the World" (Yo no fujintachi e) (Hiratsuka), 69
Transcendence, 112, 117, 123–25, 128–30, 138–42
True self, 7, 9–10, 13, 45–46, 49–50, 58, 68, 89–90, 94, 99, 102, 104, 110, 112–13, 115, 119, 121, 123, 125, 130, 144
Tsūzoku shōsetsu (popular fiction), 15, 50, 60–62, 116, 139
"Tsukushi no joō Akiko" (Akiko, Queen of Tsukushi) (newspaper series), 72–73
Tsurumi, E. Patricia, 186*n*20
"Tsuru wa yamiki" (The crane is sick) (Okamoto), 118
Tsushima Yūko, *Yama o hashiru onna* (Woman Running in the Mountains), 144
Tuberculosis (TB), 96–98, 131
Turner, Victor, 135, 193*n*43
The Twilight Years (Kōkotsu no hito) (Ariyoshi), 144
The Two Gardens (Futatsu no niwa) (Miyamoto), 80, 82, 102–3, 184*n*59

Two Virgins in the Attic (Yaneura no nishojo) (Yoshiya), 42–54

Unification of spirit and flesh (*rei-niku itchi*), 14, 69, 111
Unification of written and spoken language (*genbun itchi*), 7, 39–41
Uno Chiyo, 76
Urmutter, 135–36
Ur Mutter, 123, 135–43. *See also* Eternal mother; Great Mother

Vagabond, 125–27
Van Gennep, Arnold, 193*n*43
Venus, 129, 134
Vicinus, Martha, 36
Views of Love in the Modern Era (Kindai no ren'ai kan) (Kuriyagawa), 17, 68, 70–71, 74, 89–90, 93, 110
Virgin groups (*shojokai*), 52
Virginity Debates (*shojo ronsō*), 52–53
Virgin (*shojo*), 26, 51–54, 172*n*49, 172*n*52

"Wakaki sedai e no ren'ai ron" (Theories on love for the young generation) (Miyamoto), 103
Wanderer, 125–27
Wanderer's Poems (Hōrōsha no shi) (Takamure), 126
Watakushi shōsetsu. See I-novels
The Well of Loneliness (Hall), 56, 57
West: adolescent sexuality in literature of, 38; concept of love as from, 3, 8–9; fairytale trope in, 43; as norm, 6, 131–32; opposition to, 112, 115, 130–33, 138, 186*n*18, 186*n*20; self-development in literature in, 2; sexology in, 25–26, 56
Wheel of Life (Shōjō ruten) (Okamoto), 18–19, 119, 122–45, 189*n*14
White Birch School (*Shirakaba ha*), 7
White Birch (Shirakaba) (journal), 7, 156*n*19

"White Lily" (Shirayuri) (Yoshiya), 36
"White Magnolia" (Shiro mokuren) (Yoshiya), 38
Wife, as identity, 82, 94, 101
Womanism (*josei shugi*), 111, 186*n*16
Woman Running in the Mountains (Yama o hashiru onna) (Tsushima), 144
"The Woman Who Rode Away" (Lawrence), 128
Women: development of, 3, 5–8, 13–14, 27, 30–32, 35–39, 42–45, 48–54, 60–62, 81–82, 86–88, 103, 109, 122, 129–35, 142, 172*n*46; divine connections of, 112–13, 127–28, 133; dualistic conception of, 4, 28; healthy bodies of, 130–31; modernity and, 2, 4–7, 12, 119, 128–35, 141–43, 147–49; and the nation, 1–6, 18, 19, 27, 71, 87, 92–94, 98, 100, 104, 108, 113–17, 119–20, 124, 127–49; and origins of civilization, 136–37; power of, 128, 137–38; as premodernity, 4, 127–28, 138; progress of, 2–3, 5–8, 12, 14, 18, 49, 76, 78, 82, 85, 86, 87, 93–95, 102, 103, 109–13, 124–25, 149; as symbols, 2, 4, 28; and the war, 114
Women and Literature (Fujin to bungaku) (Miyamoto), 102, 143
Women's Battlefront (Fujin sensen) (journal), 111
Women's literature, 10–11, 15. *See also* Women writers
Women's magazines, 60
Women's Newspaper (Fujo shinbun), 24
Women's rights (*joken*), 109, 186*n*16
Women writers: autobiographical traces of, 15–16, 75–76, 169*n*27 (*see also* I-novels); and love marriage, 75–78; and love marriage ideology, 75–78; and maternal love, 115–16; and modern love ideology, 15, 104, 148; and motherhood, 115–17; and Okamoto's *Wheel of Life*, 144; and

same-sex love, 29–32, 35, 59–60, 165*n*28, 179*n*6. *See also* Women's literature

Working woman (*shokugyō fujin*), 6

Writings about Love and Marriage (Ren'ai to kekkon no sho) (Kikuchi), 100

Yamada Bimyō, 41

Yamada Kakichi, 32, 171*n*41

Yamada Waka, 32, 108, 171*n*41

Yamaguchi Aisen, *Nihon no haha* (The Japanese mother), 114, 115

Yamakawa Kikue, 26, 108, 112

Yamamoto Senji, 26

Yama o hashiru onna (Woman Running in the Mountains) (Tsushima), 144

Yanagihara Akiko. *See* Byakuren

Yanagita Kunio, 127–28, 134; "Imo no chikara" (Power of women), 128

Yaneura no nishojo (Two virgins in the attic) (Yoshiya), 42–54

Yasuda Satsuki, 52

Yasuda Tokutarō, 26–28

"Yellow Rose" (Kibara) (Yoshiya), 40–42, 55

Yoakemae (Before the dawn) (Shimazaki), 124

Yomiuri shinbun (newspaper), 77

"Yo no fujintachi e" (To the women of the world) (Hiratsuka), 69

Yosano Akiko, 26, 35, 86, 108, 158*n*32, 162*n*5; *Midaregami* (Tangled hair), 10

Yosano Hiroshi (Tekkan), 86

Yoshikawa Toyoko, 50, 171*n*41, 175*n*8

Yoshiya Nobuko: *Arashi no bara* (The rose in the storm), 60–62; "Aru orokashiki mono no hanashi" (A tale of a certain foolish person), 54–59; autobiographical traces of, 59–60; background on, 15, 34–35, 167*n*45, 169*n*27; and *Bluestocking*, 17, 32–33, 166*n*41; and Byakuren, 73; *Chi no hate made* (To the ends of the earth), 43; and Christianity, 46; "Dōsei o aisuru saiwai" (The happiness of loving one of the same sex), 36–37; "Hamanadeshiko" (Japanese pink), 39–40; *Hanamonogatari* (Flower tales), 17, 33–42, 167*n*4; and Hiratsuka, 17, 32, 50, 166*n*41, 171*n*41; and Key, 32, 72; "Kibara" (Yellow rose), 40–42, 55; on Kuriyagawa, 72; *Kuroshōbi* (Black rose), 54–55, 59–60, 72, 173*n*59; and modern love ideology, 15, 17, 33, 35, 42–43, 48–49, 53–54, 57, 62; "Moyuru hana" (Burning flowers), 73; and Okamoto, 142, 195*n*60; *Onna no yūjō* (Female friendship), 60; *Otto no teisō* (The husband's chastity), 116; and same-sex love, 16, 17, 32–62, 147; "Shirayuri" (White lily), 36; "Shiro mokuren" (White magnolia), 38; writing style of, 39–43, 45–47, 60, 169*n*23; *Yaneura no nishojo* (Two virgins in the attic), 42–54; *Yoshiya Nobuko zenshū* (Collected works of Yoshiya Nobuko), 54; *Zoku onna no yūjō* (Female friendship continued), 60

Yoshiya Nobuko zenshū (Collected works of Yoshiya Nobuko) (Yoshiya), 54

Yuasa Yoshiko, 165*n*28, 179*n*6

Zoku onna no yūjō (Female friendship continued) (Yoshiya), 60